POLICING THE POOR

POLICING THE POOR

From Slave Plantation to Public Housing

N E I L   W E B S D A L E

Northeastern University Press

BOSTON

Northeastern University Press

Library of Congress Cataloging-in-Publication Data
Websdale, Neil.
Policing the poor : from slave plantation to public housing / Neil Websdale.
p. cm.
Includes bibliographical references and index.
ISBN 1-55553-497-X (cloth : alk. paper) —
ISBN 1-55553-496-1 (pbk. : alk. paper)
1. Discrimination in law enforcement—Tennessee—Nashville.
2. Community policing—Tennessee—Nashville. 3. Police-community
relations—Tennessee—Nashville. 4. Racism—Tennessee—Nashville.
5. African Americans—Tennessee—Nashville. 6. Nashville (Tenn.)—
Race relations. I. Title.
HV8148.N27 W43 2001
363.2'3'0976855—dc21 2001034539

Designed by Gary Gore

Composed in Trump Medieval by Binghamton Valley Composition, Binghamton, New York. Printed and bound by Thomson-Shore, Inc., Dexter,
Michigan. The paper is Writers Offset, an acid-free stock.

MANUFACTURED IN THE UNITED STATES OF AMERICA
05 04 03 02 01 5 4 3 2 1

For Molly and John Websdale
and in memory of Leon Fisher

CONTENTS

ACKNOWLEDGMENTS

Policing the Poor is the product of a one-year sabbatical spent partially at the Vanderbilt Institute for Public Policy Studies (VIPPS), Vanderbilt University, Nashville, Tennessee. I am grateful to the staff at VIPPS, who helped in many ways with the project. I especially thank Byron Johnson, who at the time was director of the Center for Crime and Justice Policy. Heather Moss contributed much to this project, providing documents, setting up focus groups and some of the interviews, arranging schedules, and offering sharp insights into the research. I thank her. Nashville Police Chief Emmett Turner and Assistant Chief Deborah Faulkner provided important access to the Nashville Police Department during the early stages of this project. Rank-and-file police officers at the Nashville Police Department kindly allowed me to ride with them, talk with them on and off the record, observe them in the field, and learn from their grasp of street life. I thank all of these police officers. I conversed with many people on the street, in small diners, coffee shops, stores, hotels, and elsewhere. I am grateful to those folks. Others probably did not appreciate my presence, and I do not blame them. However, I still owe them. I also talked with people in more "formal" interview settings in places like prison, jail, court, shelters for battered women, homeless shelters, and other institutions. This pastiche of viewpoints, opinions, experiences, and insights constitutes the backbone of the book. I thank those who told their stories.

Several key informants helped tremendously. I particularly thank Sumayya Coleman, who not only introduced me to many women of color, but also educated me about the deeply compromised position of black battered women. Brenda Ross offered other insights on race and gender from her experiences in New York and elsewhere. Alexis Stewart opened the doors of the Tennessee State Penitentiary to me and, in so doing, allowed me access to much more. Through her capacity as crime writer at the *Tennessean*, Beth Warren, now a reporter with the

Atlanta Constitution, provided me with invaluable information, documentary sources, and leads. I am also grateful to Willy Stern at the *Nashville Scene* for helpful background information. Gwen Hopkins at the mayor's office in Nashville also provided valuable assistance. I'd also like to say a big thank-you to Philip Jenkins, who encouraged me during the book's formative stages and passed on numerous newspaper and magazine articles relevant to the project. Claire Renzetti and Virginia Burden read the entire manuscript and provided helpful feedback. I cannot thank them enough.

Nearer to home, I want to thank Ray Michalowski, Mark Beeman, and Eric Gross with whom I discussed various aspects of the research. A special thanks to Alex Alvarez for suggesting many interesting leads and for sharing many cups of tea. As usual, Jeff Ferrell provided great support and encouragement as we wrote what at times seemed like parallel manuscripts. I want to thank Andrew Bush for various stardust memories, including Rome, the British Sailor, Kyoto, the swans on the Thames, and horseback riding in Leeds. If a writer's biography informs the words that eventually see the light of day, then I must thank Don Rogers for his magical goal in the League Cup Final in 1969.

Thanks also to Ingrid Davis and Cathy Spitzer for friendly and efficient administrative support and to John Censioso for assistance with recalcitrant technology. The staff at Northeastern University Press helped throughout and I especially want to thank Bill Frohlich, Sarah Rowley, Jill Bahcall, Ann Twombly, and Sarah Richards-Doerries.

I would like to thank my wife, Amy, for "keeping on keeping on" and our daughter, Mia, my polestar. I would also like to thank our cat, Kisker, for scratching at the screen door and keeping me on my toes. Finally, *Policing the Poor* is dedicated to my parents, Molly and John Websdale, and all their hard work on my behalf.

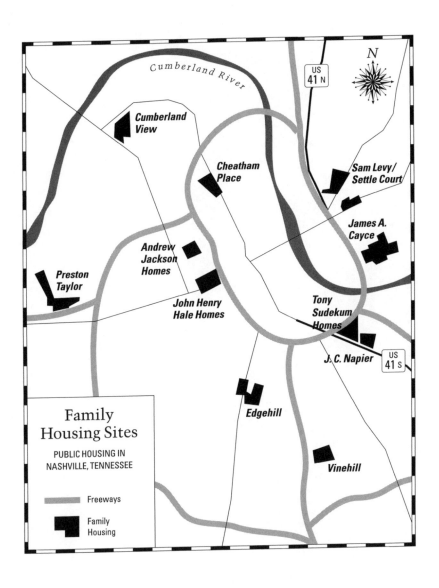

Cumberland River

Cumberland
View

Cheatham
Place

Sam Levy/
Settle Court

James A.
Cayce

Andrew
Jackson
Homes

Preston
Taylor

John Henry
Hale Homes

Tony
Sudekum
Homes

J. C. Napier

US
41 N

US
41 S

N

Edgehill

Vinehill

Family
Housing Sites

PUBLIC HOUSING IN
NASHVILLE, TENNESSEE

Freeways

Family
Housing

POLICING THE POOR

INTRODUCTION

We ate dinner earlier in the evening at Luby's Cafeteria. Detective Bronson and I were getting to know each other.[1] I was working as an ethnographer and consultant criminologist on a project to evaluate the effects of community policing on domestic violence. Bronson worked as a detective in the Nashville Police Department. He was not too keen on being a police officer. He told me, "I'd rather buy several acres and never see anyone except my family." Bronson and I drove around for hours; he had little to do other than generously provide me with a sense of the city, the high-crime areas—the lay of the land, so to speak. Bronson's desire to withdraw from social life reminded me of a good friend, Alan Dunn, a police captain in Florida. Occasionally, Alan and I drink beer together in an English-style pub on the Florida coast run by a cockney proprietor from London. Like Bronson, Alan Dunn tells me he has just a few years left before he will retire to his log cabin in North Carolina, where he will rarely have to deal with the public again.

Earlier that day, I toured the neighborhoods of Nashville in my rental car, getting out at times and just walking around, somewhat lamenting that American cities are less amenable to walking than the English ones that I grew up in. About three hours after sunset, Bronson and I pulled into the Sam Levy public housing projects. He asked me to look at the Dollar General Store to our left. I glanced over and saw a solid, gray brick building on the edge of a parking lot. Beyond the parking lot was a crowd of black juveniles and young men playing basketball under bright lights. The air was humid and the brown-walled housing very dense. A message came over the radio that a young black male last seen in our vicinity had just knifed someone. I remembered these projects from my afternoon reconnaissance, but they were different at night. The energy was different and the sultry night hid some of the desperation. There were hundreds of people on the street, many crowded around a bus stop. All the faces in the crowd were black. I

3

wondered what they were waiting for; maybe they looked at me through the window of the unmarked police vehicle and wondered what I was doing. I asked Bronson if there were any Caucasians living in these projects. He replied, "A few, and they don't do too well." At that moment, I could almost taste my skin color. As we continued to drive, Bronson pulled into a parking lot at the edge of the Sam Levy housing area. He told me he would not get out of his vehicle at night here. His precise words were "They don't like white boys 'round here." He told me: "We had one of our officers chase a suspect into this area a year or so ago. The officer shot him dead. Within a few minutes the community was up in arms. They looted the Dollar General Store. Then they burned it to the ground. We couldn't do anything. Eventually, we came in and arrested some of those involved in the burning, but it took us a while."

The incident Bronson refered to was the looting and burning of the Dollar General Store in response to Sergeant Hickerson's fatal shooting of Leon Fisher, a twenty-three-year-old black man. Fisher fled police after being pulled over on a traffic stop and was shot during an ensuing altercation (see chapter 3). As I listened to Detective Bronson, I was reminded of the Detroit riots of 1967, which were triggered by a routine police raid of an after-hours club. Forty-three people died and rioters destroyed $500 million in property.[2] The Miami riots of 1989 erupted after a police officer killed an unarmed black motorcyclist, also causing the death of his passenger. Finally, the infamous Los Angeles disturbances erupted after the brutal beating of Rodney King and the failure of the Simi Valley jury to find the perpetrators criminally culpable. As we rode around Sam Levy, I felt a growing sense of unease with the blatant apartheid that infects American cities. It was as if the Supreme Court in *Brown v. Board of Education* (1954) had never reversed the "separate but equal" doctrine of *Plessy v. Ferguson* (1896). What happened to the Civil Rights Act of 1964? The world was still black and white in Nashville, just as it had been black and white in Detroit in 1967, in Miami in 1989, and in Los Angeles in 1992.

My mind began to leap all over the place. I pondered the institution of slavery, with all its violence, paternalism, prohibitions, and segregation, and I wondered what had really changed. Of course, much has changed, but much remains the same. My mind jumped back to a ride-along several years ago in Miami. The detective I accompanied was investigating a burglary connected to a domestic violence case. In the heat of the night we came into the gated projects and saw about a dozen or so black men sitting around a Dumpster. Three or four other men on a second-floor balcony watched us. I contemplated the rich irony of gated public housing projects. In a sense, the second-floor watch seemed like a curious inversion of the old watchman system used to guard the walled cities of preindustrial Europe. These men seemed agitated as we moved in. Two guys approached us and told us that their only infractions were vehicular offenses and that they had done minimal time in jail. As the detective and I walked toward the apartment where the burglary had occurred, he turned to me and said, "Watch your back in here." I remember feeling vulnerable and thinking of how my clean shirt would look with blood all over it. For the Nashville research, I bought a bulletproof vest. The retailer told me the vest would not protect me against most machine-gun fire, the kind of firepower, he added, that some of the local drug dealers possessed.

On another ride-along in Miami several years ago, I asked an officer whether he might consider stopping at a grocery store in Overtown, a predominantly black neighborhood. As in the Sam Levy projects, the streets of Overtown teemed with hundreds of black faces. The officer told me he did not want to get out of the vehicle to enter the grocery store because it was both dark and dangerous. He made a point of telling me: "Nothing against the owners of the grocery store, I'm sure they've got good stuff in there. However, nearly all these people on the street will have done time in jail or prison and it is just not safe for us to get out." When I reflect on this particular ride-along, I wonder about the enormous impact of what Diana Gordon once called the "justice juggernaut," a penal system that is able to process practically everyone on a street in Overtown.[3]

Ethnography is not just the study of ways of life. It *is* a way of life. Having spent my formative years in the British equivalent of American public housing, I suppose I may have some affinity with the lifestyle and living conditions in the housing projects in places like Nashville. However, I am not black. Slave traders did not load my ancestors onto ships on the African coast and forcibly transport them thousands of miles. Slavers did not brand my ancestors with hot iron. Such differences are immense and do not necessarily bode well for the ethnographer. On another level, I obviously stood out like a sore thumb with what is left of my British accent and my privileged demeanor as a white male college professor. Some might see my stance as ethnographer as disingenuous, romantic, or voyeuristic. I cannot take issue with such challenges. However, the work seemed important, and I was curious about the apartheid system in the wealthiest "democracy" on earth.

I wanted to learn about policing from those subject to it, not just from police officers. To do so, I had to go to the housing projects, talk with people who lived there, and, at times, feel some of the fears they lived with. During my work I observed life on the streets, talking with numerous people touched by saturation policing and the penetrating criminal justice juggernaut. People offered me drugs. For a price, prostitutes offered fleeting relief. I rode with police officers and watched them at work. What follows is my attempt to articulate what I learned. I blend my ethnographic observations with historical and contemporary research. The patterns and trajectories that emerge are not pleasant; rather, they present a disturbing picture of social life in America. I identify community policing at the heart of postindustrial apartheid. This latest form of policing constitutes just one element of a wider strategy of controlling the poor. What is new is that much industrial labor, which served as a principal means of disciplining workers, has disappeared. In its place is the service sector job, the subterranean drug trade, and the criminal justice juggernaut.

I will employ the term "criminal justice juggernaut" to refer to that growing web of prisons, jails, law enforcement, probation, and parole that regulates the lives of so many among the poor, particularly black people. I prefer to add the word "criminal" to Diana Gordon's catchy phrase because I want to distinguish clearly between criminal justice and social justice. The term "justice juggernaut" is ambiguous in this regard, although Gordon's analysis of the function of the criminal justice agencies that compose the juggernaut does not imply that they effect social justice. Through my ethnography in Nashville it became clear that in regulating the urban underclass, the criminal justice juggernaut has become increasingly central to the management of postindustrial class, race, and gender relations. Recent forms of saturation law enforcement, some of them known as community policing, serve as the lead filter for the juggernaut, providing it with new bodies, new clientele, new cases, new sources of funding, and, allegedly, new credibility. For those subject to the awesome power of the beast, the juggernaut is omniscient and omnipresent, constituting a massive strike force.

One key word here is "regulate." I do not use it to refer only to the day-to-day management of the lives of those subject to the control of the criminal justice system. Rather, I employ the word broadly to include both the minutiae of what John Irwin once called "rabble management" and the overall state management of "surplus" populations: the unemployed, the underemployed, the homeless, and the otherwise urban disenchanted.[4] Regulating a permanent postindustrial underclass requires a special punitive energy. The criminal justice juggernaut and its community policing branch provide that energy.

As an ethnographer who has observed social life in a number of U.S. cities, walked the streets frequently, and talked with people, I find that these stories of segregation, violence, crime, hopelessness, and despair are common. This book brings some of these phenomena into sharp focus. I view these phenomena through the lens of community policing and all its rhetoric about building consensus among the poor. If we could apply such consensus building retroactively, the current community policing impulse would be akin to asking black Africans if they wanted to buy tickets to the New World to work on the plantations of the cotton and sugar barons. This strikes me as an ironic point of entry because of the many contradictions between community policing and the liberal democracies it purports to protect. Much has been written on community policing; however, almost the entire discourse neglects the opinions, perspectives, and experiences of those most intimately affected by the practice. Much of this literature is also profoundly ahistorical, failing miserably to situate community policing in the context of ghetto life, the superstigmatization of the black underclass, the rise of global capitalism, and the deep history of the slave trade.

In the chapters that follow, I blend history and ethnography to make sense of the rise of community policing in Nashville. I draw on the language, perceptions, and experiences of the urban underclass, many of them African American, to construct familial, neighborhood, and social ecologies. The cultural pastiche that emerges is not social science (whatever that is), but, rather, my effort to narrate social life, and, more specifically, mine the subtle nuances, customary cultural practices, and changing forms of social control.

Chapter 1, "Policing, Society, and History," addresses some of the historical and contemporary issues involved in policing the poor.[5] It is no accident that the most urgent and intensive community policing developments emerged in poorer communities, especially black public housing projects, during what I call the twentieth-century Redemption (1980–2000). When one looks closely enough, there are remarkable and disturbing historical homologies among the control of African slaves in the American colonies, the regulation of freedmen and freedwomen during nineteenth-century Reconstruction and Redemption, and the close surveillance and punitiveness directed at blacks in postindustrial inner cities. Put simply, just as the nineteenth-century era of Jim Crow rolled back some of the gains of the post–Civil War Reconstruction, so too has the rise of the criminal justice juggernaut and community policing undone a number of the progressive developments emerging from the civil rights era stemming from the Montgomery bus boycott and *Brown v. Board of Education of Topeka, Kansas* (1954) to the findings of the Kerner Commission of 1968. The chapter closes with an outline of recent community policing developments and raises a number of questions about what the developments mean.

In Chapter 2, "The Nashville Poor," I use an ethnographic approach and draw upon various archival and documentary sources to highlight the experiences of those members of the poor subject to new forms of community and saturation policing. My research focuses largely on the nearly all-black housing projects that ring the central business district of Nashville. Through my conversations and observations, I track the rather vehement attack on black families that has attended the globalization of capital, the intensification of social quarantining, the decline of community and neighborhood spirit, and the rise of street crime and violence.

There seems to have been much more police brutality before the rise of community policing in Nashville. For example, jailers sometimes hosed the blood out of the jail elevator in the morning after police beat suspects in it the night before. My interviews also identify long-standing police failure to serve and protect black inner-city communities.[6] Since the emergence of community policing, incidents of police brutality appear to have declined, although this is difficult to gauge.[7] Given the long legacy of police oppression and failure to protect, it comes as no surprise that Nashville, like urban areas across the United States, has witnessed its fair share of social disturbances, "rioting," and "looting."

Chapter 3, "Policing Social Upheaval," closely examines the looting and burning of the Dollar General Store in August 1997. I contrast the perspectives of police and governmental agencies with those of the closely policed poor. Ultimately, I explore the political construction of crime, rioting, and social protest, bearing in mind the peculiar circumstances of black families, the globalization of capitalism, and the deep and profound legacy of racism.

Chapter 4 "Black Kin and Intimate Violence," focuses on the regulation of black kinship systems and confronts the acute compromises faced by black battered women. I link these contemporary compromises with the history of slavery and emancipation. Black battered women living in the Nashville housing projects display a deep suspicion of police. So too do their communities. The community and certain members of it might label a battered woman a "snitch" if she calls to seek protection for herself or her children. Community policing, with its emphasis on greater surveillance of public space, seems to make little difference to domestic violence. This is particularly unfortunate because the use of actual violence, as opposed to threatened or implied violence, is much higher in domestic disturbances than it is among confrontations on the street.

Chapter 5, "Crack and the Cracks in Neoliberal Democracies," draws upon documentary sources and interviews with police, prostitutes, drug addicts, street people, and other nomadic souls. One might expect that community policing, with its emphasis on eradicating visible illegalities, would reduce vice. On the contrary, my ethnography shows joblessness, men's power over women, and the deep historic oppression of black people at the root of the urban drug trade and prostitution. Put differently, I find that community policing cannot compensate for or counteract the deeply rooted social forces that underlie both the need to sell drugs and sexual services and the desire to purchase the experiences these commodities offer. I point to "cracks" in the foundations of American democracy and civil rights and argue that the saturation policing of the crack cocaine trade bodes ill for us all, since it feeds off what Paul Gilroy once called a "racially exclusive conception of civil rights."[8]

Chapter 6, "From Elmina to Edgehill," blends historical and sociological insights with my ethnographic observations to interpret the rise of saturation policing and the criminal justice juggernaut. I note a close chronological correspondence between the gearing up of this punitive apparatus and the loss of jobs through the global expansion of capitalism. However, arguments that reduce community policing to its role in managing class relations fall well short of the mark. They do not explain the concentrated intervention of police in places like the virtually all-black Edgehill housing projects. Many American people are poor; why target primarily black neighborhoods? The answer, I argue, does not lie only in the fact that the residents of Edgehill are the most impoverished and degraded "underclass" of capitalism. Indeed, women and children represent the vast majority of the residents of Edgehill and other housing projects. The majority of these women receive meager state welfare supports. The heightened responses of community police in these acutely poor neighborhoods greatly compromise the African American family and contribute to the backlash against the civil rights victories of 1954 through 1968.

My ethnography exposes the utter devastation of black family life in the projects. At the risk of sounding melodramatic, I would claim that developments in neighborhoods like Edgehill constitute a eugenic intervention against black people. Put differently, the saturation policing of poor black neighborhoods meant to confront the threat from "violent" black men represents little more than a selective breeding program that separates young black men from black women, or stringently mediates their interactions and intimacy. The selective breeding program cleans up communities, removes undesirable and "dangerous" men, drug-addicted women, ineffective mothers, and deadbeat dads. This purification process is akin to the building of Christian chapels on the African coast during the slave trade. It remains to be seen whether the new emphasis of George W. Bush's administration on faith-based initiatives will continue the ritual cleansing commenced at the close of the twentieth-century Redemption.

Doubtless, some will be offended by my argument, so let me be clear: it is not my position that community policing works monolithically to oppress blacks or any other group. Many residents in the Nashville housing projects want a greater police presence because they fear the violence in their neighborhood streets. In addition, and this is often overlooked, those same residents also complain about the patent failure of political authorities to create living conditions in which they might thrive without reliance upon saturation policing. I refer here to the historic loss of jobs from the inner city and the failure to invest in inner-city communities. Neither is it my argument that political authorities "deliberately" introduced community policing as a "soft" means of incarcerating and stigmatizing blacks. Rather, the consequences of community policing, especially the dire effects on black families and kinship systems, appear largely unintended. However, I find it hard to believe that a number of well-informed politicians and legislators could not have reasonably anticipated the devastating impact of the crack cocaine laws upon poor communities and particularly young black men (see chapter 5). Put differently, I do not suggest there is a conspiracy to destroy the black family. Indeed, the motives of those who introduced racially biased laws, manage the criminal justice industry, and drive the chaotic economy of postindustrial capitalism matter much less than the effects produced by such onerous developments.

Obviously, community policing differs from place to place. Susan Miller writes of community policing in "Jackson City," an urban area in the Midwest with a population of 200,000. According to Miller, the Jackson City police enjoy "a solid reputation with the citizens, many of whom indicate an overall satisfaction with the treatment they receive from police." However, as Miller goes on to observe, Jackson City "has not been ravaged by the disintegration wrought by poverty, homelessness, and drug use that has plagued most larger American cities."⁹

There is a dearth of systematic ethnographic research into community policing in major U.S. cities. My work confronts this deficiency. Ethnography allows us to learn about policing from those subject to it rather than from official sources that rely on the various elements of the criminal justice juggernaut for data. Voices of people on the street provide a much more complicated picture of the role of the juggernaut than do official figures. Ethnography strikes me as a particularly important alternative to mainstream criminological analysis, which relies largely upon formal data, often without questioning or challenging their veracity. To the extent that professional organizations such as the American Society for Criminology seek legitimacy and credibility through appearing to be "scientific," we would do well to consider the extent to which such "objectivist" posturing excludes the experiences and perceptions of those subject to the juggernaut. It strikes me that mainstream criminology often serves simultaneously as mouthpiece and apologist for a criminal justice system run amok. Michel Foucault, talking about the "garrulous discourse" of criminology with its "endless repetitions," notes, "I fail to comprehend how the discourse of criminology has been able to go on at this level. One has the impression that it is needed so urgently and rendered so vital for the working of the system, that it does not even need to seek a theoretical justification for itself, or even simply a coherent framework. It is entirely utilitarian."[10]

It is difficult to generalize from the Nashville experience of community policing. Nevertheless, piecing together preliminary evidence from larger U.S. cities, I argue that community policing and its various mutations constitute central components of the criminal justice juggernaut. I extend these observations with findings from history and contemporary sociology to argue that the juggernaut is a vital element in postindustrial social control initiatives in the United States, simultaneously serving to stigmatize and scapegoat surplus populations, especially young urban blacks, and artificially lower the unemployment rate. This punitive approach to the management of surplus populations represents a historic choice on the part of U.S. policy makers, differing significantly from the placative initiatives found in most European societies.

Weaving in evidence from the annals of history and contemporary sociology alongside my ethnographic observations is risky. Juxtaposing massive societal forces with the choices of various individuals to engage in street crime, drug use, welfare fraud, and the like runs the risk of presenting individuals as passive. I must state at the outset that my conception of social actors is that they always exercise choice. I do not subscribe to what Dennis Wrong once identified as the "oversocialized conception of man."[11] Put differently, I do not see individuals as the mere product of social forces—cultural dupes, if you will. At the same time, I am at pains to point out that human nature is not only about free will, and that the conceptual distinction between free will and determinism that underpins classical, conservative, and positivist criminology constitutes a false dichotomy. As Karl Marx once put it, people may make their own history, "but they do not make it just as they please; they do not make it under circumstances chosen by themselves, but under circumstances directly encountered, given and transmitted from the past. The tradition of all the dead generations weighs like a nightmare on the brain of the living."[12]

These observations on the inextricable interweaving of human choice and social forces inform our understandings of crime. It is not my position that criminality is a mere knee-jerk response to forces beyond our control. Such a position strikes me as absurd. One theme that emerges time and again through my ethnography is the rational calculus that some people engage in to begin a life of crime, negotiate a life debilitated by victimization, or support agencies of social control against criminal elements. Neither is it my suggestion that if we provide well-paid and meaningful labor to urban ghettos people will somehow magically cease to commit crime. Again, such a position strikes me as ludicrous. White-collar criminals and corporate criminals, who often wallow in privilege, serve to remind us that the tendencies to criminality do not arise simply out of social disadvantage.

Policing, Society, and History

■ From the fifteenth century, European explorers and traders ventured into uncharted waters and found "new" land to exploit. These developments extended existing markets, created new ones, and led to the mass movement of populations. They also resulted in the colonization, subjugation, and death of large numbers of native peoples. As Walvin notes, the diversified diets of the eighteenth-century British family reflected these developments. People began increasingly to consume "tea from China, sugar and coffee from the West Indies, tobacco from Virginia, chocolate from Africa and America, rum from the Caribbean."[1] In many ways the labor power of slaves facilitated the diversification of the modern-era diet in nations such as Britain.[2]

Slave traders forcibly transported roughly 20 million Africans to the New World, the first slaves landing in Jamestown, Virginia, in August

1619.[3] The steady stream of confiscated blacks intensified in the eighteenth century, with at least 6 million transported during that time. The kidnapping and forced transportation of Africans tapered off in the nineteenth century. Slavery was officially eliminated in British colonies in 1834, in Dutch colonies in 1863, and in the United States in 1865.

Africans provided the labor for the slave-based agricultural production systems in the Caribbean, South America, and the United States.[4] A small, white European minority dominated these emerging social systems, rationalizing and justifying their social supremacy through claims of religious ascendancy and racial superiority. The confluence of these religious and racial ideologies became particularly acute in Europe in the eighteenth and nineteenth centuries, during which time "race" became firmly established as a cultural signifier of inherited characteristics.[5]

Policing Slavery and Nineteenth-Century Reconstruction and Redemption

From the seventeenth century onward, European settlers arrived in the Americas in huge numbers. The majority engaged in agricultural production, eking out a living from the land. The agricultural economies of the New World thus reflected the dispersion of various European traditions to New World settings with their different climatic conditions, natural resources, and growing seasons.[6] In spite of widely accepted religious and racial beliefs that depicted blacks as inferior, these emerging agricultural economies still had to police slaves closely.[7] Africans did not come willingly to the New World and resisted the institution of slavery in many ways. Most Africans captured in wars or kidnapped by slavers were from sedentary (nonnomadic) West African societies characterized by hard agricultural labor. Once the Africans were captured or kidnapped, traders and those in their employ, including black African natives, tied slaves together with rope and often marched them hundreds of miles to the African coast. Today, people visit the remnants of the slave forts that are scattered along the coast of West African states such as Ghana. Elmina Castle is one of the most infamous of these forts. Built originally by Portuguese traders in 1482, Elmina boasts one of the oldest Christian chapels in Africa. The Portuguese originally sought gold and ivory from local tribes. However, by 1600 Europeans from the Caribbean and North America craved cheap labor, and Elmina Castle soon became a holding pen for captured Africans. The housing of one of the oldest Christian chapels inside the Elmina slave fort was no mere coincidence. Wealthy Europeans justified their exploitation of black labor through the ideology of Christianity. Ideally, Europeans would transform primitive black savages into civilized, God-fearing agricultural workers. Work was the fulcrum and the Christian god the guiding light.

John Blassingame describes how, once on the coast, "the Africans were made to jump up and down, had fingers poked in their mouths and their genital organs handled by a doctor. Those chosen by the Europeans were then branded." Many died on the march, others committed suicide, especially while still on the African coast, with their eyes trained on their homeland. Shackled together in cramped, diseased conditions with little nourishment for anywhere from several weeks to several months, many died.[8] Harvey Wish notes fifty-five known mutinies on slave ships from 1699 to 1845; this form of resistance was common enough for slave-ship captains to take out "insurrection insurance."[9] On slave ships crossing the Atlantic, Hugh Thomas observes, "There was probably at least one insurrection every eight to ten journeys. On French ships, though, there seems to have been only about one every twenty-five voyages." Among all the insurrections, few succeeded in overthrowing the traders.[10]

Slaves' resistance continued in the New World. The scope and form of this resistance depended greatly upon the social organization of the plantations and the surrounding country. Full-scale uprisings were more common in countries such as Brazil or in the Caribbean, where plantations were much larger, usually having at least 150 slaves, and where owners were absent and whites relatively few. In the American South, half of the slaves lived on farms, not on plantations. Indeed, only one quarter of Southern slaves lived on plantations with more than fifty slaves.[11] Among the white population, those who did not own slaves outnumbered those who did by six to one.[12] The majority of whites lived in poverty and often deeply resented the privileged planter class, which also dominated colonial governments and state legislatures. The relatively small number of slaves on Southern plantations, compared to their Caribbean and South American counterparts, lived in proximity to their masters and the masters' families. Slaves themselves lived in family units, with individual family members sometimes dispersed between neighboring plantations. In these situations slaves experienced the ties, loyalties, pressures, and solidarity of both family and community life, the qualities of which often provided a buffer against the dehumanizing influences of slavery. Planters, especially in the later antebellum period, encouraged slave family life. Indeed, Southern paternalism underpinned the management of slave populations, and planters genuinely believed that the slave-owning system was the pinnacle of social organization. Slaves resisted and negotiated this paternalism carefully, knowing that white people outside the plantations were usually armed and hostile to them. Escaped slaves faced the hazards of the countryside, including overseers and masters who often knew the land well and were skilled hunters. Punishments for escaping were severe, including the cancellation of passes to see family members, the sale of the escapee to a new master, a flogging, or other coercive treatment. Given these conditions, Southern slaves engaged in little mass rebellion; historians have recorded only a small number of uprisings compared with insurrections in South America and the Caribbean.[13]

Southern society defined slaves as chattel. Masters used slaves to further their own production goals. Yet slaves knew well the virtues of freedom. While slaves in the South did not engage in mass uprisings against their owners, they nevertheless resisted slavery in a variety of ways. From shirking to stealing from owners, lying, killing owners and overseers, fleeing plantations, visiting family on neighboring plantations without passes, and engaging in acts of violence and hatred, slaves refused to submit. In the many ways slaves negotiated Southern paternalism, they undermined the very essence of slavery itself. Eugene Genovese observes that "the slaves' accommodation to paternalism enabled them to assert rights, which by their very nature not only set limits to their surrender of self but actually constituted an implicit rejection of slavery."[14]

The plantation system gradually expanded after the American War of Independence. The invention of the cotton gin in 1793 spurred cotton production. Howard Zinn estimates cotton production in the South grew from a thousand tons a year in 1790 to a million tons in 1860.[15] This upsurge in cotton production required the gradual removal of Indians from their native Southern lands, particularly from 1814 to 1824.[16]

Slave patrols played an important part in this daily performance of unpaid labor, since they limited slave resistance and insurrection. The slave patrols enforced customary cultural beliefs and practices, many of which became embodied in the slave codes introduced by colonial and, later, state governments. According to the slave codes, blacks and whites occupied different social positions that reflected blacks' basic inferiority to whites. Masters sold and bartered slaves, wagered them at gaming tables, and bequeathed them through their wills. Masters enjoyed what Foucault once called sovereign power over the bodies of slaves, whom they whipped, tortured, branded, and killed as punishment for a range of perceived offenses.[17] The ideology of slavery deemed that masters should provide slaves with clothing, food, shelter, and other material provisions. As slavery grew, particularly in the first half of the nineteenth century, masters usually provided a modicum of these material provisions for slaves, thus contributing to the collective "calling" and "duty" of the planter class to raise civilized, God-fearing slaves. President Andrew Jackson owned a cotton plantation called the Hermitage, near Nashville. Jackson owned at least 130 slaves. His was one of the largest plantations in Tennessee's central basin. Recent archeological excavations at the site revealed that enslaved families lived in roughly four-hundred-square-foot, single-room brick buildings clustered in three different locations to the rear of the mansion house. Writing about his own paternalistic style of plantation management, President Jackson observed, "One willing hand is really worth two who only does what labor he is forcibly compelled to perform."[18]

Notwithstanding President Jackson's paternalism, the enforcement of discipline in work and daily life was an essential component of the management of slaves. They could not leave plantations without passes. The passes specified the reasons for slave absence, the duration of their excursions, and their destinations. It was the duty of all whites to check slave passes. Whites who failed to do so could find themselves subject to punishment such as fines. Masters or those in their employ could whip slaves without appropriate passes or turn them over to the courts. For example, Herbert Gutman details how one slave was whipped for visiting his common-law wife without a pass.[19] Apparently, it was common practice on Saturday nights for men to visit wives who were owned by different masters and who therefore lived on other plantations. Some of these men traveled without passes. "My pa," explained Millie Barber, "come sometimes widout de pass. Patrollers catch him way up de chimney hidin' one night; they stripped him right befo' mammy and gave him thirty-nine lashes, wid her cryin; and a hollerin' louder than he."[20]

Slaves and their masters negotiated the slave codes. Some masters sent their slaves on errands to local stores without passes. If patrollers knew the slaves and were in awe of the master, then they might let the transgression pass. Formally, the slave codes forbade slaves gathering in groups of more than four to five without whites present. This especially applied to religious gatherings. However, some masters allowed slave groups to engage in religious activities and worked this out with patrollers. Similarly, the slave codes forbade slaves to learn to read and write. Nevertheless, the children of some masters taught house slaves these skills. However, in the final analysis, the inferiority and subjugation of slaves underpinned race relations. So too was the lowly position of the majority of whites who worked the land, engaged in craft work, or peddled their wares. Slave codes required all adult whites to regulate slaves. Many wealthier whites bought themselves out of slave patrol duty.

Overall, the slave codes worked to the advantage of the big planters and drove a wedge between poor whites and slaves. These two disadvantaged groups occupied lowly but different positions in the Southern production system. But on a day-to-day basis, the law sometimes worked against planters' short-term interests. For example, if poor whites stole from a plantation and slaves witnessed the theft, those slaves could not testify against or contradict the whites in court.[21] In such a situation, the only recourse available to the planter was to find white witnesses or to settle the matter privately, perhaps with violence.

Slave codes arose in a legal tradition saturated with notions of honor, status, and duty. Southern judges applied the law carefully to preserve its "credibility." For example, Keir Nash reports a study of appellate courts in nine Southern states between 1830 and 1860, noting that blacks received reversals of convictions in 136 of 238 appeals. These cases speak to the meticulous application of legal principles rather than the haphazard application of law against slaves. Commenting on Keir Nash's work, Randall Kennedy notes: "When juries were improperly constituted, even in cases where actual guilt appeared to be clear, appellate courts reversed convictions. The Supreme Court of Alabama overturned a guilty verdict against a slave charged with murdering a white man on the grounds that one of his jurors had only a share in an undistributed estate of slaves, whereas state law required a juror in a case against a slave to be a full owner of at least one slave."[22]

Besides maintaining legal distinctions between whites and blacks, the slave codes reinforced notions of purity and pollution by dictating proper deference and distance between races. For example, some codes required blacks to step aside if whites walked toward them, prevented blacks from walking with canes in the manner of an old Southern gentleman, and did not allow slaves to make loud noises. By criminalizing these types of social infractions, the codes provided avenues of redress and punishment for everyday departures from what Douglas Massey and Nancy Denton would later call "the American Apartheid."[23]

Most counties in the South had slave patrols. In some states the militia or army performed slave patrol duty. In others, patrol initiatives emerged out of colonial or state government legislation, only to slowly permeate the fabric of county and municipal government. As early as 1667, white planters in New England introduced legislation to regulate "the Negroes on the British Plantations." The code referred to blacks as being "of a wild, barbarous, and savage nature to be controlled only with strict severity."[24] Like the English planters, the other European slave-owning societies introduced similar codes. In most areas patrols checked the passes of slaves as they moved off plantations. They also conducted routine checks of slave quarters, searching for stolen property and contraband. The frequency of these visits varied tremendously and their focus sharpened in the aftermath of threatened, actual, or perceived slave insurrections.

During the eighteenth century the intensity of slave patrolling increased. For example, the Tennessee Patrol Act of 1753 required county courts to appoint searchers to survey slave quarters four times a year to check for weapons and contraband. By 1799 patrollers searched slave quarters monthly. From 1806 these searchers evolved into an elaborate preventive patrol force. County governments paid patrollers one dollar per shift, with a five-dollar bonus for each slave caught and returned to the slave's master.[25] One early legislative act creating a police system dates back to 1690 in South Carolina.[26] The act required all persons, under penalty of forty shillings, to arrest and chastise any slave away from his home plantation without a proper ticket.[27] After 1721 a merger between militiamen and appointed local civilians created a police system based on regular patrol. These patrollers received salaries and toured plantations once a month to search for guns and contraband. Patrollers also administered whippings for a variety of infractions.

Just as modern-day police officers and private security guards come largely from working- or lower-middle-class families, so too did slave patrollers emerge from the ranks of less well-to-do whites. They shared with slaves similar positions as exploited subordinates. There is evidence to suggest that poorer whites interacted with slaves in a number of ways that hurt planters. Genovese notes how poor whites would incite slaves to steal from masters, with poor whites acting as "fences" for the stolen property.[28] Some whites would encourage or aid slaves to escape. Other whites traded with free blacks and escaped slaves who had set up maroon communities in the South. Wintersmith notes the existence of maroon communities at various times in mountainous, forested, and swampy areas of South and North Carolina, Virginia, Louisiana, Florida, Georgia, Mississippi, and Alabama between 1672 and 1864.[29] These communities survived through agriculture and illegal trading with white farmers. According to Blassingame, maroon communities constituted "one of the gravest threats to the planters."[30] Not only did such communities undermine planters' authority and encourage other slaves to flee plantations, they also served as a base for guerrilla incursions against planters.[31] More significantly still, the "unholy alliances" between poor blacks and whites ran counter to the divide-and-conquer tactics of many among the planter class.[32]

The introduction of slave codes and slave patrols helped amplify divisions between poor whites and slaves. On another front, the planter class also had to contend with the rise of industrial capitalism in the North and its reliance upon wage labor as opposed to slave labor. Southern planters saw northern capitalism as ungodly, corrupt, dishonorable, and a major threat to Southern social organization. Cotton production in the South grew dramatically during the first half of the nineteenth century. Southern planters needed more land to avoid exhausting their soil and to better respond to the demand for increased cotton production. They eyed the new land of the westward expansion to extend their slave-based agricultural system. Industrialists in the North opposed them and sought to limit the westward spread of slavery. These mounting political and economic tensions culminated in the Civil War, which the North, with its superior industrial might, won.[33]

Nineteenth-Century Reconstruction (1865–1877) and Redemption (1877–1896)

In the immediate aftermath of the Civil War, some Southern states passed segregation legislation designed to separate the races in public settings.[34] Under federal pressure, state governments removed these laws during Reconstruction. This period of so-called Radical Reconstruction included passage of the Thirteenth Amendment (outlawing slavery, ratified 1865); the Fourteenth Amendment (affirming citizenship rights to all those born or naturalized in the United States, ratified 1868); the Fifteenth Amendment (asserting the right of black men to vote, ratified 1870); and the first Civil Rights Act (1875), which undertook to secure for the Negro "full and equal enjoyment of the accommodations, advantages, facilities, and privileges of inns, public conveyances on land or water, theatres, and other places of public amusement," as well as the right to serve on juries. In particular, the passage of the Fourteenth Amendment extended citizenship and equal protection under the law to blacks. Many white men violently resisted these legislative changes and the undoing of slavery. Howard Zinn notes the murder of forty-six Negroes in Memphis, Tennessee, in May 1866, most of whom were veterans of the Union army or sympathizers. During the melee, white rioters burned ninety homes, twelve schools, and four churches.[35] Bobby Lovett notes that racial violence in Nashville was a means of perpetuating white supremacy in the wake of the South's defeat in the Civil War. The Ku Klux Klan was especially active in Nashville immediately after the Civil War, and members commonly attacked Negroes, especially after dark.[36]

Congress responded with legislation to protect blacks and outlaw attempts to overturn the gains of radical reconstruction. The Enforcement Acts of 1870 and 1871 provided federal protection for the Negro right to vote, and the 1871 Ku Klux Klan Act made it a federal offense to conspire to deprive Negroes of the equal protection of law. The federal government briefly stemmed the tide of racial violence, and social intercourse between blacks and whites increased in many areas. However, the South was eventually "redeemed" after 1877, and the political forces that backed the Confederacy and the traditional racial hierarchies of slavery reassumed control without restoring the formal mechanism of slavery.[37] The word "redemption" implies salvation, as if Southern elites "salvaged" the South from ruin. The unwritten agreement between North and South was that President Hayes, Congress, and the North in general would steer clear of the "Negro problem," leave Southern whites to decide how to govern the South, and provide blacks with limited civil rights.[38] By the 1880s new segregation statutes appeared as elements of the old Southern ways of life began to reassert themselves. In 1881 Tennessee passed the South's first Jim Crow law, segregating the races on railroad cars. Two years later, in 1883, the U.S. Supreme Court nullified the Civil Rights Act of 1875, which outlawed discrimination against Negroes in public facilities. The justices reasoned that the Fourteenth Amendment of the Constitution applied only to the actions of states and not to individual acts of discrimination. Other states acted similarly, the process culminating in the famous separate-but-equal doctrine issued by an eight-to-one decision of the U.S. Supreme Court in *Plessy v. Ferguson* (1896). In *Plessy*, the Court upheld the removal of a black man from a supposedly whites-only first class railroad carriage. The separate-but-equal doctrine remained in effect until overturned by the Supreme Court in *Brown v. Board of Education of Topeka* (1954).

Lynching was an integral aspect of the nineteenth-century Redemption of the South. Angry whites lynched more than one hundred blacks a year between 1889 and 1918. Since blacks made up the bulk of lynching victims, authorities rarely brought the perpetrators to justice.[39] Whites lynched many blacks who tried to assert their rights as sharecroppers. They lynched a smaller number of blacks for breaches of social etiquette, such as failure to step aside for whites on the sidewalk.[40] Local police also targeted blacks after the Civil War, arresting them for minor charges and releasing them to local employers as cheap sources of labor, thus re-creating, in many ways, old forms of servitude without reinstating slavery.

Policing in the North: The Bureaucratic Surveillance of the Poor

The bureaucratically trained and organized London Metropolitan Police model became the philosophical forerunner of modern bureaucratic police systems in the United States. The London model derived from patrol-oriented private policing designed to protect the slave-produced commodities of merchants on the docks in London in the seventeenth century. The newly bureaucratized American police systems that emerged during the middle to late nineteenth century modified the London model, tailoring it to a social system more concerned with local democracy and ward politics and highly suspicious of the potential threat posed by uniformed social control agencies.[41]

The army, militia, or yeomanry, groups typically drawn from social classes superior to the small farmers and laborers they controlled, traditionally quelled disorder in rural England. The yeomanry's response to food riots, machine breaking,[42] and other forms of political protest was often swift, bloody, and highly visible.[43] One of the most infamous excesses of the yeomanry occurred at St. Peter's Fields, Manchester, where an orderly crowd of working men and women had assembled to demand parliamentary reform. Local magistrates sent in the yeomanry, who killed a dozen people and maimed several hundred others in a highly visible display of bloodletting.[44] In the ensuing period, people sent threatening letters to yeomanry officers active at Peterloo, causing them to resign their positions.[45] More significantly, as Alan Silver notes, tragedies like Peterloo directly exposed the privileged landed gentry to the anger, resentment, and political radicalism of the impoverished, disadvantaged, and disaffected masses.[46] In rural communities and small towns, these vicious social control tactics sometimes brought the differences between the haves and have-nots into sharp focus and "made rioters more embittered."[47] Eric Hobsbawm and George Rudé note that by 1830 the English government had become increasingly reluctant to resort to brutal and mass violence as a form of social control because of the "rumbling discontent and agitation in the large industrial towns."[48]

Rising urban industrialists sensed that drawing the manpower for social control from the socially privileged presented grave problems and exacerbated class turmoil.[49] Traditionally, in times of social upheaval the landed aristocracy called out the yeomanry. However, neither the yeomanry nor the landed aristocracy had sufficient interest in protecting the property and lifestyles of the urban industrialists.[50] Consequently, the urban bourgeoisie promoted the idea of the London Metropolitan Police Force as a "class-neutral" social control apparatus.

The London Metropolitan Police Force emerged in 1829 as the first bureaucratically trained police force. Authorities presented the new police as a "preventive" as opposed to "reactive" force, emphasizing the need to build consensus with communities. The London model strongly influenced the rise of bureaucratic law enforcement agencies in the United States, where waves of immigrants had produced a cultural heterogeneity not present in England. These immigrants flooded into U.S. cities, bringing with them their own lifestyles, desires, needs, and expectations. Some police historians link much of the rising social disorder during the first half of the nineteenth century to this cultural pluralism. For example, Roger Lane attributes rising social disorder in mid-nineteenth-century Boston to "increases in the proportion of immigrants and the children of immigrants that continued to create social problems and friction."[51] Lane describes the Broad Street Riot of 1837, the third major riot in Boston in three years, in which a mob beat members of the Irish community.[52] Mayor Eliot restored order by using the militia. Because of these disturbances, Boston moved toward a regular, professional, preventive police force modeled on the London force. The new, full-time Boston police received salaries instead of fees and searched for trouble rather than merely responding to calls for service.

As James Richardson argues, the new preventive police in New York emerged in response to rising crime and urban rioting rather than simple population growth. From the mid-1820s, crime and disorder in the city increased rapidly. On February 15, 1840, the *New York Weekly Herald* noted nineteen riots and twenty-three murders in the preceding ten months.[53] Richardson traces calls for the reorganization of policing in New York to the period from 1841 to 1844 and notes the influence of the London preventive model on the eventual formation of the New York City Police Department in 1845.

Eric Monkkonen contends that the introduction and dispersion of the new police "was not a function of elite demands for class control, changing urban riots, or rising crime."[54] He goes on to argue that "if each city had adopted a uniformed force only after a riot, changing crime rate, or the need for a new kind of class-control agency, many places would not today have a uniformed police force."[55] Small cities adopted modern preventive styles of policing based upon what they learned from their larger urban counterparts. If the new police did end up targeting the proletariat, the unemployed, and the otherwise impoverished masses, it was only because these people committed the bulk of the offenses the public feared and condemned. If the new police did engage in class control, it was an unintended consequence rather than a deeply rooted master plan.

Other historians see the rise of modern preventive styles of law enforcement as a means to discipline and regulate discontented workers.[56] Such disciplining included undermining or breaking strikes and the moral management of working-class vice and recreational activities. Sidney Harring and Lorraine McMullin inform us that the local bourgeoisie dominated the ranks of command personnel at the Buffalo, New York, police department from 1883 to 1905. The department hired officers following strike activity, a telltale sign of their class-control function. Other researchers document a similar relationship between police hiring practices and strikes.[57]

Bruce Johnson argues the new bureaucratic police of the nineteenth century did not benefit employers to anything like the degree that state and private police have done.[58] He notes, "If criminal justice and police work in the United States constitute a system, it is not a unitary one. ... Today and over time, local public police have been accessible to the viewpoints and preoccupations of the American working class; many of their activities have and do serve to defend or extend the (modest) social privileges of this class."[59] Citing a number of historical examples, Johnson argues that local police sometimes sympathized with and supported working-class interests. During the Pullman Strike of 1894, the American Railway Union (ARU) brought the city of Chicago to its knees. Johnson argues local police and the public in general had tremendous sympathy for the strikers. For example, Chicago police "actively supported strikers' relief committees. They sought to interfere with an inflammatory anti-strike publicity campaign carried out by newspapers. ... Finally, these local police failed on numerous occasions to prevent railroad property from being damaged by protesters."[60] Eventually, Governor Altgeld had to call in the state militia and federal marshals, who killed thirteen people and seriously wounded fifty-three others. For Johnson, the management of the Pullman Strike epitomized the inability of large employers to rely upon local police to undermine labor radicalism.

Northern industrialists hired private police to thwart labor agitators. Indeed, Johnson notes the role of the Pinkertons, a private police agency, in breaking seventy-seven strikes between 1869 and 1892, including their work in providing evidence to convict Irish labor organizations such as the Molly McGuires.[61] Likewise, through their growing influence in state and national politics, industrialists called on federal forces against labor. Barton Hacker documents the strike-breaking role of the U.S. Army from 1877 to 1898.[62] Federal law enforcement agencies became more active during the Progressive Era (1900–1920), challenging the likes of labor radicals, anarchists, communists, and "dangerous" aliens, constructing them as a threat to American ways of life.

William Preston notes the confluence of these growing antilabor and antialien themes during and immediately after World War I and their culmination in the Palmer Raids of 1920.[63]

During the Great Depression police undermined, beat, and killed labor organization members, the unemployed, and the unaffiliated. Richard Boyer and Herbert Morais note the swirl of labor radicalism in the early to mid-1930s that attended mass hunger, poverty, unemployment, and despair. They note that "from the first, too, the demonstrations and hunger marches were regarded by police and government as initial steps in revolution. The police in a score of cities jailed and clubbed the unemployed with an almost unprecedented ferocity, justifying their actions on the grounds that the jobless were trying to overthrow the government." In particular reference to the 110,000 protesters in New York in March 1930, they note that "the vast throng was attacked by 25,000 police. Hundreds were beaten to the ground with nightsticks, scores trampled by the charge of mounted police. The police went as insane as they had fifty-six years before when they clubbed the unemployed at New York's Tompkins Square, and their excuse in 1930 was identical with that of 1874. The jobless . . . were communists."[64]

An eyewitness account by a Dr. Lewis Andreas recalls the police massacre of steelworkers and their families as they picketed Republic Steel on the far South Side of Chicago on Memorial Day 1937:

> The police were standing in line in front of Republic Steel. . . . It was a hell of a hot day, about ninety. They had their winter uniforms on. The sun was strong, and all I could see were their stars glittering. All of a sudden, I heard some popping going on and a blue haze began rising. I said, "My God, tear gas." . . . About three minutes later, they started bringing the wounded, shot. There were about fifty shot. Ten of them died. One little boy was shot in the heel. I took care of him. One woman was shot in the arm. They were lying there, bleeding bullet wounds in the belly, in the leg and all over. All sorts of fractures, lacerations. . . . I had absolutely no preparation at all for this. . . . I made charts of these gunshots. A great majority of them were shot from behind. The police weren't all bad. Some of them quit the force because of the incident. They couldn't stand what happened. . . . They were told to do this thing. They were told

these people were armed. They were scared, they were trem-
bling and they were shooting, at whom they didn't know.[65]

The policing of slaves, wageworkers, and the unemployed typically
perpetuated the advantages of slave owners and employers. However,
the idea of preventive policing was to discipline communities and nip
disorder in the bud. Foucault identifies the modern police as vectors of
a new discipline that sought a subtle form of compliance with law and
social rules. For Foucault, modern-era police reflected a much broader
shift away from the brutal and bloody power of the sovereign to exe-
cute, mutilate, torture, and otherwise brutalize their subjects. Authorities resorted to capital punishment, branding, flogging, and other brutal and public punishments much more frequently in the sixteenth
through the eighteenth centuries than their modern counterparts have.
According to Foucault, disciplinary power supersedes sovereign power
in the modern era. The detailed surveillance capabilities of postindustrial community policing present a classic example of the deployment
of disciplinary power.

Policing and Domestic Violence

Residues of sovereign power remain within families and kinship
systems in some Western societies. The patriarchal rights of men vis-
à-vis women and children, including the resort to violence to maintain
male authority, serve as examples. Patriarchal authority is a central
theme in Western history. As one historian notes: "In societies without
social welfare systems, police forces, or penitentiaries, father figures—
patriarchs—filled the roles of all three. They did not own wives and
children; dependents were persons at law, but could interact with the
state only—with rare exceptions—through the person of the independent male."[66] In some families, men used violence to control women.
That men's violence against their intimate female partners contravened
both the law and social mores does not mean that police, prosecutors,
and judges confronted it.[67] Policing typically addressed perceived infractions in public spaces as opposed to the private spaces of the family.
Neither slave patrols nor the newly bureaucratized police of the nineteenth century systematically confronted domestic violence. Historical
research in Eugene, Oregon, shows minimal levels of police intervention, arrest, and prosecution of abusive husbands.[68] Community polic-

ing does not seem to have increased law enforcement intervention in domestic violence cases. It is noteworthy that domestic violence receives little attention in community policing "promotional literature." For women of color, particularly black women, saturation community policing may appear to hold some promise for protecting them and their children against abusive men. But, as I will argue in chapter 4, battered women from the Nashville housing projects have not found this to be the case.

Reflecting upon the meaning of domestic violence in slave communities, Christopher Morris argues, "No matter how bad it was, it was never a slave's worst problem; that was slavery itself. Partners and parents could be vicious, but a troubled family life only made the primary ordeal for slaves—the relationship with the master—harder to endure."[69] It fell to the master and his overseers to confront domestic violence. Masters often had an interest in keeping slave families "harmonious," in order to reduce the number of runaways. Slave patrols did not see intervening in domestic violence among slave families as an important aspect of their work. Elizabeth Fox-Genovese notes the way Christian churches could censure or expel slave "husbands" who victimized their wives; however, it appears they rarely intervened.[70] Morris cites examples of anti–domestic violence advice in journals such as *Southern Agriculturalist* and *Southern Cultivator*.[71] Like Fox-Genovese, Morris notes that black men had limited authority over black women. With emancipation and the legalization of black marriage, the black family became more formally patriarchal, as black men assumed new legal and economic rights. Morris argues emancipation gave black men more power over black women and may have encouraged woman battering.

Police did not confront violence against slave women partly because the law did not elevate those transgressions to the level of crimes. Masters had free sexual access to their female slaves, who resisted them at their peril.[72] Some overseers also forced sex upon slave women under their supervision. This sexual tyranny continued a tradition predating the arrival of black women in the New World. On slave ships, traders and those in their employ raped black women as a means of instilling fear and effecting control. Some black drivers coerced slave women into sexual relations. Eugene Genovese remarks that "some drivers forced the slave women in much the same way as did some masters and overseers. It remains an open question which of these powerful white and black males forced the female slaves more often."[73] Although records exist from colonial Virginia of slave men prosecuted for raping slave women, this practice was unusual. Courts mostly ignored the rape of slave women, although some legislation protected younger slaves from rape by black men or mulattos, but not from white men.[74]

Slavery greatly restricted black men's control of black women and children. However, some male slaves still beat their female partners. Doubtless, these beatings influenced how slave women experienced their own home lives. Barbara Omolade traces an unbroken line of gender oppression back to slavery when she talks of the contemporary battering of black women. "Now, long after the chains have been removed, slavery continues in a new form inside the minds and hearts of Black people. Far too many Black women have become 'the slaves of slaves,' and their slave masters are Black men. Physical and mental abuse is a major reason Black women leave their husbands and mates."[75] However, although many slave women worked a double shift in the fields or the master's household and then in their own homes, Omolade argues many still saw their own home lives as a respite from slavery and a means of reproducing their people. She notes, "The very traditional experiences of motherhood and sex within marriage were not necessarily viewed as oppressive to black women. Marriage and motherhood were humanizing experiences that gave her life meaning, purpose, and choice."[76]

These observations about the historical condition of black women under slavery resonate loudly today in the housing projects of Nashville. Black women remain torn between loyalty to their people and maintaining black kinship systems, and the need to protect themselves and their children from violence meted out by their black partners. On the one hand, they seek police protection from interpersonal violence; on the other, many in their communities and they themselves see police as both agents and symbols of oppression and racism. In addition, it has been only in the last thirty years that police patrols have become regular features in many black communities. In the past police typically responded to "trouble" only if it got out of hand or spilled over into white neighborhoods.[77] In chapter 4 I return to the issue of domestic violence and all the compromises it involves for black people.

Policing Ghettos

Historically, police policies and practices perpetuated the advantages of slavers over slaves, employers over workers, and men over women. Political authorities mostly failed to define many other egregious social harms as criminal or violent. I refer here to diseases, injuries, and fatalities caused by occupational hazards, employer negligence, misleading advertising, and the like. In one classic study, Edwin Sutherland examined the histories of seventy large U.S. corporations and found that authorities handled a large majority of their offenses informally or through civil law.[78] This noncriminal approach stemmed in part from the high status of corporate leaders. Marshall Clinard, Peter Yeager, Jeanne Brisette, David Petrashek, and Elizabeth Harries found a similar situation with 582 of the largest U.S. corporations.[79] For most breaches of federal statutes, corporations received warnings. Over 80 percent of the fines were for less than $5,000; only sixteen corporate officials received prison sentences, and most of these spent less than a month behind bars. W. G. Carson reveals how under the Factory Acts in nineteenth-century England authorities "inspected" the great employers of the Industrial Revolution rather than "policing" them like street criminals.[80] Corporate offenses include, but are not limited to, the pollution of the environment, industrial accidents that cause the injury and death of workers and others, the production of unsafe consumer products, corporate fraud, and large-scale tax sheltering and evasion. It lies beyond the scope of this book to consider these offenses. They cause much more death, injury, and financial loss than losses traceable to street crime. A case could easily be made for identifying these offenses as forms of callous violence written off as a simple cost of production.[81] That authorities do not define such offenses as violent crime doubtless reflects the ascendancy of corporations over legislative deliberations and, particularly, the political construction of law.

We also witness the selective gaze of police in their historic failure to provide adequate services and protection to black ghettoes. Paradoxically, political authorities and the police have always targeted the offenses of black males more than those committed by whites. These two seemingly disparate historical themes are part of what some writers call "black control."[82] Although police arrested blacks for serious crimes, the bulk of black arrests reflected minor or trumped-up charges such as vagrancy, petty larceny, and disorderly conduct. Randall Kennedy notes how local police, during the aftermath of the Civil War, arrested unemployed black men and put them to work for employers who faced labor shortages.[83] David A. Gerber notes how white police in Cleveland interpreted black men's "hanging out" as loitering.[84]

Throughout the twentieth century, the brutal police treatment of blacks acted as the trigger for rioting and social upheaval in black ghettos.[85] The Kerner Report (1968), written by "representatives of the moderate and 'responsible' Establishment—not by black radicals, militant youth or even leftists,"[86] identifies white racism and the legacy of slavery at the heart of that disorder. President Johnson commissioned the Kerner Report to explore the roots of urban rioting and offer preventive recommendations. Significantly, the report notes: "the rioters—those ominous looters and arsonists— . . . tended, curiously, to be somewhat more educated than the 'brothers' who remained uninvolved. By and large, the rioters were young Negroes, natives of the ghetto (not of the South), hostile to the white society surrounding and repressing them, and equally hostile to the middle-class Negroes who accommodated themselves to that white dominance. The rioters were mistrustful of white politics, they hated the police, they were proud of their race, and acutely conscious of the discrimination they suffered. They were and they are a time-bomb ticking in the heart of the richest nation in the history of the world."[87] The report goes on to attribute the events of the summer of 1967 largely to the culminating effects of three hundred years of racial prejudice. More specifically, it adds that rioters wanted not so much to overthrow the U.S. government as to gain greater access to the perceived fruits of society. The report highlights various grievances in order of importance, including police practices, unemployment and underemployment, inadequate housing, inadequate education, poor recreational facilities, the lack of effective political mechanisms for dealing with grievances, racist and other disrespectful white attitudes, and the discriminatory administration of justice.[88]

The Kerner Report essentially recommended community policing alongside a number of other broader societal changes. With regard to law enforcement in the ghetto, it called for

- a review of police operations to ensure officers were behaving properly and not resorting to "abrasive practices"

- more protection for residents to "eliminate their high sense of insecurity . . . and belief in a dual standard of law enforcement"
- the introduction of fair and effective mechanisms for the redress of grievances directed at police
- the development of "innovative programs to ensure widespread community support for law enforcement."[89]

The report also recommended that local officials assign experienced and well-trained officers and supervisors to police the ghetto; develop detailed contingency plans in case of civil disorder; provide alternatives to the use of lethal weaponry; establish intelligence systems that would allow public officials and police to better anticipate and deal with disorder; develop continuing contacts with ghetto residents to make use of the forces for order that exist within the community; and establish mechanisms for neutralizing rumors and getting at facts.[90]

Community Policing as Twentieth Century Redemption (1980–2000)

In the chapters that follow, I identify community policing as a principal means of rolling back or undermining civil rights gains made by blacks from 1954 to 1968. I do not suggest that this is community policing's only function. Clearly, many people I talked with welcome some of the changes brought about by a heavier police presence in Nashville. Their main reservation is that those changes do not go far enough. In this sense, the concerns of citizens are in tune with those expressed by the Kerner Commission, which recommended a multipronged attack on the many disadvantages faced by inner-city blacks, not just a criminal justice initiative.

Community policing is more decentralized than the professional, hierarchical, paramilitary models of law enforcement that preceded it. Officers target communities within clearly defined geographical boundaries, attempting to strike up intimate ties with citizens, families, schools, neighborhood associations, and merchant groups. Community police officers have more autonomy than patrol officers and use more of a problem-solving approach to their work. These officers supposedly encourage citizen feedback and incorporate it into subsequent policies and practices. At the same time, community police officers interact more closely with other governmental agencies to broaden the scope of urban management strategies.

Some jurisdictions claim that new community policing programs lower crime, improve relations with the community, and refine intelligence gathering.[91] New York mayor Rudolph Giuliani initiated a get-tough community policing program in 1994, which some think substantially lowered violent crime rates.[92] However, by 1998 some residents of New York were complaining about increased policing, overly oppressive tactics, and violations of civil rights. Indeed, street sweeps, the harassment of youth, dubious searches and seizures of property, drug crackdowns, and various forms of brutality accompanied the initiatives in New York under the Giuliani administration.[93]

Skeptical criminologists emphasize that unemployment, poverty, and discrimination lie at the root of much crime.[94] These skeptics do not expect community policing programs alone to lower crime. Some critics go further and contend that community policing assumes a consensus about what the community needs when there is in fact no consensus—and perhaps no community—to speak of.[95] According to Peter Manning, the police, as the last line in formal social control mechanisms, can never realistically share power with citizens.[96] Indeed, liaison and consultation with the public appear to be highly selective. For example, recent research reveals that community police "gravitate toward those who were more receptive to police and whose problems may have been more tractable."[97] Put differently, there are clear limits to the extent of liaison between police and those on the street who regularly break the law. Reports from citizens in Chicago housing projects reveal that various combinations of community policing, housing authority initiatives, and federal drug enforcement interdictions have resulted in few positive long-term changes to their perceptions of safety and security.[98]

The cautions raised by the skeptics bring up important questions about the nature of social control strategies in the United States. In Nashville, the discourse on community policing developed alongside broader discussions about how best to manage the poor. Policing, urban planning, welfare-to-work initiatives, drug policies, housing regulations, and the historic loss of jobs all came under scrutiny. This book seeks to make sense of these interwoven social phenomena. Is community policing just old wine in new bottles, or does it represent a significantly more rigorous, invasive, and insidious form of social control? And perhaps most important, what do people think about policing strategies old and new? How do community and saturation policing contribute to the criminal justice juggernaut's assault on surplus populations?

The Nashville Poor

■ To the expression "the good die young" we might also add "the poor die young." Indeed, the citizens of poorer nations on average live many years fewer than those of wealthier nations.[1] Within all societies, the economically disadvantaged and their children have lowered life expectancies and suffer more disease than the privileged. A recent United Nations report on progress in 174 countries finds the gap between rich and poor widening, with the life span in sub-Saharan Africa only half that in the developed world. The Human Development Report notes that the top two hundred billionaires had a combined wealth of $1,135 billion in 1999, up by $100 billion from 1998. In stark contrast, the total income of the 582 million people in all the developing countries is worth just over one-tenth of this massive figure: $146 billion.[2] For the first time in its history, the UN argues that these disparities constitute human rights violations, which the report's main author, Richard Jolly, contends "must include economic, social and cultural rights, not just political and civil rights." As Jolly goes on to argue, global inequalities have increased during the twentieth century "by orders of magnitude out of proportion to anything experienced before." In a stinging attack on the divisiveness of global capitalism, the report points out that the gap between the incomes of the richest and poorest countries was about three to one in 1820, thirty-five to one in 1950, forty-four to one in 1973, and seventy-two to one in 1992.

In the United States infant mortality among the poor is twice that among the wealthy. Indeed, in the United States over the last four decades, the health and mortality gap between the wealthy and the poor increased greatly. These observations are nothing new. In medieval Europe the plague killed mostly the poor, who, unlike the wealthy, did not have the resources to flee the cities.[3] Living in overcrowded housing with rats, fleas, and domestic animals, the poor were exposed daily to veritable breeding grounds for the plague. Later, during the Great Plague of London in 1665, roughly three-quarters of the prosperous residents of the inner city fled. In his diary entry for July 30, 1665, Samuel Pepys wrote, "It was a sad noise to hear our Bell . . . toll . . . so often today, either for deaths or burials," and, later, on August 8, 1665, "The streets mighty empty all the way now, even in London, which is a sad sight. And poor Will that used to sell us ale at the Hall door—his wife and three children dead, all I think in a day." Pepys notes that 6,102 people died from the plague in one week, although the number was probably much closer to 10,000.[4] Sometimes the wealthy referred to the weekly *Bills of Mortality* that logged plague-related deaths. This information enabled them to gauge the extent of any outbreak, weigh their personal risk of infection, and make plans to leave the city. Fernand Braudel informs us that members of the royal court left London for Oxford in 1664 to avoid the emerging plague. Daniel Defoe noted the social distribution of the plague in his *Journal of the Plague Year:* "The misery of that time lay upon the poor, who, being infected, had neither food nor physic, neither physician nor apothecary to assist them."[5] According to Pepys, "the plague making us cruel, as doggs, one to another," brought out the most narcissistic of human tendencies, diminishing bucolic sentiments as the panic for personal and familial survival assumed center stage in peoples' minds. In many ways, the withdrawal into self and family when death was so close is understandable. In the streets of London, as the numbers of dead increased rapidly, people threw corpses onto carts, removed and burned them. During the day the number of people walking the streets diminished greatly. Pepys observed how those few people walking the streets were "walking like people that had taken leave of the world."[6] Similar desperation emerged during the plague of Genoa in 1656. Amidst the opulence of this very wealthy Italian port, a center of banking and trade, Braudel identifies "clandestine looting because its rich palaces were abandoned" as the wealthy fled the plague.[7]

That the rich could escape many of these problems was also obvious to the poor and probably engendered considerable anger and resentment. As Philip Ziegler argues, "As the poor of Genoa, Florence, Paris or London saw the rich and privileged bundle up their most precious possessions and flee the cities it would have been astonishing if they had felt no resentment, no sense that they were being deserted and betrayed."[8] It is also the case that the wealthy sometimes make use of the poor to enhance their own chances of survival, thus exacerbating class antagonism and conflict. For example, Braudel notes that, in the aftermath of the plague in Savoy, the rich would send a poor woman into their newly disinfected houses for several weeks "as a sort of guinea pig" to see if the plague had disappeared.[9]

The quarantined Nashville poor do not suffer from the plague. However, the disenchantment etched into some of their faces recalls Pepys's observation of victims of plague, who walk "like people that had taken leave of this world." In my travels, I interviewed a prostitute, Melanie, on Dickerson Road in Nashville, who told me she worked to provide for her two young children. Speaking very quietly and pointing to an old injury on her kneecap, she told me a john had shot her in the room of a nearby motel. As we talked, a pimp, adorned with a gold necklace, pulled up in a fancy car and eyed us up and down. Another man tried to sell me jewelry and was none too happy when I said, "No thanks." On another occasion, I talked with a crack addict, Ralph Bell, whom the police had picked up around midnight in the Edgehill housing projects. Ralph was near my age (midforties) and had been using crack for about fifteen years. Officer Smiley knew Ralph and told me, "He's lost a lot of weight in the last six months and probably won't last much longer." Both the prostitute and the crack addict had a distant look in their eyes, a deeply tired demeanor evincing what I perceived as a profound disengagement from or disenchantment with the world. Both were highly visible, intermingling with others on the street. Both were the objects of an insidious quarantine, a quarantine that does not remove them from physical circulation but instead bestows a pariah status on them that serves to powerfully limit their social participation, material options, and long-term life chances.

In the Nashville projects, plagued as they are by violence, drug use, and disease, one does not see corpses piled up on carts. The scale of death, dismemberment, and disease is much more modest than that observed in 1660s London. Nevertheless, in or around these housing projects, a significant number of young black men die from a plague of violence that offers a rather chilling twist on the meaning of the term "Black Death." Even larger numbers of black men have been incarcerated. Many of the army of the imprisoned belonged to quarantined communities in the housing projects, their formal incarceration merely serving to confirm that quarantine and amplify it by removing the "freedom" of physical circulation in wider society. This is not to say that the ultimate form of quarantining—early death—does not await many of these individuals.

The wealthy of cities like Nashville have long inhabited the safe suburbs, relegating blacks and a significant number of the nonminority poor to crowded, dilapidated, and increasingly segregated ghetto housing tracts. During the Great Plague, what remained in London was a profoundly disadvantaged and disenchanted population of the poor with greatly diminished life chances. What remains in the housing projects of contemporary Nashville is a similarly despondent, desperate, and quarantined group—albeit a group imbued with the virulence of joblessness, crime, drugs, violence, and disease rather than overcome by the rats, fleas, and plague germs that wreaked such havoc in medieval Europe.

Those who inhabit the housing projects in Nashville are subject to various rituals of exclusion marking them off as undesirable, undeserving, and even menacing. I am not talking just about the historical exclusion of Nashville's blacks from suburban housing or their lack of access to meaningful labor. I am also referring to the lack of access to daily services, consumables, and conveniences that mainstream society takes for granted. Just as the wealthy knew the poor would die in great numbers during the plague, suburban Nashvillians know the housing projects to be desperate, dangerous, and off limits.

One day, a pizza deliveryman joined me in the elevator in a Nashville hotel. I asked him if he delivered to the projects. He smiled a knowing smile and said, "Only during the daytime. We stop at around four P.M." Newspapers do not deliver to homes in some housing projects. Likewise, taxi companies are reluctant to service these areas. One woman, Tracy Barker, who performs volunteer work for a local Nashville battered women's shelter, told me: "I know there are sections of town that we cannot send a cab to in the middle of the night. The cabs won't go there. Pizza companies won't deliver a pizza. Where I work on Eighth Avenue North is like the edge of it, and we can't get pizza delivered to our office in the middle of the day. Something else, the newspaper. I know there was a point where they wouldn't go in there."

I investigated these rituals of exclusion. A customer service representative at the *Tennessean* told me that it is company policy not to deliver newspapers in the projects: it is too dangerous.[10] Similarly, I placed a call to a local Pizza Hut franchise to inquire if they would deliver to the projects. A surly gentleman told me emphatically, "The projects are 'red zones'; they have drug dealing, gang bangin', and everythin' else. We don't deliver there." A dispatcher at Allied Taxis in Nashville told me something similar, although she attributed the reticence to the employees: "Drivers don't want to go to the projects and won't go there." Of all the workers in the United States, taxi drivers are the most likely persons to die from homicide. Nashville taxi drivers know of these dangers, and one can hardly blame them for avoiding high-crime neighborhoods. Occasionally the newspapers enlighten us further on the deaths of taxi drivers. For example, police suspect a customer shot and killed Hiawatha Bennett, a sixty-one-year-old black taxi driver, in 1996. Hiawatha worked for Diamond Cabs and was apparently willing to drive to riskier parts of town where other drivers refused to go.[11]

These rituals of exclusion in contemporary Nashville, underscored by fears of contagion, notions of impurity, and ideas concerning good and evil, constitute the daily lifeblood of quarantining. This stylized form of segregation recalls Braudel's observations of parts of plague-ridden Europe: "The poor remained alone, penned up in the contaminated town where the State fed them, isolated them, blockaded them and kept them under observation."[12] Braudel's words seem startlingly relevant to the quarantining in major urban areas in the United States today. Indeed, the social reaction to the plague in medieval Europe is an apt metaphor for the regulation of the modern poor in the Nashville housing projects and the rise of community policing surveillance. Housing experts in contemporary Nashville would like to turn back the clock and scatter housing for the poor among well-to-do communities, thereby diluting and dispersing the effects of poverty. However, it is too late for this. The political reality is that while the municipal government can float bonds to build a nearly $300-million stadium, it cannot come up with the funding necessary to tear down the existing public housing structures and relocate families to safer, more upmarket facilities. As Gerald Nicely, head of the Metropolitan Housing District Administration for Nashville, told reporters, "It would cost five to six hundred million dollars to effect such a dispersion and relocation program." This is more than what is apparently available. He also noted that there was considerable political resistance to scattered-site public housing, an observation that recalls the long-standing historical resistance to integrated housing across the United States. Nicely told reporters that scattered-site housing units for the poor were "accepted in the neighborhoods pretty well. That's the better way to go, no question. If we were starting over again, that's the way we'd do it. Unfortunately, we can't start all over."[13]

Dense, drab public housing reflects the poverty of its residents. Residents have little personal space. People living under these conditions can hear the disputes of their neighbors. Street crime looms large. Discontent with these conditions has taken many forms. On my travels in the Edgehill projects, I could not help noticing the charred interiors of some of the communal Dumpsters. Dumpster burning was something that the first community police officers had to contend with. These fires alarmed area residents and city authorities. According to police officers I talked with, city authorities first assumed the Dumpster fires to be an expression of the irresponsible, careless, and antisocial behavior of some of the residents. Officer Olsen explained that residents actually torched Dumpsters because the contents festered in the summer heat and humidity to produce an unbearable smell; an odor only temporarily relieved with the once-a-week garbage pickups:

> We would have Dumpster fires two and three times a week. They would set them on fire and the fire department would come over here to put these things out. Well, when we were on our bicycles riding around over here, we found out why the Dumpsters were being lit on fire. It wasn't that people had

nothing better to do with their time and they wanted to cause havoc or chaos. It was because the Dumpsters stunk. In the summertime, when you put all that trash in there, they started stinking bad. Well, the quickest way to get rid of that stench was to light it on fire. Well, that's what they did. So I said to some of the people in the community, "Well, how often do they pick the trash up over here?" They said, "Once a week." They said it was nowhere near enough. In two or three days those things are full, and then they start stinking in hot one-hundred-degree weather. So, what I did was call the public works division. We had a real good relationship with public works and still do. I asked them how often do they pick up the trash Dumpsters. They said once a week. I asked them if there was any way to increase that to twice a week. He says, "Well, why?" And I explained that we were having to pull the fire trucks out of service that could be helping someone who really needed EMT protection. We were having to pull them over here to put out these Dumpster fires two and three times a week. We're expending a lot of resources on that. Can't we empty the trash twice a week? And the director of public works said, "Never thought of it that way. A good idea." He did it, and the fires over here have pretty much ceased.

Not only did the fires "pretty much cease" in the wake of increasing garbage pickups, children in the community began painting the charred Dumpsters. Residents have not set the painted Dumpsters on fire. Likewise, the wall that cordons off the south end of the John Henry Hale projects from Charlotte Avenue is painted beautifully, reminding us that artistic inner-city energy coexists with crack pipes, fatigued faces, and street violence. These commemorative signs and symbols speak to the transforming beauty that accompanies urban misery.

Studying the Poor

It is not my intent to offer a precise statistical description of poverty among Nashvillians.[14] Neither is it my purpose to scrutinize the more "objective" aspects of poverty. Doubtless such objective and statistical approaches are helpful in discerning broad patterns of disadvantage. Indeed, many studies of poverty resort to statistical ways of knowing about the social world, identifying income, the value of housing, the concentration of population, the number of dependent children per household, and other so-called variables. However, amidst this plethora of variables we lose something crucial about the social condition of the poor—namely, the historically and socially situated meanings attached to poverty by the poor themselves and those who encounter them. This loss is lamentable but not new. Writing nearly a century and a half ago about the social condition of the London poor, Henry Mayhew emphasized. "One of the most remarkable and distinctive features of the present age is the universal desire for analytical investigations. Almost every branch of social economy is treated with a precision, and pursued with an accuracy, that pertains to an exact science. . . . Figures and statistics everywhere abound, and supply data for further research. . . . The science of investigation is admirable as far as it goes . . . but it must become the pioneer to tangible results, or its utility will by no means be apparent."[15]

Sociologists frequently use the term "underclass" to describe that group of acutely impoverished inner-city residents who typically do not work for wages, who receive benefits, and who often live in public housing in households typically headed by single females. The underclass also often includes the intimate male partners of these women or those male friends who rely on subterranean criminal activity for income. Like the women, these men are marginal to capitalist production. Violence, drug dealing, antisocial behavior, and social despair blight underclass neighborhoods. In Nashville these neighborhoods are largely African American. Black fathers are typically absent from the family home because of death, incarceration, or the unavailability of well-paid work.[16]

Writing in the nineteenth century, Karl Marx used the term *"lumpenproletariat"* to refer to that "social scum, that passively rotting mass thrown off by the lowest layers of the old society."[17] It is unlikely that Marx saw the *lumpenproletariat* as a distinctive class, since it had little potential for developing class consciousness or engaging in collective action. Marx's judgmental description of the *lumpenproletariat* is consistent with Victorian middle-class values.[18] "Social scum" and "rotting mass" are hardly terms of endearment!

In many ways, the current debate about poverty does not focus on social class, certainly not social class in the sense intended by Marx, who believed that classes form at the point of production and are structured by the ownership and/or control of the means of production. Marx's two great classes of capitalism were the minority bourgeoisie, which owned and/or controlled the means of production, and the majority proletariat, which consisted of the growing mass of exploited laborers who had nothing to sell but their labor power. Today, people talk much less of the evils of capitalism. When conservative and liberal politicians talk of the worldwide spread of democracy, they are really referring to the expansion of capitalism.[19] Politicians typically take the existence of American capitalism for granted. They interpret social problems in terms of the loss of manufacturing jobs, the decline of educational provisions, moral decay, the imperfections of democratic representation, and the ruination of young black males through drug use, drug dealing, violence, and mass incarceration. They are most reluctant to interpret black urban unemployment for what it is—a product of global capitalism. The dominant viewpoint is that all is well with the U.S. economy and that anyone could find meaningful labor if he or she would just look.

Accompanying this dominant media view is the retinue of academic apologists who abhor the plight of the poor while recommending piecemeal reforms that reproduce the domination of the very wealthy. For William Julius Wilson, whose latest book's jacket contains promotional statements from Senator Daniel Patrick Moynihan, the world of the "new urban poor" stems from joblessness in the inner city.[20] By joblessness, Wilson is referring to the loss of relatively well-paid manufacturing jobs and the accompanying rise of poorly paid service sector jobs. These changes in urban centers have accelerated since 1970 and represent a major break with the past, signaling serious social malaise at a time when the U.S. economy appears to be very strong. Wilson comments, "Despite increases in the concentration of poverty since 1970, inner cities have always featured high levels of poverty, but the current levels of joblessness in some neighborhoods are unprecedented."[21] In short, he argues that the concentration of poverty in inner-city neighborhoods has increased greatly since 1970, with young black males the most adversely affected. For Wilson, the concentration of poverty, joblessness, and the accompanying social malaise in certain inner-city neighborhoods is not simply a product of historic segregation, as some authors have suggested.[22] Doubtless, he notes, enduring patterns of racial segregation have played a significant role. However, it is the loss of wage work that has wreaked havoc and produced a "new urban poverty," which is accompanied by a plethora of what he calls "social pathologies," including crime, family breakdown, and poor educational provision for children. In relation to Chicago, Wilson notes, "In 1990 only one in three adults ages 16 and over in the twelve Chicago community areas with ghetto poverty rates held a job in a typical week of the year."[23]

Wilson's vague focus on people's life chances in the marketplace fails to develop three essential points. First, the plight of black men and others stem from an increasingly inhumane global capitalism. Just as capitalists used blacks as cheap sources of labor and as strikebreakers, the globalization of capital disproportionately affected its less skilled and more vulnerable workers, namely young black men. Second, the deep historical forces of racism also inform the contemporary degradation and marginalization of blacks. These forces predate colonialism, although colonialism witnessed an amplification of racist ideologies, particularly as a means of justifying the exploitation of native labor.[24] In their contacts with other peoples, Europeans typically depicted non-Christian others as uncivilized pagans. Indeed, this logic formed the cornerstone of slavery. Cornel West traces the portrayal of white/black dichotomies as good/evil, true/false, pure/impure back to the biblical account of "Ham looking upon and failing to cover his father Noah's nakedness and thereby receiving divine punishment in the form of blackening progeny. Within this logic, black skin is a curse owing to disrespect for and rejection of paternal authority."[25] Third, we cannot explain the peculiar plight of impoverished black families and black women only through race or class relations. We must explore gender relations as well. In many ways, the relationship between black women and the postindustrial state recalls that between slave women and their masters. It is also essential to examine the power relationships between black men and women, taking care to explore the attenuated patriarchal privileges of black men, which are mediated and limited by the criminal justice juggernaut and echo their previously limited rights over black women under slavery.

Identifying the precise extent of ghetto poverty is not as easy as it might appear. A number of ghetto dwellers earn good money. Doubtless, we could include some drug dealers in this group, even though their income is not easy to quantify using standard statistical approaches. Paul Jargowsky and Mary J. Bane define ghetto neighborhoods as those in which at least 40 percent of the residents are poor. They comment, "the areas selected by the 40 percent criterion corresponded closely with the neighborhoods that city officials and local Census Bureau officials considered ghettos. . . . We are convinced that the 40 percent criterion appropriately identifies most ghetto neighborhoods." These researchers found that as the proportion of the poor increased, so too did the proportion of minority residents in these ghetto poverty tracts. In Memphis, they found that the ghettoes were nearly 90 percent black; in Philadelphia, blacks and Hispanics constituted nearly 85 percent of ghetto residents.[26] Other researchers point to a similar concentration of minorities in urban ghettoes.[27]

The vast majority of the American population is in debt, predominantly in bloated mortgages and inflated credit card bills. Most academic debates about poverty fail to point out these basic fault lines in the capitalist economy. Government researchers and academics dwell endlessly on gradations of income within the population, never really coming to grips with the fundamental idea that social classes form at the point of capitalist production. The bourgeoisie own or substantially control the capitalist economy; the mass of workers does not. Put simply, a few do very well while the majority struggle. Michael Zweig attributes the growing inequality in U.S. society to the increased power of capitalists and the reduced power of workers. He notes that between 1980 and 2000 the American working class has not only experienced a reduction in real income, but also spent more time at work, enjoyed fewer protections through either labor unions or governmental regulation, and experienced inferior schooling for its children. For Zweig, the capitalist class constitutes about 2 percent of the working population. The middle class, about 36 percent of workers, consists of professionals with a fair degree of autonomy, small-business owners, and middle managers. The working class (those who take rather than give orders), defined by their lack of power in the workplace, represents 62 percent of workers. Zweig challenges the myth that in postindustrial America people have become mostly middle class.

Official governmental interpretations of poverty treat us to a plethora of statistical obscurities about who is really poor, what educational levels these folks have attained, what kind of housing they live in, and so on. The hallowed unit of analysis is the "census tract," a bewildering category that seems to bear little resemblance to actual social life or, more simply, real neighborhood boundaries. Put bluntly, census-tract analyses obscure the fundamental class divisions of capitalism between those who run the economy and those who run in place.

The most impoverished and alienated people in contemporary society often live in urban ghettoes. This does not mean that those in rural areas do not experience acute poverty. However, it does mean that the spatial concentration of poverty and the social amplification of misery tend to be much more acute in the inner city. Edward Luttwak notes the inevitable presence of what many call "underclass pathologies." According to Luttwak, these pathologies stem from what he calls "turbocapitalism," or capitalist enterprise freed from government regulation, unchecked by labor unions, dismissive of the needs of employees, with unrestricted investment options, and increasingly less burdened with taxation. He notes, "The vivid drama of suicidal addiction, endemic crime and chaotic families conceals a much simpler and in a way an even more brutal reality: as the total economy becomes deregulated, computerized and globalized, it has less and less need for non-creative, routine labor of any sort, blue collar or white collar, no matter how sober, stable or hard working."[28] For this displaced army of the disenchanted, crime and other opportunities beckon. We ought not be surprised.

Drug use and drug dealing are common in ghetto communities, as well as in many other communities. Drug use is one way of dulling the pain of acute poverty and disenchantment. Drug dealing is an economic survival strategy, the fruits of which filter down to many in the community, although the bulk of the harvest accrues, like capitalist wealth itself, to the privileged few.[29] One woman in Nashville, recently shot in the crossfire between drug dealers, told me that the young men who lived three doors down from her "dealt drugs to make a fast buck." Authorities have packed the jails and prisons of America with young black men convicted of crimes related to the drug trade. One consequence for these men is the acquisition of a criminal record, thus making it more difficult for them to compete for increasingly scarce jobs. With roughly 5 percent of the world's population, the United States incarcerates roughly one-quarter of all the world's prisoners and holds a higher proportion of its own population in jails and prisons than does any other country. Currently, over 2 million people are behind bars in the United States, with another 3.7 million on probation or parole, making a total of at least 5.7 million citizens under the auspices of the criminal justice system.[30] Of those incarcerated, at least one-third are black males. The removal of these men from the streets is probably one reason why crime in the ghetto is not at much higher levels. The constant turnover of street-level drug dealers creates job vacancies for up-and-coming young men. Perhaps, in a rather warped and chaotic fashion, this turnover sharpens the aspirations of some youth, who admire the gold jewelry, nice cars, and other status trappings of success, however illegal.

The lucrative, safe, and respectable employment opportunities in the incarceration industry reside far from the ghetto. Duncan Campbell reports estimates that companies such as Goldman Sachs and Merrill Lynch "write between $2 billion and $3 billion in prison construction bonds every year. . . . So much money is invested in incarceration that politicians would find it difficult to reverse the trends against the wishes of their financial backers and lobbyists. . . . The annual bill for incarcerating prisoners is up to $35 billion. The prison industry employs more than 523,000 people, making it the country's biggest employer after General Motors."[31] Numbers like these provide us with some sense of the economic underpinnings of the American criminal justice juggernaut. These kinds of investments provide a sense of the economic and political inertia underlying postindustrial punishment. As I will argue in later chapters, the criminal justice juggernaut manages what John Irwin once called the "urban rabble."[32] In so doing, it artificially lowers official unemployment figures without providing the kinds of welfare services made available in European capitalist economies.

The crack cocaine trade really took off in the mid-1980s. Cheap and easy to smoke, crack has hooked many into the pursuit of transient states of ecstasy in neighborhoods short on hope and traditional aspirations. Elijah Anderson shows how the drug trade negatively affects entire communities in cities such as Philadelphia and Chicago.[33] In short, those who research these neighborhoods agree that they are places that make raising children a hazardous venture at best. At one time networks of mothers and older women in the black community provided mutual support.[34] Ironically, as the proportion of single-female-headed households increased, the support networks among women in public housing projects seem to have deteriorated. This deterioration of support in the matrilocal housing projects stems from the rise of a more hostile criminogenic culture on the streets. As I will argue later, the criminal justice juggernaut was the direct cause of this erosion of support among mothers, making it more difficult for them to raise children. At the same time, the authority of these female heads of household decreased, making it much more difficult for them to discipline neighborhood children, act as sources of support for their own daughters, and serve as role models for what Anderson unfortunately calls "decent" behavior. As Anderson notes, "These women universally lament the proliferation of drugs in the community, the 'crack whores' who walk neighborhood streets, the drug dealers who recruit the youth of the neighborhood, the sporadic violence that now and then claims innocent bystanders."[35]

The violence, drug use, and family breakdown in the projects accompanied the growth of more acute forms of apartheid in those neighborhoods. From the New Deal of the 1930s, federal housing policies encouraged whites, but not blacks, to buy their own homes, which helped confine blacks to inferior housing in the inner cities.[36] The Housing Act of 1949 authorized construction of 810,000 public housing units in the following six years in a bold move to replace many urban slums with more acceptable homes. In urban areas across the country, racially segregated housing projects emerged within central cities. Local builders, realtors, and moneylenders worked together with local government officials to keep old and emerging neighborhoods racially segregated.[37] The Housing Act of 1954 made funds available for urban renewal. City fathers across the country used these funds to tear down slums and the homes of the poor and sell the cleared land to private developers. Jill Quadagno notes that by 1960, authorities had torn down 400,000 homes, many of them inhabited by blacks, and replaced them with only 10,760 low-rent units. In the newly cleared urban spaces, developers erected "enterprise zones" comprising shops, hotels, and office blocks. "Urban renewal," as Quadagno notes, became a euphemism for "Negro removal."[38] "Enterprise zones" have a long history in the provision of American housing and have resurfaced in Nashville as part of the community policing initiatives, particularly in Edgehill. As I will argue later, the rise of enterprise zones is part of an ongoing diaspora or dispersal of black populations, which limits community cohesiveness and dovetails with the rise of the best-funded of federal housing programs—the confinement centers of the criminal justice juggernaut.

Before the passage of the 1964 Civil Rights Act, suburbanization continued swiftly, with over half of new industrial buildings, stores, hospitals, and schools being built outside central cities. During these years, transportation costs increased greatly, and new jobs in the suburbs became essentially inaccessible to many blacks. Although the Civil Rights Act banned discrimination in housing receiving federal assistance, this did little to undo segregation; by 1963, the Federal Housing Authority (FHA) and the Veterans Administration (VA) financed less than one-fifth of new housing. In addition, authorities weakly enforced the ban on discrimination. In 1968 the Kerner Report noted that "fifty-six percent of the country's non-white families live in central cities today, and of these, nearly two-thirds live in neighborhoods marked by substandard housing and general urban blight. . . . In the Negro ghetto, grossly inadequate housing continues to be a critical problem." The report also noted that "Thousands of landlords in disadvantaged neighborhoods openly violate building codes with impunity. . . . Yet in most cities, few building code violations in these areas are ever corrected, even when tenants complain to municipal building departments."[39] As noted in chapter 1, residents of urban ghettoes that exploded in violence and destruction during the summer of 1967 identified dissatisfaction with housing at the center of their overall discontent, along with unemployment, underemployment, and inappropriate policing strategies.

The 1968 Housing Act encouraged the FHA to reimburse lenders who made somewhat riskier loans to the poor so that they could buy homes. The legislation required buyers to contribute only 20 percent of their income toward the mortgage. Builders seized upon this opportunity to inflate the prices of homes they sold to the poor, skimming the difference from the federal government. The owners themselves still contributed only one-fifth of their incomes regardless of the price of the house. These developments applied only to federally funded housing, a form of housing rejected by suburbanites, who employed an array of tactics to make it very difficult for denser housing for the poor to penetrate their neighborhoods.[40] The suburbs remained almost exclusively white. As Quadagno notes, by 1973 President Nixon had declared "a moratorium on all subsidized housing programs, pending a re-evaluation."[41] Within months, Nixon recommended a shift of federal monies to the rental market, with families paying up to 25 percent of their income to private owners as rent. The development of Section 8 housing shifted responsibility for providing low-income housing to the private sector and its links with local and state housing authorities.[42] In the early years of the Reagan administration, when U.S. turbocapitalism really took off, the federal government dramatically reduced subsidies for housing, from $26.1 billion in 1981 to $2.1 billion in 1985. Again, as Quadagno notes, Reagan asked that housing recipients increase their rental contributions from 25 to 30 percent of their income, a raise few challenged.[43] To initiatives such as these, early in Reagan's first term, we can trace the rather rapid demise of "social caring" in this country.

The disappearance of manufacturing jobs and the rise of lower-paying service jobs have made it more difficult for families to put food on the table, pay rents and mortgages, and meet other financial obligations, thereby pushing some people into homelessness. The abandonment of cheaper inner-city rental properties by landlords has added to the shortage of affordable housing. Gentrification increased the cost of some inner-city housing and displaced less desirable rental properties.[44] Homelessness stems from rising poverty and the lack of affordable housing. The decarceration of mental health patients without sufficient aftercare increased the ranks of the homeless.[45] Studies suggest that women comprise about a quarter of the total homeless population, a significant shift from a few decades ago, when nearly all the homeless were male.[46] For some of these women, their exposure to domestic violence is a significant cause of their homelessness. Rather than remain in the violent home, they seek some kind of shelter housing or try to survive on the streets.[47] As we will see in chapter 4, interpersonal violence against women in the housing projects creates special compromises, difficulties, and fears for very poor women.

The Nashville Poor

Across the country, HUD policies were at the center of civil rights unrest. Quadagno notes the complaints of civil rights groups "that the Nashville Housing Authority employed few African Americans, that less than 15 percent of the public housing units were integrated, and that the Housing Authority had failed to adopt a satisfactory plan for assigning tenants to housing."[48] Modern-day segregation of public housing in Nashville traces a line back to slavery. Blacks came to "Nashborough" from the time of first settlement in the late 1790s, representing roughly one-fifth of the early population.[49] Although free blacks suffered discrimination, they were important labor sources in the early local economy. During slavery, blacks and whites lived near each other, even though they had their respective socially segregated spaces in churches and other settings. It was not until the Civil War, when fugitive slaves entered the town in large numbers, that a "black centre" emerged in Nashville.[50] In October 1865 the Freedmen's Bureau relocated thousands of blacks from Nashville, Memphis, and Chattanooga to work for white farmers in the surrounding countryside.[51] The bureau allowed white farmers to pay off the fines of blacks arrested for infractions, including "talking too loud," "using bad language," "speeding in a wagon," "driving a wagon on a sidewalk," "having a party without permission," and "running and drumming."[52] At the start of nineteenth-century Reconstruction, Nashville had five Negro areas (Edgefield contraband camp, Black Bottom, Edgehill contraband camp, Trimble Bottom, and northwest contraband camp) besides the "black centre."

The northwest contraband camp consisted of plank buildings and was "heavily black and poor." Between 1925 and 1965, urban renewal saw the disappearance of all but three churches, a nightclub, and a community center. Lovett describes Black Bottom as a "foul area . . . because of frequent flooding and the ever-present black mud and stagnant pools of filthy water."[53] The blacks who inhabited Black Bottom lived in crowded tenement housing and originally labored for the Union navy on the nearby Cumberland River. Black Bottom residents also lived among brothels, gambling joints, and saloons, constantly negotiating crimes of vice, a situation that earned Black Bottom the reputation of the most hated slum in downtown Nashville. As the plantations began to break up during Reconstruction, blacks moved into the Edgehill contraband camp on the southern border of Black Bottom. In Edgehill, Lovett notes the development of an aspiring working-class community, more respectable than its degenerate neighbors in Black Bottom.[54] The Edgefield contraband camp was the fourth Negro neighborhood and grew out of a Union army encampment on the eastern side of the Cumberland River (later East Nashville). Trimble Bottom was the fifth Negro community to appear in Nashville. Built on low-lying land, Trimble Bottom was subject to flooding and disease. Black residents of nineteenth-century Nashville lived in crowded, dilapidated housing that was often not completely weatherproof, without proper sanitation, surrounded by unpaved gullies and stinking brooks and creeks, and, at times, transected by railroads. Trimble Bottom, Nashville's oldest surviving black neighborhood, did not get sidewalks or sewers until the 1970s. Today blacks occupy the worst housing in Nashville, just as they tend to across the country.

As Nashville expanded and suburbanization continued, Lovett notes that "the city's inner core became blacker because the suburban movement caused outlying county properties to increase in value, forcing poor Negroes to relocate to cheap inner city rental districts."[55] The growth of Nashville did little to improve the general living conditions for most blacks. Their mortality rates were much higher than those of whites. The homes of the Nashville poor at the start of the Great Depression had no indoor plumbing, electricity, natural gas, or furnaces. As Don H. Doyle notes, "All but a few relied on outdoor toilets, kerosene lamps, coal stoves for cooking and heating, and a hydrant down the street for water. . . . Health conditions . . . were appalling. . . . The city's death rates remained high, especially among the poor black population."[56]

At the turn of the century, four out of five black families rented their homes. Black men still performed mostly menial, poorly paid labor, with at least half of black women servicing the homes of whites, just as they had done under a somewhat different social regime during slavery.[57] Nevertheless, historians describe a rich community life in black Nashville in 1930, with much street life, social intercourse, and men and women playing out their respective social roles at the same time as working hard at demanding, albeit not well-paid, jobs.

Historically, the city fathers used the railroad tracks (roughly an east-west axis) to separate blacks from whites. A minimal number of roads crossed those tracks to join the two communities. With few blacks owning cars, their only option was to walk into white neighborhoods. Even today, reaching the largely black-occupied public housing projects such as John Henry Hale, north of Charlotte Avenue, is a challenge. While it was problematic to walk from the black community across the railroad tracks to the nearby white community, the city fathers made it very easy for black domestic servants to travel by bus to the "posher areas of west Nashville and Belle Meade from these same black quarters. . . . It was meant to be this way, for the bus routes, as they had been in countless Southern cities, were drawn up to ferry maids to and from middle- and upper-class white homes, where black women could find work."[58]

Segregation in housing extended to the new public housing projects; Cheatham Place for whites and Andrew Jackson Court for blacks,
both completed with Public Works Administration funds during the
New Deal. Local landlords and realtors opposed the extension of public
housing in Nashville, arguing that it was a threat to the private market.
In spite of their resistance, over the next three decades public housing
projects developed around the declining central business district, often
being sandwiched between freeway links or other main thoroughfares
to the much wealthier suburbs. The ring of public housing was essentially a spatial, racial, and social-class buffer that served to segregate
the very poor, many of them blacks, and, from the 1960s, growing numbers of single-female-headed households.[59]

Urban renewal in downtown Nashville began in earnest in the late
1940s. Like other medium and larger cities across America, Nashville
witnessed a steady process of suburbanization as wealthier inner-city
residents moved out to independent municipalities like Belle Meade
(incorporated in 1938). Owners of the old nineteenth-century mansions
that originally ringed the business district sold them or turned them
into rental units. These units became slums surrounded by brothels
and gambling dens. The Federal Housing Act of 1949 facilitated "urban
renewal," cleared many of the slums, and replaced them with parking
lots and office buildings. As across the country, most of the homes torn
down belonged to impoverished black residents. In Nashville, as in
other cities across the United States, urban renewal did mean "Negro
removal."[60] Some of the established residents moved into emerging
public housing, others made alternative arrangements. Urban renewal
diminished community cohesion in black neighborhoods, continuing
the diaspora and the unsettling of blacks dating back to the capture of
slaves from Africa.

Wherever blacks lived in Nashville, most were likely to suffer abject poverty. As David Halberstam notes, the 1960 census revealed that
ordinary blacks in Nashville in the late 1950s got the worst jobs, housing, and education. Although the median annual income for the city
was $3,816, most black families managed on $1,500.[61] Heavily underpaid black domestics caught buses into wealthier white neighborhoods,
where they worked a five- or six-day week for fifteen dollars.

In the proliferating and mostly African American housing projects,
a sense of community still flourished. Neighbors knew each other,
women commuted to work as domestics or remained at home to raise

children. Men worked for wages, albeit lower wages than their white peers. Ironically perhaps, in the decades following the 1964 Civil Rights Act and the 1965 Voting Rights Act, certain things began to deteriorate for blacks in Nashville. As U.S. capitalism successfully infiltrated global markets, relatively well-paid jobs began to pass beyond the reach of inner-city blacks. Over subsequent decades, the housing projects became less sociable places. Crime became endemic, drug dealing and drug use rampant, violence flourished, and despair proliferated. Black women found it increasingly difficult to settle into stable relationships capable of providing sufficient resources for raising children.

The sharpening of existing inequalities between blacks and whites in Nashville seemed even more glaring given the extension of formal political rights in the shape of the Civil Rights Act and Voting Rights Act. Community life in the projects declined. This decline was painfully evident in housing projects such as Sam Levy, Settle Court, Andrew Jackson Homes, Preston Taylor, Edgehill, Vinehill Towers, J. C. Napier Homes, Tony Sudekum Homes, James A. Cayce Homes, and John Henry Hale Homes. Tracy Barker, a woman who worked in those areas back in the mid 1970s, described this decline:

Tracy: I used to work in those places . . . in 1974. My husband and I had little ice cream trucks. Soft-serve ice cream trucks. We had two. And we drove through those projects and sold ice cream. . . . And while I didn't sit in there at night, we went everywhere. I did Vinehill. I did Edgehill. He did Settle Court because it was a little more dangerous than the others . . . I'm a woman, and I had my daughter with me. Oh, I met some really great women, mostly women and kids, in there, and Vinehill, Edgehill, were racially mixed. . . . The other one on Murfreesboro Road [J. C. Napier] was mostly black. I never had any problems there. If I felt uncomfortable, I would leave. I never let myself get blocked in, I was in an ice-cream truck and I had cash. I never felt that my children were at risk. We didn't stay late, you know, eight-thirty we were done at the latest. The projects were not terrible places back then.

Websdale: Yeah. I wonder what's happened over the last twenty years, because it seems things have changed.

Tracey: Drugs. Drugs.

Websdale: Yeah?

Tracey: But they were around then. But I never felt harassed or bothered in any way. Back then my husband went to Settle Court and I remember him coming home and talking about it. He went to Settle Court and heard gunshots and just kind of backed up and left. But that was when gunshots were not the norm in those places. Now I understand that happens everynight.

Nowadays, most of the Nashville housing projects are frightening places. The specter of crime and violence looms large over the daily struggle to put food on the table, nurture family members, educate children, and hold out any hope for a brighter future. The threat posed by the streets was a self-evident truth for most of the people I talked with, and most were not concerned with how it came to be that way.[62] On street corners in public housing in Nashville, at the edges of neighborhood parks, at the ends of rows of public housing, young males stand watch for those who would buy drugs, who would intrude, or who might seek to colonize space for criminal activity.

In south Nashville, on the outskirts of the central business district and serving as a buffer between the relative tranquillity of the suburbs and that central business district, are four public housing projects: J. C. Napier, Tony Sudekum, Vinehill, and Edgehill. Interspersed between these projects are a number of smaller public housing sites whose residents typically have significantly higher incomes than their peers in the projects. Murfreesboro Pike (Highway 41) is one of the main arterial highways leading out of south-central Nashville to the suburbs. On the edge of the central business district, Tony Sudekum and J. C. Napier nestle between Murfreesboro Pike and Interstates 40 and 24 (heading east; see map). Murfreesboro Pike is a main thoroughfare for johns seeking the services of prostitutes. As one heads into the city from the serene suburbs, one passes not only the occasional prostitute, but also the odd pimp, some adorned in gold chains, and perhaps exiting a fancy car. Approaching J. C. Napier and then Tony Sudekum, one may occasionally see an ad hoc street vendor selling various items, the origins of which remain unclear. In the space of thirty minutes, I witnessed a stall go up, the vendors selling white socks. When I returned, the two black vendors had moved on, I assumed having sold their wares.

Police presence and the "upgrading" of some housing projects in the southern sector of Nashville have also affected street crime, drug dealing, drug use, and community spirit. The drug trade and the violence associated with it have declined in and around the Edgehill projects and Vinehill Towers. These areas of public housing became part of the "Metropolitan Enterprise Community" (MEC) in 1996. The national Child Development–Community Policing program (CD–CP) selected Nashville as one of five sites across the country to replicate the original work started by Yale University and the New Haven Police Department. In July 1996 the Nashville Police Department joined with Family and Children's Services, a voluntary, nonprofit mental-health and child welfare agency, and sent a team of twelve people to Yale University for training. The MEC comprises roughly three square miles and is home to four public housing projects: J. C. Napier Homes, Tony Sudekum Homes, Edgehill, and Vinehill.[63]

Community police officer Ralph Olsen, who worked in Edgehill on foot and on bicycle patrol as part of the MEC initiative, told me:

> When we started community policing here in 1996, it was basically the Wild Wild West. Drugs were dealt freely. The drug dealers had no reservations about standing on the street corner. There was absolutely no respect for law enforcement at all, and that was not only from the drug dealers' perspective, it was from the citizens' perspective as well. Because when we would do some type of operation to do a reverse sting or something, the citizens would come out and be aggressive, throwing rocks and bottles at us. That was a nightly occurrence in the Edgehill projects. You would have rocks and bottles hurled at your car. Not a positive thing was said about the police. It took us about six months to get a foothold to where people would start calling us. What we did was we went door to door and handed out our cards with our personal pager numbers on them. We encouraged residents to let us know if we could help them with anything, with any matter. I mean, it didn't matter if it was a water bill issue or electricity getting cut off. After about six months, we started to see a crack in their shell. People started calling.

When I asked why they were so hostile toward the police, Olsen replied, "Part of it was conditioning. We've got some third-and fourth-generation families, and their main goal in life is to turn eighteen so they can get their own apartment or place over here in Edgehill. If someone is lucky, or fortunate enough or smart enough or dedicated enough, to get out of the projects, they really don't want to come back.

Most of every one of them is on some type of support. There are very few male father-figure types."

The Edgehill projects see less street violence now than before the arrival of community policing. However, street crime and violence still occur, especially after dark, when police presence diminishes. Holes cut in the wire fencing in the Edgehill projects enable young male drug dealers and others to elude police, who, being somewhat better fed and carrying various protruding weapons, are apparently too large to squeeze through and continue pursuit.

Barbara lived in Vinehill Towers for a few of months before it was refurbished. Her abusive ex-husband disabled her with his violence, leaving her with serious back and neck injuries. Before coming to Vinehill she lived in a well-to-do neighborhood and told me she hated her short spell in the housing projects. Barbara told a story of the way local drug dealers took a cut of some residents' disability checks or other benefits:

> The SSI checks come in a blue envelope. I figured that out the first month I was there. I'm asking, "Why is everybody waiting downstairs?" The night before the checks arrived, a guy was standing outside of the Towers saying, "Better pay the dope man, better pay the dope man." And I'm like, "Do what? What are they talking about?" So the next day everybody's getting these little blue envelopes. They go wherever they go and cash 'em, come back, and there were certain apartments. I finally figured it out. . . . On my floor, he was called a dope man, I know his real name and everything, but he'd take every penny of your money. I lived on the eighth floor. It was awful. There was this body, a man's body lying in front of the elevator. So I go to my apartment and I called 911. The police came and they put their finger right there on my head and they said . . . "Lady, you need to learn something real quick. You don't see nothing and you don't hear nothing. You're living in Vinehill Towers now."[64]

Barbara's experience with her SSI check is not unusual. It appears that the danger of having one's SSI check stolen depends upon the setting in which one lives. It could be that older, more physically infirm citizens fall prey more often to this kind of predation. One worker at a homeless shelter told me of a man regularly beaten up when his disability checks arrived. However, Officer Walt Miller, who has worked throughout the projects in Nashville since community policing was first introduced, told me that many people simply would not put up with such intimidation and bullying. Officer Miller explained that those who would steal such checks would take "whatever they can get their hands on. If they can intimidate somebody and get all of it, they would. Most people, though, won't put up with that." These observations regarding the vulnerability of some to having their SSI checks stolen and the resistance of others to this particular form of predation remind us that drug dealers and street criminals do not have it all their own way.

Those who live in the MEC are among the most impoverished people in Nashville, although the MEC comprises what city authorities see as the more "hopeful" or "salvageable" of the housing projects. A quick demographic summary of the residents of the MEC captures this impoverishment:

- 97.7 percent of the population is African American.[65]
- Females head 67.6 percent of families with children.
- The median household income is $4,999 per annum, compared with $30,223 for metropolitan Nashville.
- 74.5 percent of the population lives below the poverty line, with 52 percent of households on some form of public assistance.[66]
- 70 percent of households are located in public housing.

In 1996 a COPS (Community Oriented Policing Services) Ahead grant allowed the police department to hire twenty-seven officers and dedicate them to working in the MEC using a community policing philosophy. The grant divided the officers among the MEC. Currently, there are eight police officers and a supervisory officer in "alert centers" in each of three zones (J. C. Napier, Tony Sudekum, and Edgehill/Vinehill). The alert centers are multidisciplinary and home to police officers, social services, health services, and other organizations working within the MEC. The coordinated approach of the alert centers allows for better collaboration and provides the community with various services. For example, in the Napier enterprise zone the police alert center shares building space with the staffs of Family and Children's Services, the YWCA, Metro Social Services, the Dollar General Training Center, and local resident retail initiatives. In Edgehill, the alert center is next to the Dollar General Store. This service-delivery design dramatically increases access to needed resources, especially for those residents without any transportation.

The northern section of U.S. Highway 41 (Dickerson Road) weaves its way toward Goodlettsville, in the direction of Kentucky. Like its southern counterpart (Murfreesboro Road), Dickerson Road is also a haven for prostitution, pimping, gambling, the fencing of stolen property, and other subterranean criminal activities. At the point where Highway 41 exits the central business district and heads north, we find the infamous Sam Levy and Settle Court housing projects. These projects, located to the east of the Cumberland River, border the eastern edge of the I-40 loop. It was in the Sam Levy projects that some residents burned down the Dollar General Store and its neighboring adult learning center after police shot and killed a young black man they had stopped for questioning in 1997 (see chapter 3).

The other housing project in East Nashville is James A. Cayce Homes. With the lowest per-capita income of all the housing projects in Nashville, Cayce suffers much criminal activity. Ronette Cooper lived in the Cayce projects for nine years, developing a nerve-racking daily regimen for running the gauntlet of drug dealers and other offenders who threatened her and her two children's safety:

Ronette: I worked. I had two kids. I wanted to get out of there. Either you shut up or you go along with their game.
Websdale: Why do you think there is so much drug using and gang stuff in those areas?
Ronette: It's the only way they can make some money. They [dealers, street criminals] knew I had a job, took my kids to the sitter, and came back and more or less just slept there.
Websdale: Yeah. And they didn't try and sell to you?
Ronette: Well, they'd try to sell to me, but I locked my doors. Just like they tried to jump in my car, but I kept the doors locked. Yeah, yeah, thank God for automatic locks. They cut off the dope right in front of you, big chunks of stuff, and I didn't want my kids to see that.

Rolanda, from the James A. Cayce Homes, like Barbara from Vinehill Towers, told of witnessing a homicide; one day she opened her front door and saw a shooting. The victim lay dead at her feet. She saw the perpetrators, although they did not appear to have seen her. When police arrived she approached and told them who had committed the offense, only to be pushed into her home by officers and told, "You didn't see or hear anything, ma'am." The intent of the officers seems to have been to protect Rolanda from the perpetrators by not allowing her to come forward.

Cheatham Place is one of the "nicest" housing projects in Nashville, originally built to house low-income white residents.[67] Residents consider the nearby Andrew Jackson Homes, originally built for blacks, as another of the relatively safer housing projects. However, street crime is still a problem there. At a meeting of Mayor Bredesen's Violent Crime Commission, Bill Thompson, president of the Andrew Jackson residents' association, said that residents knew the criminals in his projects. However, they did not call the police about illegal activities because they feared retribution. Describing a recent incident in the Jackson projects, he said a man fired a shotgun several times and then told people he would "kill anybody who told police."[68]

Projects like Cheatham Place and, to a much lesser extent, Andrew Jackson Homes appear safer. This is perhaps because they house residents who are significantly older, less reliant on government welfare, less embroiled in all the compromises that dependence and poverty appear to bring, and relatively better off than residents in most of the other projects.[69] However, from my conversations with various people, it is not so much income level as how people receive their incomes that seems to influence the rhythms of street life, neighborhood cohesion, levels of crime and violence, and drug dealing and addiction patterns. Again, the most desperate housing projects in terms of crime, street violence, police calls, and the drug trade are those with the highest proportion of residents receiving welfare and the lowest proportions of seniors.

South of the Andrew Jackson projects lies Watkins Park, bordered on its southern edge by Jo Johnson Street. The John Henry Hale projects nestle into a densely packed area of land to the south of Watkins Park. The Hale projects are much more threatening than Andrew Jackson Homes, reflecting the remarkable changes that can take place in the social ecology of American cities within very short geographic distances. The Henry Hale projects are alive with drug dealers who hang out on the corner of Watkins Park and on Jo Johnson Street, keeping watch on the entrances to the rows of project housing and strolling across to the nearby dilapidated store on the north side of Jo Johnson. At night in John Henry Hale, especially in inclement weather, criminal activities flourish. The streets are dark, since drug dealers and other street criminals shot the streetlights out. In the dark, drug dealing, drug use, prostitution, weapons sales, and the fencing of stolen property are carried on with confidence and little chance of anyone, including the police, observing. On the fringes of John Henry Hale, especially in abandoned industrial areas and under bridges, prostitutes provide sexual services; the cost of oral sex is around twenty dollars, or, if they want drugs, a couple of rocks of crack cocaine. As Officer Miller told me: "John Henry Hale is a battleground. They're extremely aggressive over there. Police don't go into those projects on their own. It's not safe. To get out on foot in those areas you're asking for trouble. We've had rocks thrown at our cars, we've had tires slashed, gunshots nearby."

Preston Taylor Homes is a crowded, decaying, unsafe public housing project in northwest Nashville. Almost exclusively black, this complex of 550 homes will be rebuilt by the end of 2001. This millennial zeal is part of a federal project called HOPE VI; an initiative, according to the *Tennessean*, designed to "replace 100,000 of the nation's worst housing units' cramped, crime-infested dwellings . . . with communities where the poor blend in."[70] HOPE stands for Housing Opportunities for People Everywhere. Currently, Preston Taylor possesses 550 homes for the "very poor." The replacement development will have 340 nicer townhouses, all but 30 of them reserved for low-income residents.

Critics of the HOPE VI initiative complain that an HUD study of ten HOPE VI projects across the country revealed that fewer than half of the original residents found places in the upgraded housing. Preston Taylor Homes is the second largest public housing development in Nashville, and its residents are poorer than those who live within enterprise zones such as Edgehill. Nashville police reported 582 drug-related incidents in the Preston Taylor projects from 1994 to 1997. Police I rode with told me that the area is not amenable to community policing or, indeed, any form of policing. If they have to go in at night, police enter en masse and with great caution. Talking about policing in Preston Taylor and other housing projects, Edgehill Officer Andy Stevens told me that "Preston Taylor is very inaccessible. Settle Court is still inaccessible. J. C. Napier and Tony Sudekum have enterprise officers, but they have not had the response that we have had in Edgehill. They still have homicides occurring on a rather consistent basis."

HOPE VI plans for Preston Taylor include the building of a Dollar General Store and Training Center, a new elementary school, a community/child-care center, and a pedestrian/bike path linking the development to the city's "greenway" system. Critic John Fox, who fought a similar development in Seattle, described the HOPE VI project as a "Trojan horse . . . a tool that can be used to wipe out existing housing serving the poorest of the poor, with no guarantees for replacement."[71] Indeed, the same 1998 HUD study found that most residents who were not accommodated in the upgraded replacement developments ended up in other projects. HOPE VI involves the selective promoting of some of the poor and the reassignment of many others to existing housing projects. Housing authorities will not permit those with criminal records to live in the upgraded HOPE VI housing facilities.[72] This is precisely the philosophy of the federal "weed and seed" project: weed out undesirables like drug dealers and other criminals and seed the revamped community with a "new" opportunity structure. Though this may be to the liking of certain upgraded project residents, it means that those with criminal records will be rehoused in existing projects; thereby in the long term creating the possibility of a superconcentrated criminal population. As the *Tennessean* put it, "Pushing Preston Taylor residents with criminal records into places like Settle Court in Sam Levy Homes should send shivers through Metro police."[73] The HOPE VI initiative and all the talk of enterprise among the very poor also ought to send shivers down our spines. I would argue that the forced relocation of blacks, some to "better" housing, others to jails and prisons, is a fine-tuning of the historic diaspora of blacks.

A gathering of Mayor Phil Bredesen's Violent Crime Commission at the Preston Taylor project's community room in 1997 provided a forum for area residents to air their many concerns about the atmosphere in which they lived. Elizabeth Jordan, president of the Preston Taylor residents' association, told the audience, "At night, you can hear nothing but gunfire. You can hardly sleep. . . . It sounds so close, you don't know if it's coming through the window. . . . It scares the daylights out of me."[74] According to Captain William Hibbs, Nashville police handle about half a dozen calls a night regarding shots fired in the Preston Taylor Homes.

As noted, residents in Cheatham Place and Andrew Jackson Homes are much less likely than those of other projects to receive welfare as their primary source of income. As evidenced by police call data, the geographical distribution of homicides and violent crime, and my own ethnographic observations, these two older projects are more peaceful, less criminogenic, and generally safer places to live. Is this because welfare recipients are more likely to commit crime? or that housing projects composed of a higher proportion of welfare clients are likely to be more dangerous? Suffice it to say at this point that the welfare recipients in the more dangerous housing projects of Nashville are mostly single females with children. Like their counterparts across the country, they do not commit much violent crime themselves. Rather, as we know from crime statistics, younger males (of all races) are far more prone to criminal behavior, especially acts of violence.

Women who receive welfare payments as their principal means of survival lead deeply impoverished lives and encounter men who are also extremely disadvantaged. Among and between some of these men in the Nashville projects is much crime and violence. On numerous occasions, poor women told me they needed to supplement their incomes to raise their children and survive. For many, welfare payments are wholly inadequate, leading a number of them into relationships with men who deal drugs either on a small scale, as street dealers, or, in rarer cases, as owners of houses outside the projects from which they supply street-level dealers. Others have relationships with men who gamble in the women's homes or on their porches or back steps, paying them a portion of the "take" to do so. For a price, other women make their homes available to men as places out of which to sell drugs. In these so-called crack houses, younger women might offer up their bodies for prostitution. Sometimes johns pay prostitutes in cash, other times with drugs. Either way, the resident of the house who accommodates these activities, or the person who assents to them in her absence, receives some kind of kickback. Some women allow men to fence stolen property through their homes or store guns in them. As one woman who used to run such a house in the projects told me, "It all comes down to money and power."

Women who survive on welfare have told me how arduous it is to make ends meet. Some felt justified in deriving additional income from the subterranean economy to raise their families. The justification was the simple need to feed, clothe, and otherwise provide for their children. These women are not scroungers who have rejected mainstream social mores. Neither have they necessarily rejected the institution of marriage. Rather, many women reported that marriage was a difficult and unlikely ideal to realize given their circumstances and those of the men they met.[75] Women on welfare have few incentives to work for wages. They experience difficulties obtaining safe, affordable child care. They report wanting to mother their children and resent time spent away from them. Women also resent the low wages and the difficulties of traveling to workplaces. Work they qualify for is mundane, not satisfying, and service-oriented, reproducing their inferior social status. This type of work has a long history for African-American women, who, as I noted in the preceding chapter, worked as field hands and domestics on plantations. Given the difficulties in their lives, the commitment of these single women to their children is quite remarkable.

Many poor women I talked with expressed deep disenchantment with the welfare system. Such disenchantment has a long history. From the time of the New Deal, it was clear that government benefits were available to some groups and not to others. As part of the New Deal compromise struck between northern workers and white southerners, President Roosevelt refused to support legislation abolishing lynching or the poll tax.[76] Under the New Deal, the federal government excluded agricultural workers and domestic servants from old-age insurance and unemployment compensation, which blacks in particular relied on. The provision of federal benefits to poorly paid blacks in the South would have lessened the dependence of black workers on white employers who paid them poorly. At the same time as denying economic benefits to southern blacks, New Deal subsidies to southern farmers and landowners enabled them to buy labor-saving machinery, thereby creating further unemployment and contributing significantly to the migration of black agricultural workers to northern cities during the 1940s.

The rise of the welfare system dates back to the provision of mother's pensions during the Progressive Era. Between 1911 and 1920, forty states introduced pensions to ensure that impoverished widowed mothers did not have to toil in low-paying jobs to make ends meet, lose their children to institutional care, or be labeled as paupers. Despite laudable intentions, these programs dissolved into a stigmatizing and selectively funded initiative. The government funded women's pension programs mostly in urban centers and excluded large numbers of black women. Though they were resisted from the outset as a drain on scarce tax dollars, pension programs were federalized under the Social Security Act, thereby creating Aid to Dependent Children (ADC).

A 1939 amendment skimmed off what Theda Skocpol calls "worthy widows," so that social security's old-age and survivors' insurance covered these women. This left poorer caretakers (often black) as the principal recipients of ADC (which later became Aid to Families with Dependent Children, or AFDC), a group, as Skocpol notes, "without morally approved family histories."[77] During the 1940s and 1950s, states, especially those in the South, tightened eligibility requirements for ADC receipt. For example, Quadagno notes that "seasonal employment policies cut ADC recipients off the welfare rolls during cotton-picking season."[78] The addition of "man-in-the-house" rules enabled social workers to make unannounced policing visits to check for cohabiting men. Finding a man in the house provided a reason for removing female recipients from the welfare rolls. As the number of unmarried southern black women increased among ADC/AFDC recipients, so too did state policing of this acutely impoverished and stigmatized sector of the population. This selective policing of mostly poor black women provides yet another example of the state assault on black families.

Eventually, Congress loosened eligibility requirements in the face of much larger numbers of female-headed black households, with some legislators expressing concern that restrictive access to ADC caused an increase in single parenthood. The ranks of welfare recipients increased significantly, from 7.8 million in 1966 to 12.4 million in 1970. However, the Kerner Report notes 21.7 million nonelderly living below the poverty line in 1966. Therefore, two-thirds of the poor did not receive any public assistance to enhance their incomes, a fact bitterly resented by many and a testament to the futility of absolute distinctions between the working and nonworking poor. The report notes, "In most states benefits are available only when a parent is absent from the home. Thus, in these states, an unemployed father whose family needs public assistance in order to survive must either abandon his family or see them go hungry. This so-called 'Man-in-the-house' rule . . . seems to have fostered the breakup of homes and perpetuated reliance on welfare."[79]

The Kerner Commission articulated a longer-range strategy for improving the welfare system. It recommended "a national system of income supplementation to provide a basic floor of economic and social security for all Americans."[80] However, southern congressmen and representatives from chambers of commerce across the country strongly opposed President Nixon's plans for a Family Assistance Program (FAP) that would have increased the number of people eligible for AFDC benefits from 10 to 28 million and provided universal child care. In particular, the FAP would have significantly improved the economic lot of southern blacks, reducing their dependence on white employers. However, the FAP failed, and along with it the possibility of a national child-care system in the United States.[81]

The poor in the Nashville projects live well below the official federal poverty line. Making ends meet through welfare, or indeed a low-paying job, is virtually impossible and may be a setup for involvement in criminal activity. From her ethnography with low-income single mothers in Philadelphia, Kathy Edin reaches a similar conclusion. She notes, "It was nearly impossible for these women to make ends meet on either a welfare check or a low-wage job. . . . These single mothers and their children often went without items most Americans would consider necessities: adequate food or shelter, clothing, heat, electricity, telephone service, and adequate health care or health insurance."[82] Single mothers living in public housing projects are particularly vulnerable to interpersonal violence and abuse and drug addiction.[83]

Welfare reform put welfare under state control and was a major budget-cutting initiative, first projected as saving $54.1 billion by 2002.[84] The 1996 Personal Responsibility and Work Opportunity Act placed lifetime limits on the receipt of cash assistance at five years or fewer and made receipt of welfare contingent upon recipients' agreeing to engage in job training, education, or actual wage work for varying lengths of time. Temporary Aid to Needy Families (TANF) replaced AFDC benefits, and the number of women receiving welfare declined significantly.

In Tennessee the shift from AFDC to a program known as "Families First" began in concert with national welfare reform in 1996. Governor Sundquist's administration dreamed up the program's name. Readers ought not be misled and get the impression that families really matter; Families First removed roughly half of single mothers from the welfare rolls, forcing them into job training, education, and low-paid labor.[85] Given that only about 14 percent of Tennessee's children on welfare received child support, the state also proposed the installation of a $43-million computer network between state and federal agencies to track down deadbeat dads. Governor Sundquist proposed to revoke the driver's and professional licenses of parents of welfare children who do not make their child-support payments.[86] During the first two years of the program, 849 "deadbeat" parents (mostly dads) had their driver's licenses revoked for failing to provide child support. We might ask how the revocation of these licenses assisted these men in finding the work needed to make child-support contributions.

The budget for Families First totaled $71.5 million, with $50.6 million coming from the state and $20.9 million from the federal government.[87] This budget replaced the $219-million AFDC budget, which provided monthly cash assistance to 240,557 people in Tennessee. To qualify for Families First, most of the 72,814 adults on welfare in Tennessee in 1996 signed contracts saying they would agree to work, search for jobs, seek education, and train for work. In return, the state would offer support with child care. If those people did not live up to their part of the "bargain," they would be subject to removal from the rolls. For those enrolled in Families First, authorities placed a five-year lifetime limit on the receipt of benefits. For most who participate, the state eliminates cash benefits after eighteen months.

The shift from welfare to work caused considerable anxiety for the ranks of the Nashville poor. These growing anxieties received widespread attention through the *Tennessean*. Many faced with the possibility of losing benefits if they did not march to the new tune of reformers expressed their concerns. Linda Douglas, a single mother of three girls living in Nashville public housing, told a reporter from the *Tennessean* that she feared it would be difficult for herself and other mothers to make a meaningful and satisfying transition to wage labor.[88] On the one hand, she said she recognized that staying on welfare for the past ten years had kept her family poor. On the other, she predicted a possible increase in crime by mothers if the state eliminated their welfare benefits.[89] In particular, she pointed to possible increases in women selling their bodies and/or their food stamps so that their families could survive. Like many welfare recipients, over the years Douglas had worked at establishments such as fast-food restaurants and shirt factories. However, she had neither a car nor a driver's license, and the bus that serves her housing project does not run after 5:15 P.M. Missing the bus presented the added difficulty of walking home through a dangerous neighborhood after dark. Her primary reason for not wanting to pursue full-time wage work was that she wanted to be at home to greet her twin girls, LaShaunda and LaSandra, aged ten, when they arrived home from school. Linda Douglas feared for the safety of her girls in public housing if she was not with them. As an attentive and loving mother, she commented, "These days it's so hard to leave kids at home by themselves." In particular, Douglas worried about vehicles that sped past her front yard and drug deals and other crimes that occured in the streets. Under the Families First plan, authorities required Douglas to be absent from her home forty hours per week, working twenty hours and devoting another twenty to job training, education, or life-skills classes. At the end of her training, Families First required her to work full-time or lose her welfare benefits, although she would still be able to receive food stamps, subsidized housing, and medical care. Talking with great pride about what kind of example she wanted to set for her children, Douglas said, "I want them to know there are other ways of having money besides government handouts."[90]

Many women I talked with mentioned that maintaining a job in the face of the pressures of single parenting, abject poverty, and fear of crime was often beyond them. For these deeply impoverished single mothers, some of whom faced a number of other acute problems including depression, drug and alcohol addiction, and other health problems, the chances of "succeeding" at full-time wage work were slim. The *Tennessean* also informed its large readership of the story of Londa Lynn Martinez, aged thirty, who said she felt that welfare reform might help self-starters such as herself. However, she feared that many would "start selling dope, stealing," and that "the crime rate would go up." Martinez predicted, "I can see the Department of Health and Human Services office with mothers cussing, crying and screaming, 'Why are you doing this?' " Another woman, a friend of Martinez, dropped by during the interview with the reporter. She did not want to talk about her life on welfare, but she did tell the reporter that if she lost her welfare benefits, "she'll turn to prostitution for money to raise her young child."[91]

We have known for a long time that welfare does not allow a family to live above the poverty line. Kathy Edin and Christopher Jencks found that poor black women feel obligated to feed, dress, house, and love their children. However, as their work in Chicago and Cook County shows, welfare mothers develop additional sources of economic support, some of them illegal (crime, prostitution), and do not report these supports to welfare authorities.[92] Federal welfare reform legislation prevents any person with a felony drug conviction stemming from offenses committed after August 22, 1996, from receiving TANF or food stamps unless a state introduces legislation to the contrary. As Amy Hirsch notes, although twenty-seven states eliminated or modified the ban, twenty-three (including Tennessee) retain it. Given that many female drug addicts living in places such as public housing are also battered women, imposing lifetime bans on the receipt of welfare makes it more difficult for such impoverished, undereducated women to leave violent personal relationships, escape prostitution, and avoid homelessness.[93]

Some poor black women in Nashville benefit from the subterranean economy of drug dealing either directly, by letting their project housing be used as a base of operations, or indirectly, by having intimate relationships with men who deal, sell, manufacture, and distribute drugs. In some of these relationships, especially where women are the victims of domestic violence, men force them to be involved in drug running. The welfare-to-work initiative pushes more of these women to the precipice, where they will "choose" to run the gauntlet of the drug trade to feed themselves, their children, or their drug habits. Although the 1986 Anti–Drug Abuse Act established most of the drug-related mandatory sentences in operation today, the 1988 Omnibus Anti-Drug Act added mandatory sentences for simple possession of crack cocaine and increased the penalties for conspiracy, so that coconspirators drew the same penalties as those committing drug offenses. According to Nell Bernstein, "Under conspiracy laws, those who don't sell drugs—who merely have the bad fortune, or judgment, to be associated with people who do—can wind up with those same sentences. The 'conspiracies' that lead to these convictions rarely involve overt plotting and scheming to distribute large quantities of drugs. For a woman whose husband or boyfriend is involved in the drug trade, conspiracy may consist of having drugs in the house, taking phone messages from drug associates or driving the husband or boyfriend to the bank where he makes an illicit deposit."[94]

These mandatory sentences and conspiracy prosecutions increased the number of female prison inmates. Bernstein notes that the number of women in prison increased from 13,400 in 1980 to 84,400 by the end of 1998. From 1990 to 1997, the number females serving time for drug offenses almost doubled. Many women incarcerated under these laws are shipped off to prisons located far from their homes. At least half report not having seen their children while incarcerated.[95] That the Families First initiative could push more women to crime and thus possibly separate them from their children underscores its threat to black family life. At a domestic violence shelter in Nashville, I talked with Angela, a black woman who lived in public housing. She offered me these thoughts on the provision of welfare and the decline of marriage and the family in the black community:

> This way they got it set up is not helping, and the whole thing of public housing and welfare reform needs to be reformed. My suggestion for the public housing problems would be to stop giving the teenagers apartments. And instead of breaking up a home, or a family, require the family to be together before you start givin 'em . . . help. . . . If the man is willin' to be there and help his family, why not help him too, instead of sayin', "We can't help you, because the daddy is there." That's why nobody wants to be married. That's why there's no families anymore. It's "have a baby and get a project." That's what a lot of young girls are sayin . . . and they're afraid of being married because as soon as I get married, you gonna look at both our income, we can't get a job better than McDonald's . . . and you can't fault everybody for not having the education because if they're not grown up to want that education, or try and get that education, if the mother or father have not taught this teenager to want this other life . . . half of the people in public housin' drop out at age thirteen.

The state of Tennessee apparently needed its welfare mothers to fill expanding service sector jobs. Dr. Bill Fox, a University of Tennessee economist, told the Tennessee House Health and Human Resources Committee that "65,000 to 70,000 jobs will be created in the state each year over the next five years, and the state's labor force simply is not big enough to fill them. AFDC clients could be a very important source of the labor force that we, as a state, need in order to maintain the kind of economic growth we have become accustomed to. Tennessee has outpaced the nation in employment growth. Our labor market is very tight."[96]

To help move more people from the welfare rolls into low-paying service sector jobs, the state clamped down on welfare fraud. In July 1997 Department of Health and Social Services (DHS) investigators began arresting sixty people charged by a grand jury with various counts of food stamp and welfare fraud. Larry Evitts, director of investigation for the Tennessee DHS, told reporters, "This is only the tip of the iceberg. . . . These are the worst of the worst," but "by no means everyone who is committing welfare fraud in this county." The DHS investigators invited local media to accompany them to witness the arrests. Those indicted had allegedly "redistributed" welfare moneys that exceeded $500,000. As Evitts pointed out, "With this much taxpayer money involved, it is a public issue." Another motive was deterrence. Evitts reminded readers that "We may arrest sixty people today, but two to three times that number will call in and have their case closed as a result of this." At the end of the article reporting the fraud, the *Tennessean* duly printed the names of arrestees.[97]

In mid-July 1997 the Edgehill Center began offering extended child-care services until midnight and on Saturdays. This level of service is rare in Tennessee. After the introduction of welfare reform, roughly 1,500 Edgehill mothers with children under six required child-care services. However, in Sam Levy Homes, where the average annual household income in 1997 was $4,908, well below the federal poverty level of $15,600 for a family of four, there was no group child care offered for Families First mothers with children under eighteen months. This dearth of child care presented major problems, since roughly three-quarters of the families in Sam Levy, including 622 children under six, became Families First clients in 1996. These new difficulties in the lives of Sam Levy mothers emerged under the growing shadow of the new stadium for the Tennessee Oilers football team, built on land next to poor sectors of town, including Sam Levy. A symbol of prosperity in the city of Nashville, the stadium cost nearly $300 million, a sum several times more than the money spent on Families First.

Authorities cut the welfare rolls in Tennessee from 91,500 to 58,476 by the end of 1997. On assuming full-time jobs, many mothers complained about losing day care, food stamps, transportation assistance, and subsidized rent.[98] The Middle Tennessee Chapter of Jobs with Justice argued strongly for employment that paid more than mere subsistence wages. During 1997, requests for emergency food assistance in Nashville increased 20 percent; half the people seeking assistance were the "working poor." Area relief agencies reported that they expected the increased need to continue because of rising housing costs, low-paying jobs, and the shedding of women from the Families First program. As Jaynee Day, executive director of the Second Harvest Food Bank of Nashville, explained, "You can't pay your rent, buy food, pay your utilities, provide transportation and day care on $5.82 an hour. So even though the economy is doing very well, there are a lot of people that are just barely getting by." She added that business downsizing and plant closings contributed to the increased demand. Ironically, the increased efficiency of food manufacturers in packaging and handling food provided fewer surplus items for organizations like Second Harvest. Luckily, perhaps, Second Harvest had experience with cuts in social programs and the increased need of the poor. After the cuts in social spending in 1981, Second Harvest's client list soared as much as 25 percent a month. Staff at Nashville's food banks knew it was difficult for many of their clients to engage in low-wage work and support their families.[99]

With the food lines lengthening as the new football stadium began to go up, the contradictions and problems with Families First crystallized. As the 1997 Christmas holiday season approached, state officials announced a new $22-million program to extend the eighteen-month transition from welfare to work for the "toughest cases" already enrolled in Families First.[100] Tennessee's transition period came up short compared to those in other states. In addition, state officials also acknowledged the problems many women faced securing satisfactory child care and transportation. As demands for emergency food support grew in Nashville and across the country, especially among working women with children, Jaynee Day commented, "I think that's pretty startling. . . . It just seems deplorable when people have to choose between paying medical bills and rent or feeding their children." Ms. Day attributed the increase to the low wages working people were receiving and the dearth of affordable housing.[101] I heard these complaints from numerous women. Nevertheless, Governor Sundquist claimed success for the welfare-to-work initiative. He told the *Tennessean*, "Unemployment numbers are down. More people are working. That indicates to me that people are doing better and we're reducing poverty, and probably more importantly, people are feeling good about themselves. . . . I think Families First is very compassionate, but it's also tough love."[102]

The tough-love approach that denied many women the chance to be with their young children soon ran into trouble. Complaints surfaced about the failure to provide qualified child-care staff. Phil Acord, executive director of the Tennessee Children's Home in Chattanooga, observed, "The economic boom and the increased demand because of welfare reform has forced us to put too many children under adults without adequate training." The *Tennessean* pointed to several high-profile cases involving children being harmed in inadequate child care. In one case, a child-care worker left two toddlers in child-care center vans in hot weather in Memphis; both children died of hyperthermia. Linda O'Neal, the executive director of the Tennessee Commission on Children and Youth, linked these kinds of incidents to poor government funding. She noted, "I think they are related and are symptomatic of inadequate financial support, which translates into overworked, underpaid and inadequately trained staff."[103] Given the miserable history of child-care provision in the United States, deaths like these should come as no surprise.

Just as the failure to provide adequate child care took its toll, so life on the street caused the deaths of ten homeless Nashville citizens. In freezing temperatures and light snow, people gathered at Nashville's Riverfront Park for a memorial service for the ten homeless people known to have died in Nashville in 1995. The number of known deaths among the homeless was down from the 1994 total of thirty-five, perhaps because authorities displaced the homeless from the downtown areas and its periphery through more intensive policing. The vulnerable among those displaced probably died elsewhere. The memorial service added the ten new names of decedents to a list of one hundred or more people who had died on the streets; many from drug and alcohol problems, some the victims of murder.[104]

Dennis Brazen, who has worked with the homeless in Nashville since the mid-1980s explained that the refurbishing of downtown streets and the construction of a convention center and parking garages pushed out the homeless, scattering them far afield and rendering them less visible in areas of commercial activity. "When Nashville decided they were going to put a convention center in, upgrade some things, they started changing the face of downtown. Downtown used to have a lot of flophouses. . . . They parked a paddy wagon on the end of Broadway, and bobbies on bicycles two-by-two went up and down. And it pushed the homeless out of the downtown area. You can find homeless folks now out in Antioch and in West Nashville, by St. Thomas's Hospital, which is just before you get to Bellemeade and the governor's mansion. Broadway for a while was kinda like a skid row. And that's kinda where they hung." In many ways the homeless of Nashville are the most disadvantaged of those living in poverty. Not only does society shun the homeless, they are also the targets of stringent policing.

This is particularly so when the homeless occupy space earmarked for commercial development.[105] However, the plight of the Nashville homeless derives in large part from the lack of affordable housing and decent jobs.

On occasions in Nashville, particularly when the weather turns colder, some emergency shelters turn the homeless away because of a lack of space.[106] During tourist season it is also more difficult to find emergency shelter for the homeless in spill-over hotels, which sometimes set aside rooms for them. When room rates are at a premium, it is harder to make emergency placements.[107] In addition to facing the rigors of the street and the hostility of police, business owners, and much of the public at large, the homeless often fear each other.[108] Tracy Shepard, homeless for two years, described the Union Rescue Mission as the "house of pain." He told a reporter, "It's not safe."[109] The executive director of that shelter, the Reverend Carl Resener, acknowledged that there was violence at the mission, attributing it to the mix of people who were war veterans, mentally ill, and simply down and out.[110]

The availability of well-paid work directly affects levels of homelessness. In Nashville the new arena, built at a cost of $144.5 million, was touted as a workplace for those in financial trouble. However, most of the jobs offered at the arena are part-time. Only 10 percent of the 225 jobs created were full-time. The arena's cleaning service offers jobs to thirty to forty homeless men staying at the Union Rescue Mission. One man, Maurice, aged thirty-one, reported that he pocketed twenty-two dollars one night for a few hours of cleaning after an arena event. However, those casual employees often work until 2:00 A.M., and then the mission forces them to check out at 6:00 A.M. Carl Resener explained that "you can't make enough at the arena to get off the street. Plus, that's not enough work for anybody—three, four nights a week. The arena and the football stadium were supposed to result in a lot of jobs. That's pure political hogwash."[111]

In the shelter for homeless women in Nashville, residents told me they feared the violent male partners they had fled more than they ever did their female coresidents. One woman who lived in a shelter for five months before getting her own place told me:

> We worked together. So when I left him I left what I did for a living and that whole way of life. . . . Housing is a big piece for women, and women do not want to go in the projects. I don't

care what color they are. If they've not lived in them they don't want to go there. If they're there they don't want to stay there. . . . Housing is a huge impediment. Child care is huge. The sorry transit system we have in this town is another problem. If you don't have a car, where do you start? I left my partner in January. Of course I couldn't apply for a job until the black eye went away. So in March I got a job and didn't get my own place until May. So that's five months. And I had family to help me, I had resources, I had community support, I had a car, which is huge to these women. And it still took me five months to get my own place.

We cannot separate the rise of saturation community policing in Nashville, first in Edgehill, then elsewhere, from the politics of poverty. One of the principal jobs of community police in Edgehill was to re-move the visible eyesore of homelessness from the streets. Before the rise of community policing in the Edgehill enterprise zone, some home-less people would light fires in winter to keep warm. In this zone, with its mixture of businesses and homes, some dilapidated and a few crack houses, the homeless created makeshift dwellings out of pallets and other materials from businesses. They stole cushions to sleep on and gasoline to light their fires. For years this neighborhood, which borders Edgehill and blends into downtown Nashville, was a contested area where businesses struggled with the ranks of surplus labor, the un-employed, street alcoholics, the urban insane, and the homeless. Sig-nificantly, it was in these neighborhoods surrounding Edgehill that we see the first policing initiatives to extend the "gains" of community policing beyond the projects. Although the homeless still walk the streets and a few drunks still beg for beer money, these areas peripheral to Edgehill have undergone major changes in the few years since com-munity policing appeared. This shift did not come without costs to the homeless. Authorities moved them on, incarcerated them, and de-stroyed their makeshift homes. The homeless lost their friends, who were replaced by yuppies with social consciences and gentrified homes. In a way, the sprucing up of the Edgehill borderlands parallels those HOPE VI initiatives by which projects like Vinehill have been "cleaned up," with the "problem element"—criminals, drug dealers and addicts, and those unwilling to accept jobs or job training—being removed.

The changes to the periphery of Edgehill would likely not have occurred without saturation policing in the projects during the day and, to a much lesser extent, at night. However, these developments also feed off the desire of some suburbanites to move into the city to avoid a long commute. There is a rich irony in people's beginning to reverse the suburbanization trajectory in favor of living closer to the city center and its racially segregated poor. Saturation community policing facilitated this reversal. Officer Olsen reflected on these changes: "The housing values have increased tremendously. There are some properties over here that are in the $180,000 to $200,000 range. Now, has it become chic to move closer to town? Yes. There are a lot of people that are moving back into town that had moved to the suburbs and they got tired of it. Is that part of it driving the market? Very well may be. But . . . you see right there this lady playing with her dog right out here? You would not have seen that three to five years ago on this street." I asked if this was due to the proximity to the Edgehill projects. "Proximity to the projects and proximity to the violence that was constantly going on over there," replied Olsen. "The gunshots that you would hear every night. Would you want to live near it?"

For someone who spends a lot of time in the comfort and luxury of the ivory tower, this was an easy no answer. However, for those who live in and around the projects in Nashville, or have children with women who live there, it is not possible to "just say no." Alex Hayes, a black man of twenty-two, is one such person with whom I talked. He lives on the edge of J. C. Napier Homes, has two children with one woman in those projects, and is currently living with another woman and helping to raise her child. Alex had spent time in jail for a domestic violence offense and was on probation when we talked. He knew the projects well and talked at length about the compromised position of poor black people. His remarks bring closure to this chapter and offer a bridge into the next one.

For Alex, the American Dream is hollow rhetoric. "You think of all . . . this stuff they broadcast. 'You can get a better home, better apartment.' You dream of having something nice, man, you just don't always want to look at these bricks in here, see the projects . . . but you know the hype's a trap." Alex even thought that some of the drug dealers themselves lived sad, disillusioned lives:

> They get mad a lot in the projects because they're tired, some of 'em get tired of what they do. It's a disguise, man. Yeah, you

can go out and get champagne, be happy, laugh, but you're not really happy with your life ... because you doin' what you doin', uh, a lot of frustration come because you know, you got to live like this to support your kids, and take care of a woman. And you be pissed and mad at everything, now that's just not right. You want shit to be right so much and it don't happen. But you want that money so bad, you know. You know it's fucked up when you got a home and even if you don't have a job, you out there, outside. It's just like a damn job especially if you sellin' dope, because you out there eleven to twelve to one, and the wee hours of the night. . . . They not really happy with the livin' style because you ain't really got what you want. You know, where you wake up in the mornin', see some nice grass, you know, smellin' good air and shit, you know. Instead you takin' the trash out and walking all into the Dumpster where it's just burned up and shit and stink, and you tired of seeing this shit. You don't wanna hear the gunshots and shit, and police "vrrrmmm" and fire engines round your house all the time, and then, somebody bustin' and shootin', then next-door neighbor blastin' music and shit, you tired of that shit.

Lack of money, social quarantining, and the lure of the drug trade constantly affect Alex's life. He wants to provide for his children, perform meaningful labor, and live safely. He knows the rituals of exclusion that keep him from rising above his station. Alex knows all about burned-out Dumpsters and sees little to wonder at if someone paints them. For him, community policing is business as usual, perfectly in step with the gulag mentality of a criminal justice juggernaut that increasingly incarcerates huge numbers of the poor, particularly those of his skin color. Growing up as he did in the 1980s and 1990s, crack cocaine, gang violence, prostitution, and urban disenchantment permanently cloud his horizons. Alex needs no data to tell him that politicians fixed the welfare system so that people stay poor, that authorities chase deadbeat dads, or that child care is inadequate. That people disappear sometimes in the projects, whether they are homeless or not, does not shock him. The perspectives espoused by men like Alex are crucial to our understanding of policing and the alarming rise of the criminal justice juggernaut.

C H A P T E R R

Policing Social Upheaval

■ The remains of at least thirty slave forts punctuate the coastline of Ghana. These forts held slaves awaiting transportation to the Americas. The first slave purchase recorded in Africa was in 1503. From then until the mid-1850s, roughly 60 million Africans lost their freedom to slavers. Approximately two out of three died in captivity, either in the slave forts or on the long journey west. At Elmina Castle, enslaved Africans passed through what became known as the "Door of No Return" before they boarded slave ships. One observer noted, "The centuries-old stench of mold and human waste still rises from the small cell with a narrow, barred door that opens to the harbor—the last spot where African slaves touched the continent before being shipped to the Americas."[1] Portuguese traders originally built Elmina Castle in 1482 to store goods between visits by trading ships; gold and ivory were the principal commodities of interest to the Portuguese. From 1600 Elmina was fully operational as a staging post for dispatching Africans to the New World. Traders and those in their employ branded slaves before loading them onto ships. Elmina Castle is of immense historical significance. The chapel found within its walls is the oldest Christian church in Africa outside Ethiopia. The Dutch captured Elmina in 1636 and converted the chapel into a large slave-trading hall, expanding the slave trade.

Today, approximately twenty thousand foreigners visit Elmina Castle each year. Most of them are African Americans. Eugene Vickerson, a retired real estate salesman from Atlanta, told of his experiences at Elmina: "I cried yesterday when I visited some of the other places, so today I'm doing pretty well. . . . I am just overwhelmed with emotions. It is all so much more real when you see this. . . . It was something I felt I had to do. It was my first time here physically, although I have been here many times before in my mind. My overwhelming sense is that the racial question still exists, the oppression continues. Not that much has changed; that is what is so sad. We know bad things happened and there was terrible suffering, but it continues in different forms, in different times."[2]

From time to time slaves did overrun ships. On plantations in the New World, resistance varied according to the plantation's organization, the numbers of slaves present, the presence of owners, and the relative hostility of populations beyond plantations. The policing of slaves restricted the likelihood of rebellion. In spite of the limitations and tight social control used to regulate black populations, whites feared slave uprisings out of all proportion to the threat posed by them or the likelihood of their taking place. These fears carried over into the post–Civil War discourse on crime and penalty that constructed the African male as a dangerous threat to "ordered" white society.[3] This ideological construction was particularly ironic, since, as Fox Butterfield and others have shown, the southern code of honor and its ultimate reliance upon the violent resolution of disputes originated among whites.

Can we explain contemporary African American crime rates in terms of ongoing oppression and the history of slavery? It is difficult even to begin to address this question because criminology and social history provide us with few analytical tools that address the historical relationships between race, ethnicity, and crime. In what follows I explore rioting, disturbances, and various forms of crime through the lens of social history and ideas such as "social banditry" and "social crime." Insofar as these notions recognize the political construction of criminal law, they are helpful. However, because of the social quarantining of the black underclass, concepts such as "social crime" provide only a segue into making sense of the relationship between policing, race, and social upheaval. My aim in introducing this literature is to provide a possible framework for reflecting upon the killing of Leon Fisher by Nashville police and the social upheaval and rioting that followed his death. As I noted in chapter 1, police killed Fisher after an altercation arising out of a routine traffic stop. Fisher's death became the center-piece of a heated public debate. Was Fisher a social bandit? A common thug? A murderer? Did his acts constitute common forms of street crime, or did they mean more? Did Fisher's crime, in his own mind or those of others, constitute some form of embryonic social protest?

Historically, those who broke unpopular laws did not necessarily see themselves as criminal, immoral, or even as breaking socially agreed-upon rules. Eric Hobsbawm sketched the typical career of what he calls the social bandit: "A man becomes a bandit because he does something which is not regarded as criminal by his local conventions, but is so regarded by the State or the local rulers." He goes on to note how important it is that the "incipient social bandit should be regarded as 'honourable' or non-criminal by the population, for if he was re-garded as a criminal against local convention, he could not enjoy the local protection on which he must rely completely." The notion of "social crime" developed by the English cultural Marxist historians resembles Hobsbawm's much tighter notion of the social bandit. Hobs-bawm refers to those who break unpopular laws as "social criminals."[4] Examples of social criminals from the annals of history include poach-ers who broke the unpopular game laws that basically permitted only the wealthy landed aristocracy to hunt wild animals;[5] wreckers who plundered merchants' vessels that went aground along the coast of En-gland;[6] coiners who, among other things, minted their own money;[7] rioters who popularly agitated for the availability of cheap bread or, more generally, for the restoration of lost rights;[8] and smugglers who illegally trafficked in commodities such as wool and tea, avoiding cus-toms officers and the tariffs due the government, thereby providing goods well below market price.[9] Poachers, wreckers, coiners, rioters, and smugglers enjoyed a popularity within their own communities and farther afield, snubbing the law, questioning its moral basis, and identifying it as an alien regulatory code. This code emanated from privileged groups that often took advantage of the lower social orders. Although the principal focus of these infractions was the acquisition of property on terms favorable to social criminals and their wider communities, it is also clear that from time to time these individuals used violence to further their goals.

Social Upheaval during Nashville's Twentieth-Century Reconstruction

Racial violence originated with the theft of Africans during slavery. The slave codes, post–Civil War convict leasing, and lynching continued this violence. Whites used lynching, other forms of extralegal violence, restrictive covenants, and redlining to keep blacks in their place. Blacks did not endure these hardships without resistance, and Nashville became a prominent center of black resistance during the 1960s. The civil rights movement in Nashville did not merely mirror national initiatives or simply replicate those in places such as Greensboro, Little Rock, Birmingham, or Selma. As Don Doyle explains: "Just as Nashville had stood on the northern edge of the Confederacy, was the first city to fall to the federal invasion, and became a center for education and economic change after the war, so Nashville became an important force in what became known as the Second Reconstruction. . . . Nashville . . . was the first major city in the South to experience widespread desegregation of public facilities. Out of the Nashville movement came a cadre of skilled leaders for the civil rights struggle."[10]

With its own image as a progressive city of the New South, a center for religion and education, Nashville was more accommodating of shifts in race relations than other cities that witnessed much more systemic violence and intimidation. As elsewhere, desegregation in public schools became a principal focus for controversy and political maneuvering. In the wake of the 1954 U.S. Supreme Court decision in *Brown v. Board of Education of Topeka, Kansas*,[11] and in response to a local lawsuit,[12] the Nashville School Board began a plan for desegregating public schools. The idea was to desegregate one grade at a time, beginning with the first grade. This strategy, as one reverend who was active in the civil rights movement in Nashville later told me, was to delay the day when blacks and whites would mingle in high school, mix socially, date each other, and intermarry. Those in favor of continuing apartheid policies intimidated those who would break with the past. Doyle reports some black parents with children due to enter white schools receiving threats such as, "We'll beat your little girl to death and string her up by her toes. Then we'll burn your home."[13] On the first day of school, September 9, 1957, mobs jeered the small number of black parents who turned up at white schools with their children. Some of the mob hurled sticks and stones at the parents. That evening a wing of the Hattie Cotton School, an integrated school in East Nashville, was bombed. A Jewish Community Center was bombed in March 1958 and the rabbi, William Silverman, received a warning after the blast saying that other Jewish institutions would be bombed as well as any other "nigger-loving place or nigger-loving person in Nashville."[14] In 1966 the Nashville School Board voted to do away with the one-grade-at-a-time policy for desegregating its schools; however, by 1970, all formerly black schools were still educating blacks only, and most of the formerly white schools were still educating nearly all whites.

Resistance to segregation moved beyond the highly charged issue of public schooling to places such as lunch counters in downtown stores, where blacks were free to spend their money but not entitled to eat at the same counter as whites. In 1960 segregationists beat protesters as Nashville police stood by and watched. David Halberstam reported the Nashville Woolworth's demonstration in the *Tennessean*: "For more than an hour the hate kept building up. . . . First it was the usual name calling, then spitting, then cuffing; now bolder punching, banging their heads against the counter, hitting them, stuffing cigarette butts down the back of their collars. The slow build-up of hate was somehow worse than the actual violence."[15] The same year, whites beat four black students for eating at a lunch counter at the Greyhound bus terminal in Nashville. Greyhound officials who allowed this de facto desegregation received threats and the next day two bomb detonators were found at the terminal. In later picketing campaigns to desegregate lunch counters, segregationists bombed the home of black leader Z. Alexander Looby. Proprietors eventually desegregated lunch counters and movie theaters. By 1964 most other public places followed suit, much to the chagrin of segregationists. Major race-related disturbances did not resurface in Nashville until 1967, when, in the aftermath of a speech by Stokely Carmichael, the spokesman for the Black Power movement, students squared off against Nashville police in a riot of considerable proportions, with rocks thrown, shots fired, and Molotov cocktails hurled into buildings. When Martin Luther King Jr. was assassinated in April 1968, similar violent protest reared its head.

The Reverend Dorie was active in the Methodist Church in South Nashville from 1966 and offered some insightful observations regarding police-community relations and urban renewal. Urban renewal in Nashville led to the creation of a massive public housing complex in and around Edgehill.

> Edgehill became so concentratedly a public housing community. We will try to remedy this for future generations. It was a horrible answer. . . . to think that you could put multiproblem families all up together, and then, and then have laws saying you can't have an employable male in the house and still get the subsidy. . . . I came to really hate public housing projects. When I came to Edgehill in sixty-six, the civil rights movement was boiling, Vietnam was heating up a little, the war on poverty hatched in sixty-four . . . and I think at that time with the civil rights movement and hoses and dogs and, especially in the South, use of law enforcement to quell civil rights demonstrations and so on, it was a very tense, antagonistic atmosphere at that time. . . . King died on Friday. On the following Sunday afternoon, I was driving down toward the church on Edgehill and some rocks went over the hood of my car, and there were a few kids standing around, throwing rocks. Cities all over the country were burning. Memphis was burning as a result of his death. I came on home . . . it was four o'clock in the afternoon, I was watching TV or something, and I began to feel the house rock, and, I looked out at Sixteenth Avenue, which I saw as kind of a main thoroughfare. There was a line, two city blocks of half trucks, armored cars, police cars, all heading toward Edgehill.

The Reverend Dorie left his house for a six o'clock meeting only to be called from that meeting by his secretary, who told him that things were spiraling out of control in Edgehill and that the police were conducting antiriot maneuvers there. Dorie and others returned to Edgehill: "When we got back into the project we could hear gunfire and all kinds of yelling and noises. . . . They were doing their antiriot thing.

... They shoot out streetlights because snipers could see you down below, there weren't any high-rise buildings, but they were shooting the streetlights out. They were just going indiscriminately into the apartments and pulling telephones out of the wall, turning over mattresses. One woman said that this old lady across the court was sitting on her porch, before dark, and guardsmen came through, saw her sitting there, said, 'Get your ass in the house. You don't belong out here.' And she said, 'My son is fighting for your freedom in Vietnam, and how can you talk to me like that?' " Later that evening the Reverend Dorie was leaving the Edgehill projects with his friend Jim to go to Juvenile Hall to retrieve a resident's son when a small boy came running home late:

> This kid came runnin' across in front of us, looked like he was ten or eleven years old, and immediately behind, just one second later, four or five national guardsmen thumping and running, one dropped on one knee and fired a rifle, didn't hit the kid, the kid froze.[16] Jim and I jumped out of the van and went over. What happened was the kid was coming home at curfew. They had pronounced a curfew, and when he saw all this, he ran; he hadn't committed any offense of any sort. . . . A week after that, a civil rights attorney named Avon Williams called me and Jim and asked, "Will you come to the city council and testify about what you saw?" And we did, and I said, "You know, there was a rock thrown over the hood of my car, there was some provocation, but this was incredible overkill." And I had to leave my phone off the hook for a week after that. The phone calls were just awful. Called me names and, you know, that kind of stuff. And it all had to do with the use of law enforcement to suppress and subdue social movements, especially associated with race—poverty and race. There was no question that the police were the enemy. The predominant mood was "these are the enemy."

The white-supremacist opposition to desegregation and the authoritarian and brutal policing of the Edgehill projects in 1968 provide the recent historical backdrop for contextualizing the contemporary rioting directed at police by mostly black males in the housing projects. The "overkill" that the Reverend Dorie described in Edgehill in 1968, the rolling artillery, the shooting out of streetlights, all tactics directed at quelling civil rights demonstrations, returned to Nashville once more in 1997, triggered by the police shooting of Leon Fisher.

The Dollar General Riot of 1997

In the early morning hours of August 10, 1997, police attempted to stop three black men in a Chevrolet Suburban for speeding on Meridian Street. The men pulled into the parking lot of the Dollar General Store in Settle Court/Sam Levy Homes and fled on foot. Sergeant Randy Hickerson gave chase and caught up with one of the men, Leon Fisher, aged twenty-three. It was Leon's birthday. During the chase, Hickerson reported hearing someone firing a gun behind him. He also noted that Fisher jumped up on a curb and faced him, assuming an aggressive stance. According to the sergeant, Fisher seemed to make eye contact with or signal to an adult male bystander, who proceeded to circle around Hickerson in what the officer saw as an "obvious attempt" to get behind him. According to Hickerson, he told Fisher to "get down," but Fisher did not comply. The officer delivered one or two baton strikes to Fisher's arm. Allegedly, Fisher still did not respond to the officer's commands. Hickerson testified that at the time he confronted Fisher he felt Fisher may have been on some kind of stimulant that made him more violent. During the altercation, Fisher reportedly reached in his pockets in a manner suggestive to Hickerson that he may have been reaching for a gun. Consequently, the officer drew his gun. Fisher then revealed his empty hands, and Hickerson reported that he put his gun away. When a second police vehicle arrived at the scene, Fisher allegedly lunged at Hickerson, grabbed him by the collar, and knocked him to the ground. In response, Hickerson hit Fisher twice on the head with his baton. Hugh Nelson, the second officer at the scene, discharged pepper spray at Fisher, who apparently avoided it by turning his head. Fisher then started to punch Hickerson in the temple with his fists. Hickerson reported feeling faint and threatened and believed that Fisher was trying to disable him in order to grab his gun. Hickerson then pulled out his gun and fired two rounds, the second of which hit Fisher in the upper chest above the bulletproof vest he was wearing. It was only after shooting Fisher that Hickerson reportedly handcuffed him to prevent further assault by him and to assess his injuries. In a statement made soon after the shooting, Police Chief Turner reported that Hickerson administered emergency first aid immediately after the shooting. Hickerson removed the cuffs when emergency medical personnel arrived. Fisher died shortly after arriving at Nashville General Hospital. Police reportedly found a small amount of cocaine and marijuana in Fisher's clothing.[17]

A crowd formed near the Settle Court parking lot. Some of them threw rocks and bottles at police, who immediately put on riot gear. After aggressive posturing on both sides, the crowd broke up and the police left.[18] News of the police shooting spread like wildfire through Sam Levy Homes, and, according to various sources, a larger crowd composed of anywhere from four to six hundred people gathered. Some of these people looted and then burned the Dollar General Store and the adjoining YWCA learning center. Authorities charged two teenagers from East Nashville, Desmond Royzelle Robinson and Anthony Lee "AWOL" Williams, with arson. A jury later acquitted the boys after less than one hour of deliberation.[19] Robinson's mother and Williams's aunt testified that the boys were at home in bed when the fire broke out at around 5:00 A.M. Judge Cheryl Blackburn held that prosecutors had insufficient evidence against a third suspect, Jenera B. Higgins, aged twenty, to show that he had "knowingly" set fire to the building. Higgins had already pleaded guilty to charges of burglary and theft, acknowledging his part in the looting of the store. He told police his only involvement in the fire was to pick up an already-burning T-shirt and throw it.

Only two witnesses, Toria Buchanan and Treva Cunningham, testified against Robinson and Williams. Buchanan told the court that she had seen Robinson shoot out the windows of the YWCA learning center, while Williams used a tire iron to smash windows. Cunningham stated that she witnessed the juveniles attempting to remove a metal gate from the front of the Dollar General Store, noting that they lifted it sufficiently high so that people could enter and begin looting. Cunningham also later observed the two boys pour lamp oil into a large trash can, onto the floor in the store, and around the outside of the store. Moments later the building was ablaze. According to Ralph Kooster, a lawyer close to this case, jurors viewed the testimony of the sisters as suspicious because the two women had been involved in a local feud with Robinson and Williams. The sisters claimed that the boys shot into their Sam Levy apartment on September 2, 1997. It was after this shooting incident and, indeed, because of it, that the sisters came forward to testify against the boys. Apparently, the sisters were sick and tired of the boys and wanted to put a stop to their intimidation. For Kooster, the evidence was convincing that Robinson and Williams had set the fire. In particular, Kooster noted the high degree of correspondence between the evidence given by the sisters and the findings of the fire marshal. After the prosecution had failed to prove its case on the arson charges, Assistant District Attorney Jim Todd, who prosecuted the boys, told reporters, "The saddest thing about this case is that half the project was out there, but only two people would talk."[20] His observation concurred with that of witness Toria Buchanan, who testified about the extent of looting. "Everybody was going in the Dollar Store and getting stuff. . . . It was probably half of Sam Levy."[21] Treva Cunningham described a frenzy of activity. "Everybody was knocking everybody else down trying to get in there and take things."[22]

There will probably always be some conjecture about the nature and extent of looting in Sam Levy on the morning police killed Leon Fisher. Clarice Aleman, a longtime Sam Levy resident, told me that Toria Buchanan and Treva Cunningham also looted the store and that they had tried to frame Robinson and Williams for the burning. She also said that people came from outside Sam Levy to loot the store and there were likely only thirty or so Sam Levy residents, mostly younger women, who looted. There were a number of indictments for theft directly resulting from the taking of merchandise from the Dollar General Store. Police searched the homes of Sam Levy residents for stolen property; it is not clear how much they found. Neither is it clear whether residents genuinely consented to these searches. The state secured few convictions for theft and burglary stemming from the looting.[23]

The social postmortem of the shooting of Leon Fisher and the looting of the Dollar General Store in Settle Court revealed tremendous divisions between police and local residents and differences among local residents themselves. From a variety of sources it seems as if primarily younger women and juvenile males looted the store. The younger women were most likely welfare recipients who had the most to gain from looting. It is likely that those in regular employment were asleep at the time of the burning and looting. Probably those in receipt of social security and disability insurance were less likely to have looted, although the evidence is questionable at best. A significant number of people looted, perhaps up to a hundred, though many residents did not participate.[24]

Several younger African American men told me they had enormous rage at the oppressive criminal justice system. These men understood the reasons why Sam Levy residents and others looted and burned in the wake of the Fisher killing. For whatever reasons, their viewpoints did not receive much coverage in the local press. The *Tennessean* reported the words of Calvin Odem, aged twenty-five, whose children lived in Sam Levy at the time of the burning. Calvin said, "You've got to take your frustrations out on something."[25] It is well documented that Desmond Robinson, who was sixteen at the time he was charged with setting fire to the Dollar General Store, was very much upset at the shooting of his acquaintance Leon Fisher. His mother testified to this in court, saying that her son became unusually quiet when police shot Fisher "right in front of our house."[26] According to informants at the Nashville Police Department and the district attorney's office, Robinson was probably one of Fisher's drug mules. According to these sources, the interruption in business affected Robinson more adversely than the fact that police may have killed Fisher illegally.

Many women living in Sam Levy expressed great disappointment at the incendiarism. The store, which opened in 1993 in the wake of the South Central Los Angeles rioting as a public-private venture, provided a convenient place for the largely female residents to shop. In addition, in the year before the burning, about one hundred women passed through job-readiness or life-skills training programs run by the YWCA/Dollar General center at Settle Court. This center had a fully equipped classroom with computers and electronic cash registers. The store used its profits to fund programs at the center as well as to pay the wages of the women who participated in twelve- to sixteen-week internships at the store. Of those, forty women went on to work at various jobs outside the store. Carol Sneed first saw the charred remains of the store on her way back from church on Sunday morning, August 11, 1997. She told reporters, "That store didn't bother nobody. Now I got nothing to go to. . . . There was no reason to riot. The store didn't kill Fisher." Joyce Moore, another resident, said, "The store not only helped the community, it helped people get better jobs." Cleovonta Kirkendoll commented, "They burned up something we really needed, and it's going to be hard to get it back. They didn't hurt nobody but us." The store was also a place for community members to meet, so the destruction affected neighborhood cohesion and social intercourse. Jacqueline Vinson, assistant manager at the store, said, "I made a lot of friends out there. People in the neighborhood looked out for us. When I think of all of the good things that happened, it brings me to tears. I am mad and hurt." For Jacqueline, the store was the heart of the community. [27]

It seems unlikely that many female residents harbored concerns about the looting of the store. It is also unlikely that they experienced the same sense of violation, because the looting did not have as serious an impact on their lives as did the burning. Clearly, a large number of female residents looted the store, and others benefited from the receipt of stolen merchandise. Those working as interns or employees of the store probably had different feelings about the looting and its meaning, although their feelings appeared only sporadically in the press.

Police Shooting Black Men

In 1944 Gunnar Myrdal, using language that resonates with great power today, talked of the relationship between white police and blacks: "It is apparent, however, that the beating of arrested Negroes—frequently in the wagon on the way to jail or later when they are already safely locked up—often serves as vengeance for the fears and perils the policemen are subjected to while pursuing their duties in the Negro community. . . . Police brutality is greatest in the regions where murders are most numerous. More than half of all Negroes killed by whites, in both the North and the South, were killed by police."[28] James Fyfe examined police shootings by race of suspect from 1969 to 1976 in Memphis, Tennessee. He noted a black mortality rate for unarmed and nonassaultive suspects that is eighteen times the rate for whites. Fyfe concluded, "The data strongly support the assertion that police there did differentiate racially with their trigger fingers, by shooting blacks in circumstances less threatening than those in which they shot whites."[29] The ruling by the U.S. Supreme Court in *Tennessee v. Garner* (1985) that it is unconstitutional to shoot a fleeing felon, unless that felon threatens the lives of police officers or others, seems to have reduced racial disparities in police shootings of unarmed and nonassaultive suspects.[30] Nevertheless, the perception among blacks is that police are more likely to be trigger-happy if the suspect is black.

The latest research suggests that the ratio of blacks to whites shot and killed by police is three to one, and that blacks are "much closer to the at-risk status based on involvement in serious crime and therefore may represent a disparity rather than systematic discrimination."[31] Put differently, African Americans perpetrate more of the kinds of "violent" crime, particularly armed robberies, that draw police fire.[32] However, these more recent research findings suggest that some police do discriminate based on race. Douglas Smith, Christy Visher, and Laura Davidson's research on 5,688 police-citizen encounters in three different cities shows, all other things being equal, that police arrest black suspects more often than white suspects.[33] Similarly, Joan Petersilia's research in California revealed that police arrest blacks more often than whites, and on flimsier evidence.[34] Whatever the empirical evidence, people's perceptions that police are racist remain strong, particularly in minority communities. For example, in 1996 a poll in the *New Yorker* magazine found that most blacks "strongly agreed" that the police and the legal system were biased against them.[35]

People's perceptions of how the criminal justice system operates form the basis of their reaction to it. Incidents such as the brutal beating of Rodney King by Los Angeles police officers in 1991 teach people about police violence. More recently, the New York Police Department Street Crime Unit, which had been formed to confront violent street crimes such as rape and robbery, reinforced these perceptions of racial discrimination with the dramatic killing of street peddler, Amadou Diallo, a twenty-two-year-old black man. Diallo stood unarmed outside his apartment in the Bronx and appeared to have been reaching for a gun, but was actually reaching for his wallet, perhaps for identification, when police killed him in a hail of forty-one bullets. According to Jane Fritsch of the *New York Times*, the reduction in violent street crime in New York "came at a price. Thousands of innocent people, mostly minorities, were stopped and questioned, frisked and even arrested by the unit's officers, who dressed casually in street clothes and rode around in unmarked cars."[36] These observations on the complex relationship between policing and race/ethnicity provide the appropriate segue into my discussion of the shooting of Leon Fisher.

Public Perceptions of the Shooting of Leon Fisher

People interpreted the shooting of Leon Fisher differently. I talked with at least ten black women who told me they could easily believe that Fisher's death stemmed from excessive and unjustifiable police force. Clarice Aleman, a middle-aged black woman who had lived in

Sam Levy Homes for nine years, told me, "The police are capable of doing anything. They harass you for no reason at all." The young black men from the projects with whom I talked held the same feelings. Several individuals thought it was possible that police handcuffed and then shot Fisher. One of Fisher's relatives, Steve Monger (pseudonym), told me that the police did a good job in an earlier shooting in which someone killed Steve's brother. In that incident, the police were kind and sympathetic. However, Steve opined that the shooting of the unarmed Leon Fisher was unnecessary and excessive. Some of these perceptions also percolated through in media accounts. The *Tennessean* captured one of the main points of conjecture arising out of this shooting: "The most glaring discrepancy between police accounts and those from neighbors is whether Fisher had already been handcuffed when officers shot him. Area residents said Fisher was handcuffed before the shooting; police said the handcuffs were applied immediately after he was wounded."[37] Clarice Aleman could not speak to whether police cuffed Fisher before shooting him. She did tell me, "I believe they wanted to kill him that night." She added, "They beat 'em when they catch 'em. There is a lot of police brutality."

James Warfield, Fisher's cousin, told reporters, "I heard he did some bad things, but what they did, they still didn't have any cause for it. I think they killed him because they didn't have a case against him."[38] Warfield was referring to an outstanding homicide case in which Fisher was a suspect. Nashville police had executed a search warrant on Fisher on July 31, 1997, to obtain a sample of his blood for DNA testing. They suspected Fisher of murdering Michael Bradley, who was found shot multiple times in a grassy area near Spring Street and Interstate 65 on June 22, 1997. At the time Hickerson shot Fisher to death, the DNA results were not available from the Bradley homicide case.[39] Previously, police had arrested Fisher for possession of a firearm, selling drugs, evading arrest, driving with a canceled license, and for a string of offenses dating back to April 29, 1993, all apparently connected with his drug-dealing activities.[40]

Others expressed the opinion that police shot Fisher simply because he was black, thus continuing a long tradition in Tennessee and across the country. Fifty-three-year-old Ron Hayes told reporters that Nashville police were "happy with the gun. It ain't right. . . . When an officer shoots somebody who's black, they're already covered. We're losing so many young black men by them killing each other that when an officer kills one either by accident or on purpose it adds fuel to the fire." As he was pacing up and down in an alleyway near a Dumpster that the crowd torched the night the Dollar General burned down, Lamont Smith told reporters, "Man got killed on his birthday. . . . Police shot my bud while he had handcuffs on. Telling us to stay in our house all the . . . time, not minding their own business." Margaret Turner said, "Everybody's going to say the officer feared for his life. . . . How the hell can you fear for your life when this man is handcuffed and you done beat the hell out of him? . . . Everybody seen that he was handcuffed before he was shot. He was handcuffed and they were beating him."[41] However, another witness, Roxanne Williams, told the press that Fisher was not handcuffed when he was shot. Nevertheless, she disagreed with the official police version of the story, saying that Fisher had stopped fighting officers once he had been pepper-sprayed.

During my fieldwork, I met one of Leon Fisher's friends, Daryl Thomas, who was on probation at the time we talked. Daryl hates the police with a passion. He told me: "You know, it's like that, see, that's why, this anger, where it makes you just hate the Metro [police], so bad man, you know, um, that shit be, man, it's, it's deep, man, it's, it's crazy, you don't even know what to do no more." However, Daryl would not say that police cuffed Fisher before killing him. Daryl simply told me he was not there that night and that everyone had his own story about the shooting. I sensed that Daryl did not think that police cuffed Leon Fisher and then killed him. Daryl implied that those who claimed police cuffed Fisher and then shot him had another agenda. He put it this way: "Leo was, you know, from the community, and when somethin' like that happened to him . . . now they . . . the community, they hate the police . . . so they might be sayin' . . . 'he bein' in the handcuffs,' you know, like I said, everybody has a different story. . . . You just actually had to be there. Of course, police gonna say what they gonna say." Daryl also told me that he had seen injuries Leon Fisher had received in the past that Fisher said the police had inflicted: specifically, bruising to the stomach and chest area. According to Daryl, a "couple of cops" beat Leon in an earlier interaction:

Daryl: He got beat up by a couple of cops.
Websdale: Who did? He did—Fisher? Before the shooting?

Daryl: Yeah before. Yeah, he got beat up . . . either beat with a stick or whatever. . . . I mean, you see it, underneath his shirt, man, he was real bad, man, bad bruisin' [pointing to his own stomach and chest].

Daryl's sense that police had previously beaten Fisher led him to offer this explanation for Fisher's behavior on the fatal night: "Damn, you know, you don't really know what was goin' down for Leo to punch him [Sergeant Hickerson]. Maybe Leo did it just to be doin' it, or he had to do this shit for a reason—resistin' arrest—maybe he just got tired of them bein' fuckin' with him, you know . . . and just went off. Nobody don't really know."

I called a key informant who had worked extensively on the civil lawsuit currently pending regarding the Fisher shooting. This attorney had talked with many family members, including Fisher's distraught mother, who later lost another son in the commission of a crime. The attorney said he knew of no evidence at all from any family members that police beat Fisher before the incident in which Fisher died. This does not mean that police did not previously use excessive force on Fisher. His criminal history tells us that he had many run-ins with the police and that he evaded and resisted arrest on a number of occasions. It is possible that the injuries Daryl saw stemmed from one of those incidents of resisting arrest; it is also possible that those injuries did not stem from excessive use of force by police at all. Given the historical propensity of the Nashville police for using violence against blacks, I thought it prudent to probe a little more. One of the assistant district attorneys in Nashville told me nervously, and under strict guarantee of anonymity, that police brutality occurs "way more than it needs to. A broken arm here, a broken leg there." My source attributed this brutality to the high stress of police work, vacillating as it does between great boredom and putting one's life on the line. The political choice of city government to fund the $300 million football stadium and to leave the police force understaffed and underpaid added more stress.

Several police officers told me about the brutality used by police at the old jail at the Ben West Building. To tell a suspect that he was going to "take a ride in the elevator" was a euphemism for, as one officer put it, "We are going to beat the holy shit out of you." Another officer told me that the elevator was excessively heavy because they had had to paint over the walls so often to hide the blood. Jail authorities assigned a janitor to hose the blood down in the morning after a busy night of transporting and beating certain suspects. Black males in particular took these beatings. The motorcycle unit, known as "Newman's raiders," sometimes beat noncompliant suspects. Most officers who talked about these matters stated that these systematic abuses had ceased in the last decade or so, and, particularly since the ethos of community policing arrived. However, Sid Kimbar, an ex-convict, talked about police brutality while sitting at an outdoor lunch table of a South Nashville McDonald's. Sid was one of a small number of white men living in the predominantly black housing projects. Knowledgeable about the local drug trade and having served time for violence himself, Sid opined, "One in five of the younger Nashville police officers" uses excessive force "from time to time."

The war stories of prior police brutality are part of the socialization of recruits. Such socialization far transcends knowledge acquired at the training academy or from formal criminal justice coursework at universities, where, as one officer put it, the descriptions of police work bear absolutely no resemblance to street life. Officer Olsen vouched for the accuracy of these stories. When I told him that one could understand how the community is hostile to the police at some level, he replied:

> Oh, yes. People told me, "Well, you know Metro ain't got a great reputation." And I was like, "Well, what do you mean?" "Well, you don't want to piss Metro off, 'cause by God, Metro will tear you up." People knew that metro police officers would knock the hell out of you, for lack of better terms, if you talked back or something. When we came out and people would sometimes run, we would ask, "Why did you run?" They would say, "I was scared you were gonna beat me." This was coming from twelve- and thirteen-year-olds. Well, they had never been beaten by the police before, but they had heard stories about it. But yeah, I've heard the stories from the old-timers, from the twenty- and thirty-year veterans, that if you looked cross-eyed at a metro police officer twenty years ago, you would find yourself waking up in a hospital someplace. Does that occur any more? I haven't seen it. Now, have I heard stories about it? Yeah.

In a conversation about police brutality, Derek Hales, a black man who lived in the projects, told me: "I saw it happen. I mean . . . people be fleeing for their life. They run from the police, but they done heard so many stories about, late at night, nobody's around but you and eight, nine, ten officers. I'm gonna run. Whether if I'm dealing, or whatever, I got me like a pack of weed, you know, marijuana. . . . The police, boy, I see em, I take off runnin' . . . but when they catch you, they gotcha. They got you handcuffed now, so, on the ground, now they gonna kick on ya and stomp ya and beat ya, pick you up, throw you down. . . . You can't win against 'em, you can't win if you go to court." Rob Whittaker, a black man in his thirties who works in catering in Nashville, put it like this: "A lot of young African Americans, especially the males . . . feel that they're walking around with a bull's-eye drawn on their head. It's a very, very real sense of fear."

Whittaker's viewpoint found voice in a demonstration against the police's killing of black men in Tennessee. At Legislative Plaza, across from the state capitol, a group of approximately a dozen picketers, carrying placards referencing other cases of white police officers shooting black Tennesseans, protested the shooting of Leon Fisher. They had requested an audience with Governor Sundquist or Lieutenant Governor John Wilder but did not get it. Nashville police photographed the group. One of the demonstrators, Maxine Thomas of Memphis, objected to being photographed and called it "a form of intimidation." Isaac Richmond of Memphis, the national director of the Commission on Religion and Racism, organized the protest. Richmond told reporters, "When we look at the statistics, we don't see a statistic of black officers killing black men, or white officers killing white men. . . . We see a statistic of white officers killing black men. That's not just accident, and that's not just a unique incident. . . . Black men are being killed all over the state."[42]

There is no question that many young black men in Nashville and across the country perceive a threat from police. I imagine it would be hard for blacks to watch incidents like the Rodney King beating and reports of the shooting of Amadou Diallo and not experience a deep sense of fear. Over the years, some Nashville police officers have used excessive force against people other than blacks. In fact, the perception that police are still excessively brutal and play fast and loose with people's constitutional rights has stimulated two highly significant lines of investigation. The first, the Office of Professional Accountability, directed by attorney Kennetha Sawyers, has the power to review complaints against police officers and monitor police activities. The second is an investigation by the Department of Justice into allegations that off-duty police officers, moonlighting as private security guards, had beaten Hispanic migrant workers, stolen their money, and otherwise mistreated them. These investigations both got off the ground as I was conducting my research, and await completion.

The allegations of the mistreatment of Hispanic migrants rocked the city in the fall of 1999 and spring of 2000, with calls coming for the resignation of Police Chief Turner, himself an African American, for failure to manage the department properly. The allegations first surfaced on the front page of the *Nashville Scene*. Reporters conducted a six-month investigation into the abuse of Hispanic migrants by a private security firm with ties to the Nashville police department.[43] The company opened in 1996, and the owners disbanded it in 1999, as the *Nashville Scene* inquiry gathered steam. *Scene* journalist Willy Stern reported that a private security firm, Detection Services Incorporated, authorized the illegal towing of Hispanics' cars, robbed Hispanic migrants, and beat them. The primary focus of this extralegal activity was on illegal aliens, who officers knew could not complain because they faced the threat of deportation. A lengthy excerpt from the article helps convey the nature of the allegations and the racist venom of some of the officers:

It was a Saturday night in January 1999, and the clock had just struck midnight. Seated around a table at a Denny's Restaurant, eight private security guards smoked cigarettes, sipped coffee, munched on chicken strips, and passed the time. The guards worked for the company named Detection Services, and their job was to act as night patrolmen for apartment buildings across Nashville. But none felt like working, and the company's owner, Larry Lawson, didn't care. He was seated at the table too. As long as the men fudged their time sheets, the owners of the apartment buildings would never know the difference.

But suddenly, Lawson declared: "I'm bored. Let's go down to taco city and fuck with the Mexicans." All the guards knew what that meant. They jumped in four cars and cruised to the Ivy Wood apartment building, one of the complexes they were under contract to patrol. They parked at the main entrance, blocking it. The guards were dressed in blue uniforms, with badges pinned to their shirts and handcuffs hanging from their belt loops. Most wore guns. They turned on their bright, white search beam and the flashing green lights atop their cars. In the eerie glow, they waited for their prey. Soon, two men on their way home to Ivy Wood pulled up to the entrance in their car. Larry Lawson stopped the car. Why? Only because the men were Hispanic. He shined his flashlight into the eyes of the driver. Guards hulked around the car, shining their flashlights inside. Lawson asked the driver for identification, and when he didn't respond quickly, Lawson yanked him out of the car. Guards then hauled out the passenger. As they protested, Lawson screamed, "Shut up or you'll go to jail." Lawson shoved the two men, face down, against the car hood. Lawson and another guard, his son Mike, handcuffed the Hispanics, twisting their arms behind their backs. Then the Lawsons frisked them. After that, the guards searched the car for drugs and weapons, keeping an eye out for cash to steal.

Pointing flashlights into the eyes of the Hispanics, Lawson and his guards yelled more threats: "I'm the police around here. I'm going to throw your Spic ass out of the country unless you start doing what I say." The two Hispanics tried to resist. But the guards threw the handcuffed men to the ground and smashed their faces into the dirt. One guard kicked them in the ribs again and again. Another grabbed one of the Hispanics by his hair, yanked up his head, and screamed, "That serves you right, you Mexican motherfucker."

Outraged, one Hispanic yelled back at Larry Lawson in Spanish. Lawson whipped a can of mace from his gun belt and sprayed straight into the man's face. His victim writhed in pain, rolling in the dirt. The account of this night of terror at the Ivy Wood complex—"taco city" in the expression of Larry Lawson's sadistic humor—was told to the *Scene* by three employees of Detection Services. Fearing retaliation from Lawson or his many friends in the police department, the employees spoke only on condition of anonymity. In individual interviews, they gave the same version of what happened. They said the events—the brutality and the abuse—were repeated several times as more Hispanics drove into the apartment complex and ran into the roadblock. And it didn't begin or end that winter night at Ivy Wood.

The series of articles goes on to document how company guards beat and humiliated Hispanics, stole their money, entered their apartments without warrants and held loaded guns to their heads. Forty of the seventy-five people on the payroll at Detection Services worked as Nashville police officers. According to Stern, most officers did not mistreat Hispanic migrants. The majority worked for the company at the downtown stadium. However, sources identified officer Mike Mann, who "clearly participated in the abuse of Hispanics. . . . Mann helped stage—and sometimes supervised—roadblocks and the illegal towing of cars." According to Stern, many Nashville police officers knew of the abuses. The Nashville Police Department was allegedly compromised in other ways: two officers on the Detection Services payroll worked for the department's internal affairs division, which has apparently investigated Detection Services three times. According to Stern, two of these probes were "seriously flawed, and the third compromised by the leakage of confidential information." Larry Lawson apparently bragged that the internal affairs division of the Nashville Police Department was in his pocket. The *Nashville Scene* also alleged that it was common for Detective Services to obtain confidential information from the computer terminals of metro officers. Many of the security guards refused to talk to metro police investigators after Chief Turner set up an inquiry into the relationship between the department and Detection Services. According to Stern, the guards believe the department is "corrupt" and "dirty," and they, like many abused Hispanics, fear retribution by police.

The precise nature and extent of the recent abuse of Hispanics in Nashville are difficult to pin down. It is difficult to determine whether only a small number of so-called rogue officers abused migrants. In many ways, it is unrealistic to expect illegal aliens to come forward and identify police officers as their abusers. These foreign workers have too much to lose and fear and likely know the extent to which some rogue officers are willing to go. These factors will likely impede the inquiry by the Justice Department and the local FBI. Nashville Mayor Bill Purcell set up the Office of Professional Accountability to address some of these issues. However, the office is not well funded and has a small staff. I talked with a couple of Hispanic attorneys whose clients complain about police harassment. According to Bill Verdugo, the *Scene* stories are accurate and consistent with the street experiences of his clients. Verdugo attributed police excesses to "poor leadership, bad hiring, and cultural and legal stupidity." When pressed he told me that some of the officers considered themselves "angels of justice" and wanted to make all kinds of arrests outside their jurisdiction. At one point he said, "They can't lynch blacks anymore, so their attention is now trained on illegal aliens, who they feel they can harass." For Verdugo, the level of anti–illegal immigrant feeling in Nashville is amazing, a form of rampant hypocrisy, because those illegals contribute so much to the local economy and perform the "very jobs that Anglo-Saxon, Protestant males no longer want to do."

Public Violence and Intimidation in the Nashville Projects

I have described some of the circumstances surrounding the killing of Leon Fisher and the subsequent looting and burning of the Dollar General Store. Did this looting and burning constitute political or pre-political rebellion? Before I try to answer this question, I must address the matter of public violence and intimidation in poor neighborhoods, particularly in Sam Levy Homes. This violence and intimidation directly affect people's willingness to talk about how they feel about men like Leon Fisher and, more broadly, the community response to his killing. Put differently there may be more agreement as to the legitimacy of illegal behavior such as looting because people fear retribution if they do not express a certain level of support for the behavior. Worse still, if they criticize the behavior to authorities, they fear being labeled as "snitches" in their own communities. This climate of fear and intimidation clearly exists in Nashville's public housing projects and warrants careful consideration because it places limits on what we might learn about social solidarity and the meaning of collective actions such as rioting. A number of people I talked with would not converse with me in the projects. In some cases, we met at prearranged locations, talked on the phone, or met in other settings, such as community focus groups, coffee shops, shelters, courthouses, jail, and prison.

Treva Cunningham and Toria Buchanan, the two sisters who testified against the juveniles suspected of burning the Dollar General, had to move, along with their mother, DeVita Buchanan, out of Sam

Levy. Buchanan testified, "If you open up your mouth living in the projects, they aren't going to do nothing but come and shoot up your house." Treva Cunningham told the court she and a friend watched the Dollar General Store burn, but her friend "still lives over there and she's scared." They also testified that most residents of Sam Levy were afraid of cooperating with the police for fear of retribution. Cunningham's friend remained in Sam Levy and refused to speak with police about what she had witnessed because she was afraid of the repercussions.[44]

On a daily basis, street violence reinforces this fear of retribution, rendering life behind the doors of the family home unsafe. I was walking around in a children's play area behind a homeless shelter for women, itself located in a run-down neighborhood composed of streets where drug deals took place regularly and street shootings occurred from time to time. There was a large concrete wall separating the play area from those streets. The director of the homeless shelter remarked that because of the concrete protecting wall, "this is probably the safest place some of these kids have ever lived. They can play out there without being afraid, you know, not worrying about getting shot."

Life behind the concrete wall may protect the kids from the spray of bullets from drive-by shootings, which are particularly alarming to citizens who have children playing outside. Over the years since crack cocaine came to dominate Nashville's underground economy, newspapers have reported many such shootings. For example, on December 27, 1996, Anthony Robinson, a twenty-nine-year-old black man, was the victim of a drive-by shooting. Robinson was standing on the sidewalk in front of his house as a carload of people came by and fired multiple gunshots at him. In another incident, a person in a passing vehicle shot a seventeen-year-old black man, Derek King, in King's front yard. The perpetrator fired several rounds into a group of people gathered in the aftermath of an earlier shooting. In still another case, Victor Woods, a black man aged thirty-two, was shot multiple times in the doorway of his residence. Police suspected he was selling drugs out of the house; he had an extensive arrest history that included several drug-selling charges.[45]

Life at home in the projects is not unsafe just because of stray bullets. Daryl Thomas explained why he did not feel safe in his own home: "It's not even safe at home, because you know you got people comin' in to rob you . . . just breakin' in. Could be junkies from in the alleys . . . you know, shit like that just walkin' in, shit, it's crazy man, you know you can't really live safe now."[46]

These ethnographic examples are consistent with statistics that show violent street crime rife and highly concentrated in areas of public housing, particularly those projects with a higher proportion of welfare recipients. A 1997 police report revealed that roughly 55 percent of all homicides in Nashville occurred within a one-mile radius of the center of public housing developments. Of these homicides, police reported 70 percent as drug-related, with 83 percent of the victims being black.[47] In 1996, ninety-seven people died in Nashville from homicide or police shootings. Typically, twice as many black men die as white men, and other black men kill nearly all black victims of homicide. The highest recorded number of homicides in a year in Nashville was 106 in 1995. In cases involving the killing of black men, police identified fifty-eight suspects, fifty of them black. At least two-thirds of these killings are drug related, often stemming from turf wars between well-armed dealers and/or sellers.

The Reverend James Thomas of the Jefferson Street Missionary Baptist Church had this to say about the death of black men: "Black life is not worth that much, that's the way most people in the inner city see it." Responding to claims that some black men had not internalized the virtues of "delayed gratification," Bernard Lafayette Jr., president of the American Baptist College and pastor of the Progressive Baptist Church in Nashville, commented, "It's not so much instant gratification, it's life expectancy. . . . These guys actually have a full-blown celebration . . . 14-year-olds excited about making it another year. . . . If you ask that same group how many young people they know who have been killed, their hands go up. The whole idea is, 'I better do it now.' "[48]

On many occasions over the last decade, housing project residents have hurled rocks and bottles at police. All the housing projects contend with street crime and violence. However, the looting, burning, and violence at Sam Levy was unusual, and the possible underlying causes warrant further inspection. Sam Levy was the most crime-ridden of the twelve low-income housing projects in Nashville, and one of the most crowded, with 480 housing units and 1,545 residents in a space of just thirty acres. Rhonda Clark, who works at the McFerrin Community Center, told the *Tennessean*, "I can walk through here because I know guys hanging out and their parents. . . . But it's still infested with drugs, and that makes people stressed." As in the John Henry Hale projects, patches of Sam Levy are dark where those involved in the drug trade and other criminal activities have shot out the lights. Local residents are particularly wary about walking in those areas and report feeling more vulnerable there. Children also have to negotiate the street violence. One child, twelve-year-old Antonio, witnessed two men wearing ski masks drive down his street and shoot at a teenager. He told a reporter, "People just drive down the street and shoot."[49] While some residents told me that things have improved in Sam Levy since the rioting and looting, others disagreed. Clarice Aleman told me: "It is worse than ever. There are about a dozen crack houses in these projects. It's really ridiculous, kids can't play, old people can't walk around much. It ain't safe out. It's really rough. They ought to tear this public housing down and do like they done in Edgehill. Have stricter rules about who they let in. All these teenagers with kids just attract drug dealers. They need more jobs and activities for the kids. When we grew up we had activities, we had older people to guide us. Now there are no role models for the young men."

Social Banditry, Thuggery, and Race

Mayor Bredesen expressed the opinion that Leon Fisher was a thug and a drug dealer and that the looting and burning of the Dollar General Store was the work of an urban rabble who had little respect for law, order, and private property. Eager to play down the rather obvious parallels between Nashville and South Central Los Angeles, Mayor Bredesen told the press, "What I don't want people to think is that this is something like South Los Angeles, where the community rises up and burns something. . . . That does not appear to be what happened." The mayor quickly resorted to blaming thuggery for the events: "When thugs come in and burn and loot something that was important for this community, it's not only an affront to this community, it's an affront to all of Nashville." At a news conference outside the burned store, Bredesen articulated a rallying cry, "All of Nashville is going to assist in building this store better than ever." From early on, then, authorities juxtaposed the forces of good and evil for all to consider. Without benefit of public inquiry, Bredesen told reporters, "It's eminently clear to me that Hickerson did everything possible before resorting to deadly force. . . . Once I got the facts of the matter, it seems to be very clear there is no racial component to this."[50] Sam Levy was nearly all black. A white police officer shot an unarmed black man in a state that has a history of such shootings. The flakes of ash had barely settled from the burning; nevertheless, Mayor Bredesen was "very clear" because he had "the facts."

Homicide detective Clifford Mann bolstered the image of Leon Fisher as a "thug" when he told the *Tennessean*, "This guy Fisher, people are out there raising hell because he was killed while attacking a cop. But where did he do all his damage? Right there in Settle Court. He was paying little girls and boys to be his lookouts while he sold drugs, and they're acting like he was a saint." He went on to add that Fisher was part of a "crew of cold blooded killers and drug dealers."[51]

Members of the Sam Levy community had other things to say about Leon Fisher. Rhonda Clark knew Fisher as he grew up. At the time police killed Fisher, Rhonda had been living in Sam Levy for nine years. She told me, "He was all right, he was a good kid who took a wrong turn. He was selling drugs for a living, but he wasn't loud and vulgar, like some of 'em, and he wasn't violent toward members of the community." James Warfield told the *Tennessean* that Fisher, his cousin, had three small children and took good care of his family. In the same article, Mary Riley, an acquaintance of Fisher's, said, "It's very shocking. I've never seen him have an attitude with anybody."[52] Clarice Aleman also knew Fisher. She told me, "He was an all right guy. He did help a number of people in the community, an' his mother, sister, an' his kids. He wanted to do good for his kids. But he was a dealer and got mixed up in that stuff and either your friends gonna kill you, or the police will if you dealin'."

People did not, then, see Leon Fisher simply as a thug and drug dealer. For some he was never a thug in the community. Likewise, the looting and burning of the Dollar General Store meant different things to different people. To further explore the multiple and socially situated meanings of the upheaval in Sam Levy, I turn to the work of social historians who have studied crowds, rioting, popular rebellions, and social crime.

In preindustrial England and France of the eighteenth and early nineteenth centuries, the principal form of social disturbance was the food riot. This consisted of a local protest, usually in a rural area, village, or small town (especially a market town), in which residents col-

lectively and sometimes violently objected to the price and/or availability of bread. Protesting low wages did not appear as a systemic form
of popular and organized agitation until the rise of industrial capitalism
and the emergence of national networks of labor unions. Eventually
the strike came to predominate over the food riot. One of the hallmarks
of preindustrial protest was the destruction of property rather than life
and limb. Another was a stated desire to seek redress and restoration
of traditional rights. The poor saw these as rights lost over the years,
trampled on by their social superiors, ignored, or subverted. Protesters
also sought to preserve the reciprocal responsibilities of social superiors. This included a belief in the resort to what George Rudé once
called the "leveling instinct," or rough justice. Another characteristic
of the preindustrial riot was its spontaneity, often arising out of a small
local gathering of people and spreading rapidly to encompass activities
such as arson, property destruction, looting, and burning people in
effigy.

Gustave Le Bon reasoned that a preindustrial crowd assumed the
basest of human instincts, being reduced to something akin to a hyp-
notic state devoid of all collective intent and political meaning.[53] In
short, the crowd was a mindless entity. This viewpoint was consistent
with various myths about such a group and its members. Explanations
of preindustrial rioting that strip such behavior of any political meaning resemble the knee-jerk interpretation of the Dollar General looting
and burning offered by Mayor Bredesen. The similarities between Le
Bon's interpretation of crowd behavior and Mayor Bredesen's construction warrant careful consideration.

In talking about legends concerning crowds and rebellions, George
Rudé comments, "What . . . dies hard is the legend of the crowd as riff-
raff or . . . as a 'mob,' 'foreigners,' lay-abouts. . . . Usually these epithets
fell wide of the mark, as these rioters, in particular, turn out, from the
voluminous records that have survived in their case, to have been
mainly respectable labourers and rural craftsmen of almost unimpeachable character."[54] E. P. Thompson reminds us that in the eighteenth
century, "the men and women in the crowd were defending traditional
rights and customs; and, in general . . . they were supported by the
wider consensus of the community."[55]

Referring to the eighteenth-century crowd, Rudé makes the important point that the members "could hardly fail to be corrupted by the
example set them by their social betters. It was an age of brutal flog-

ging, torture of prisoners and public executions: in London, the desic-
cated heads of the Jacobite rebels . . . still grinned down from Temple
Bar in the early 1770s; and in Paris men were broken on the wheel
before the City Hall to the accompaniment of the consoling incanta-
tions of officiating clergy."[56] Whatever the levels of violence meted out
by protesting crowds, violence committed by "social superiors" or political authorities was always much greater, exacting a far greater toll
in terms of loss of life and injuries. How do these insightful observations about the commission of social crime apply to the Dollar General
looting and burning in the aftermath of the police killing of Leon
Fisher? Was the looting and burning akin to the leveling instinct Rudé
noted? A form of "rough justice"?

Since coming to the New World, African Americans have never
played on a level playing field. Consequently, it is difficult to interpret
the Dollar General incident as an example of rough justice or leveling.
Given the social and political quarantining of the housing projects, the
social upheaval in Sam Levy Homes enjoyed little popular or widespread support among other Nashvillians. Even if the looting welfare
mothers saw their own behavior as justifiable or protopolitical, I found
no evidence from those I talked with or from the documents and media
reports I read that dominant white society shared such sentiments.

Just as Rudé noted that the eighteenth-century crowd could "hardly
fail to be corrupted by the example set them by their social betters,"
dominant European American culture provides plenty of past and present examples of brutality and punitiveness toward blacks. If history is
a rearview mirror and a hypothetical black man is at the wheel, the
specter of slavery and all its ritualized violence looms large with every
glance to the distant past. The driver sees the image of the white mob
in September 1957 in Nashville, aroused and full of hate at the desegregation of schools. The driver sees the armored cars in Edgehill after
the assassination of Martin Luther King Jr. and the shooting out of
streetlights by the national guardsmen. More recent images include the
ritualized hosing down of the jail elevator after the brutal beating of
recalcitrant or noncompliant black suspects. Even if our hypothetical
black man chooses not to glance into the mirror, if he glances out of
the window he may see his dead brothers zipped into body bags, perhaps the result of overzealous policing. If he looks just ahead to the
horizon, as all good Americans do, things do not improve, for he sees
growing numbers of black brothers anxiously awaiting lethal injection,

endlessly contemplating the last twitch of their bodies and their last sad breath. The driver needs to keep his eyes open as he drives. He must pay attention. He must survive. Even if he lapses into a trancelike state in which he never looks in the mirror or he looks forward but does not see what lies ahead, police may soon snap him out of his trance on a "profile stop." As he negotiates the profile stop, he fears he will become part of the "imagery" for the next generation. He remembers famous names such as Emmett Till, Medgar Evers, Hattie Caroll, Martin Luther King Jr., Fred Hampton, and James Byrd and realizes that his place in history will probably seem inconsequential.

It is also the case that Nashville society did not regard the looters, burners, or Leon Fisher as being of "almost unimpeachable character" in the way that Rudé described the respectable laborers and craftsmen of the eighteenth-century crowd. The spoiled identities of the black characters at Sam Levy stemmed at least in part from their widely perceived status as unemployed, illegitimately employed, or unproductive. The dominant view of black welfare mothers is that of scroungers living, as the undeserving poor do, at the edges of legality. Neither authorities nor the media perceived rioters as "protesters" or a group assembled to claim traditional rights and customs. Indeed, blacks have no history of such rights in the New World, unless one wants to call the responsibilities of planters to feed slaves "rights." Slaves certainly never had a right to life, let alone the right to liberty and happiness. As we have seen, two-thirds of captured Africans died in the African interior on slave marches, in slave castles like Elmina, or on the slave ships.

If we construe the looting and rioting as a conscious or symbolic response to joblessness, police harassment, the erosion of constitutional rights, and welfare reform, they become much easier to see as protopolitical or political expression. As I will go on to discuss in chapter 5, some drug dealers do see their behavior as a form of survival, a rational response to their predicament. However, as Stanley Cohen observes, "We cannot take the offender's denial of criminality in *itself* as an indicator of other social meanings."[57]

Nevertheless, the dominant view of authorities in Nashville was that the undeserving poor found themselves in the housing projects through their own moral failure. They behaved "irrationally and spontaneously" in burning down the Dollar General Store, their neighborhood vehicle to the American Dream. The implicit message from authorities was that those rioters and looters had yet to make the passage from what Darnell Hawkins once called the "normal primitive" to the civilized contributor to mainstream society.[58]

There is much about the Dollar General looting and burning that resembles riots in bygone eras. It is inaccurate to remember Leon Fisher only as a drug dealer or thug. To subsume his behavior under the all-encompassing label of "criminal" is to gloss over all the other things in his life that people saw as good. It is also to ignore Fisher's crimi-nogenic living conditions and the long arm of slavery, and to conven-iently fail to consider young African American men's fear of the police, where that fear comes from, and how young blacks might partake in an ever-amplifying spiral of resistance and violence with police. At the same time, we ought to heed Stanley Cohen's caution about "rescuing today's deviants from the wastebin of social pathology" and his liken-ing of "historians' attempts to rescue machine breakers, food rioters, poachers, and smugglers from—in E. P. Thompson's ringing phrase—'the enormous condescension of posterity.' "[59]

This is not the era of the food riot. We are long past the bloody time in American labor history, from the post–Civil War period to the Great Depression, when large sectors of the workforce fought for better working conditions, higher wages, and the right to organize. Does this mean there is nothing to learn from the aforementioned studies of the crowd and popular rebellion? I think not. We cannot ask Fisher his views on drug dealing, the police, or his other offenses. If he rational-ized his offenses, he might have done so by claiming he supported his immediate family and that police mistreated him. We cannot impute political motives to his behavior. There is no evidence that he saw his crimes as a clarion call to revolution; however, there is no evidence to the contrary, either. From my research it seems accurate to say that many more people than not in Sam Levy and other projects disapprove of street violence and live in fear of it. However, without further eth-nographic work in places like Sam Levy, we must not rule out the possibilty that although people live in fear of crime, they may still construe it politically. It is not clear that a majority of people in Sam Levy disapprove of the subterranean economy and the money that it circulates through the densely packed housing projects. Just because the offenses of men like Leon Fisher might not qualify as social crime does not mean that his neighbors accept the legal code as legitimate.

The residents of Nashville's housing projects are well aware of state surveillance, the erosion of their Fourth Amendment rights, their loss of privacy, and their loss of daily freedoms supposedly guaranteed under the Bill of Rights. They certainly welcome the prevention of street violence and drug dealing, but they know crime and punishment operate within a broader ideological matrix that explains social problems in terms of individual behavior. It is convenient for the "haves" to write off the Leon Fishers of this world as drug-dealing thugs; looters as thieves; and the incendiarism in cities from Nashville to Los Angeles as dangerous social malaise. However, a closer look reveals something else.

Like rioting in preindustrial England and France, the rioting in response to the killing of Leon Fisher was spontaneous and swift, and involved mostly violence to property. In the immediate aftermath of the shooting, a crowd of a hundred or so people gathered and threw rocks and bottles at police. The police donned riot gear. There was no further loss of life on either side. Rioters may have burned the Dollar General Store because it was the nearest possible object of their wrath. However, it would be remiss not to reemphasize its symbolic meaning as a job-training center. In recent decades, the Sam Levy community witnessed jobs migrate to overseas markets and inaccessible suburbs. Residents saw community and family life greatly compromised by, among other things, a violent street economy. We could debate whether the employment readiness offered at the Dollar General is tokenistic or meaningful. The evidence suggests both to be true. Clearly, on the one hand, you can prepare would-be workers all you like, but without the presence of meaningful, accessible, well-paid labor, such preparation means little. Unless we reverse the historical trajectories of global capitalism, job-readiness programs and education will always be of limited worth.

The majority of residents in Sam Levy disapproved of the burning of the Dollar General Store. At the same time people also seemed to understand how things could culminate in such incendiarism. After the arson, one resident of Sam Levy Homes attacked the stereotypical image of those who lived in the Nashville projects.[60] Resident Faye Hall commented, "It shouldn't have had to go this far, but it took this to let people know what's going on over here. . . . Everybody who lives here ain't dope dealers, like some people want to portray us. Most of us want the best for our kids, and we want to move out of here. People say things and they don't even know our names. They need to start listening to the people who live in these communities. Our kids shouldn't be in prison in their own homes. The leaders of this city need to take time and go to the different projects to see what is going on."[61] I do not want to dismiss the regret single mothers in Sam Levy expressed about their loss of opportunities due to the burning of the store. We ought not ignore the importance of job training for young black women, some of whom are addicted to drugs, have lost their children to the courts, or are victims of domestic violence. Put differently, it is impossible to separate the regret of young black mothers at the Dollar General burning from the state assault on the black family.

As I noted, people expressed differing opinions on the appropriateness of the looting. Clearly, a significant number of women in Sam Levy participated. Whether others felt comfortable with the looting is a question not easily answered. Given the number of people who participated and the varied reactions to it, clearly more people appeared comfortable with the looting than the burning. We do not and are not likely to know the extent of approval. This would require the systematic interviewing of those involved. However, we ought not assume that just because people, in this case mostly young black women on welfare, steal from a store on a grand scale that it has no political meaning for them, especially if "political" refers to the deployment of power. Given the meltdown of welfare support into forced labor in low-paying jobs, these women deployed what limited power they had left. Doubtless their action was also a reflection of their collective anger at the shooting of Leon Fisher. The zipping of young black men into body bags is profoundly political, and we ought not minimize the seemingly chaotic, opportunistic, or self-serving responses to it.

Where do these observations leave us? Was the Dollar General riot a form of nihilistic violence to property triggered by yet another perceived form of police excess? Is it the case, as Paul Hirst once condescendingly commented, that "Criminality is an individualised response by backward and pauperised sections of the working class, not a political response by its vanguard"?[62] Indeed, can we attribute clear meaning to the behavior of those who looted and burned?

It seems at first glance as if the notion of social crime lacks currency in communities like Sam Levy Homes, a neighborhood stripped of much of the essence of family, community, and wage labor. Many poor blacks either have lost interest in voting or have forfeited the right to vote because of their status as convicted felons. Is it not just a little disingenuous of criminologists and policy makers to dismiss riotous violence as criminal, degenerate, or counterproductive, when rioters and looters have little else left? How could neighborhoods like Sam Levy *not* implode as black people endured the twentieth-century redemption, including mass surveillance and harassment by police? Putting it bluntly, the twentieth-century reconstruction reveals the limited impact of formal political rights (individual rights) over substantive social and economic rights. Blacks might well ask the meaning of fancy and ethereal notions such as liberty, freedom, and justice when it is such a struggle to put food on the table, raise children safely, and find some semblance of dignity and worth through regular wage work. Indeed, I would argue that the criminal justice juggernaut replaced the plantation master as principal oppressor and that felonious labels substituted for the property qualifications and literacy requirements that undermined black voting rights in the 1890s. Without question, the Bill of Rights is rewritten every day in places like Sam Levy. This rewriting attests to the centrality of community policing and the criminal justice juggernaut to the twentieth-century redemption, and the growing correspondence between racial demoralization and the selective production of surplus populations under global capitalism.

That community policing emerged in a postindustrial society experiencing growing disaffection among the urban poor is no accident. Indeed, as I will go on to show, the rhetoric of community policing is a powerful ideology accompanying the erosion of any pretense of community, and the writing off of a generation of young black men as breadwinners, fathers, voters, and citizens. Community policing, like the slave patrol of old, is another way of infiltrating black communities. However, the "beauty" of community policing is that it achieves this surveillance at the same time as purporting to democratically manufacture consent. In some projects, such as Edgehill, it is indeed the case that saturation community policing has meant that many more streetlights remained lit than was the case five years ago. It is also the case that a significant number of residents appreciate the decrease in visible street crime and the reduction in shootings.

There is a deeper and more disturbing historical current running through the postindustrial criminal justice juggernaut's targeting of young black men. As we have seen, these men have told of their negative experiences with the criminal justice system. They mentioned not only the constant harassment and surveillance by police but also the degradation of jail, prison, and unemployment. It is as if we have reconstructed the Door of No Return at Elmina Castle in the flourishing jails and prisons of postindustrial America. It is as if the bull's-eye painted on the foreheads of young black men re-creates the hot-iron mark branded into the flesh of black Africans awaiting passage. If the bull's-eye is too abstract a metaphor, then the label "criminal" or "felon" surely traces an unbroken line back to the shackles clamped onto slaves as they rode the oceans to the New World. If this is not political, then I do not know what is.

The Dollar General Store after the looting and burning triggered by the police killing of Leon Fisher. Photo by Sam Parrish.

Workers board up the Dollar General Store and YWCA Learning Center after it was looted and burned. Photo by Sam Parrish.

The new neighborhood camaraderie: Metro police officer Troy Smith passes out "Junior Police Officer" badges to the neighborhood children in front the burned-out Dollar General Store in the Sam Levy Homes area. Photo by Sam Parrish.

Graffiti in the Settle Court area of the Sam Levy housing project warns readers that the war on drugs is understood as a war by both sides to the conflict. Photo by George Walker IV.

Police go door-to-door in the Sam Levy project searching for stolen property after the burning of the Dollar General Store. Here they apparently found nothing suspicious. Photo by P. Casey Daley.

Police officer Dartell Treadwell watches Mohammed Elmi point his finger at his family, signaling them to pack their belongings and move out of their Settle Court apartment. The family moved to Nashville from Somalia and spent 10 months in Sam Levy. They are leaving because of their fear of violence and the drug trade. Photo by George Walker IV.

Maxine Thomas protests police shootings of blacks as a Metro police officer photographs the protesters. Photo by Bill Steber.

Rebuilding the Dollar General Store: Volunteers pick up debris while Mayor Phil Bredesen pushes a wheelbarrow in the background. Photo by Jared Lazarus.

Paint your Dumpster: Koyondra Wilson, six years old, paints a Dumpster outside the Dollar General Store and YWCA Learning Center. Photo by Jared Lazarus.

Black Kin and Intimate Violence

■ Springtime was in bloom as I pulled up in the parking lot of the Tennessee State Correctional Facility for Women. I got out of my car and headed toward the reception area. I was due to talk with a group of inmates about their lives, their families, their experiences with the police, and crime in and around the housing projects. The atmosphere at the prison was tense. Two women awaited execution on death row. As I walked toward reception, a startling juxtaposition of images confronted me. The first was a cluster of flowering Bradford pear trees, thick and creamy against the skyline. The night before I had seen similar luxurious blooms as I traveled through a wealthy new subdivision of Nashville to interview a senior police officer at his home. The second image was the concertina wire surrounding the prison complex, confining a motley collection of supposedly dangerous individuals.

Amid laughter, tears, cussing, and poking fun, rich information emerged from the conversations. At some point in their lives, these women's intimate male partners had beaten them. Holly had lived in the Nashville housing projects most of her life. She was serving time for fighting back against her violent husband. Her story provides a neat segue into my discussion of the policing of domestic violence. Holly told her story with great humor and panache. I sensed that she had told it several times before.

This man got the gun, he's talkin' about how he's fixin' to blow my brains out. I got on the phone to 911, "Please y'all, 911, somebody please hurry, please hurry." I hear the gun click . . . "Pa-ching." Dead blew up the waterbed. The woman on the other end [dispatcher] said, "Madam, what's goin' on? Madam what's goin' on? . . . [laughter] I'm sayin, "Lady help! The man got a fuckin' gun, lady help!" . . . I'm up on the big waterbed, now water goin' everywhere . . . and the woman said, "Don't cuss, lady, don't cuss." [laughter]

What the hell you talkin' about "don't cuss?" [laughter]

I was sick of bein' bruised. I can't see. Got to open my eyes with my hand. He said, "Bitch, I'm goin' to bed." He went up an' he went to bed. I pour me some grits and water, like I seen my momma do to my daddy, and I sit there, and I sit there, and grits and the water got together. I put in some sugar. I just pulled the cover back, started pouring from the top of his head all the way down to his mouth. Police come, "Lady . . . why didn't you call us?" I said, "You ignorant motherfuckers, if you check 911 I called y'all three hours ago tellin' you this man is shootin'. . . . This waterbed is blown to hell, holes all in the mattress, great big old holes in the wall, water done just messed up everythin' . . . and that was a sawed-off double barrel, he meant business." Police said, "Well, we gonna have to carry you in." I said, "Carry me in?" They carried me down . . .

Well you call them police, you call police an' you hang up the telephone, they'll get there quicker than you would callin' 'em. . . . and tellin' 'em there's somethin' goin' on. They'll call right back to make sure you're okay. . . . [laughter] Well this happened just recently. I just found this out. My uncle, he called the police station, and told them that he was gonna blow it up, and they came an' got him immediately. [laughter] They took me to jail for aggravated assault. They told me the sugary grits was the weapon. They said that sugar in that grits was just like glue—it peeled all his skin.

Elaine told her story quietly, without sarcasm, and with a deeply depressed affect lubricated with tears. Elaine perceived that she contributed to her own victimization by giving her abusive partner authority to "take that much possession over my life." She drew much support from people at the table as she recalled her abusive husband's surveillance and torture, and the resistive violence she used against him that eventually led to her incarceration.

He was possessive. I gave him that authority over me to take that much possession over my life. The jobs I had, every job I had while I was with him for eleven years, had to be to his standards, the clothes I wore . . . he had to go to the shopping mall with me and make sure that my skirts wasn't too short . . . my pants wasn't too tight, um, when we went out to eat I had to sit with my face like this in the plate and eat. I couldn't look at nobody. Somebody recognize me and he says, "Who that!?" . . . You know and stuff like that, and then, you know, a lot of times I blame myself for stayin' with him as long as I did because I figured if I hadn't stayed with him as long as I did, he wouldn't been able to continue to abuse me. But, when you in love with somebody you take stuff like that. . . . This man stabbed me in my leg with a butcher knife, he beat me up . . . and then would try to have sex with me. After he done beat me, he talk about how I look beautiful with my face all swelled. I got knots on the top of my forehead, but I look beautiful to him with all these knots and stuff. He like just to see me like that because he knew that nobody else would want me. But he beat me up one time too many, I got hurt. I did like she [Holly] did. I let him go. I made love to him. I let him go to sleep. When he woke up I was sittin' in his chair stabbin' him with a steak knife. . . .
I took him and drug him to the car, took him to Vanderbilt Hospital, called his mom, and told her, "I just almost killed your son for puttin' his hands on me." They handcuffin' me at

the hospital. He told the police, he said "Naw, I don't want to press no charges against her." And I looked at him, I said, "You shouldn't! Look at me." An' I told police, I said "Look at my damn face—he done beat me stupid, an' I'm not supposed to do anything to him? And you all gonna take me to jail?" See, that's what I can't understand. When we fight back to protect ourselves, the law wants to lock us up.

I attended domestic disturbances in poorer neighborhoods of Nashville, interviewed two groups of mostly black women from the Tennessee State Penitentiary for Women, and talked with twenty or so other women at domestic violence and homeless shelters. Many of these women had remained silent about their victimization for long periods of time. They attributed their silence to fear of retribution, love of their abusers, shame, embarrassment, wanting to keep the family together, relying on his paycheck, and hope that things might change.

Cecilia, a black woman, endured three violently abusive relationships from 1986 to 1997. She talked about domestic violence in the black community. "I heard my mom talk about how my grandfather abused her and his family. She was from a family of nine children. I've heard other stories like that. In the black community people want to keep it hush-hush. This is a family matter. This is nobody else's business."

One night at a refuge in a run-down neighborhood in East Nashville, I attended a support group meeting for ten black battered women. At the meeting Alicia told me that some black women would not automatically call the police if beaten. She told me that the projects offered little privacy. Calling the police, for whatever reason, violated that privacy. Given the street violence in the projects, one can understand Alicia's sentiment. She also observed that some black female victims of domestic violence engaged in illegal activities that made calling the police problematic. "The environment that they're living in, you don't call all the time, ya know, because everything is everybody's business and you know they don't want people to know what's going on behind closed doors. A lot of times the woman could be involved in some illegal action and she might not speak out about domestic violence."

Bessie, the support group facilitator, talked of the courage of black women coming together to share their victimization.

When you think about it historically, this whole issue of domestic violence for women of color, and black women in particular . . . was kept hidden, and unless you talked to your doctor, your pastor, unless you were able to speak to your friend
next door, you kept it between the family members. This support group is really a new way of fighting back in terms of
speaking out, to come and talk about what's going on in their
homes. We have to not only work through the mistrust of the
system, but we have to . . . trust one another. It's amazing that
we have these women who actually are very courageous to even
take the steps to enter into that healing process of speaking out
and doing whatever they can to keep themselves safe.

Many black women I talked with highlighted a deep-seated historical resistance to opening up black family life to scrutiny. Black women
passed down this resistance across many generations, which may indeed trace an unbroken line back to Africa. Black women withheld
information about familial conflict and domestic violence as a means
of preserving the integrity of black kinship systems in the face of slavery and its aftermath. Given this cultural legacy, it makes sense that
black battered women would see the family as a respite from a deeply
racist world and would hesitate before calling authorities. It is likely
that black family life alleviated the pressures of slavery in different
ways for black men and women. During slavery and beyond, black
women endured interpersonal violence at the hands of black men
within those families, just as they endured rape, sexual assault, whippings, and other forms of ritualized violence and control by white slavers.[1] Though it may have been the case that white planters prohibited
slave men from assaulting their partners, white men had the right to
beat women to maintain discipline on the plantations. How this affected black women's senses of their families as potential respites and
how these understandings influenced their willingness to report their
abusive black male partners needs more exploration.

As Herbert Gutman shows, the black family endured many hardships during slavery. Referring to evidence from Mississippi and northern Louisiana slaves, Gutman notes that "about one in six (or seven)
slave marriages [was] ended by force or sale." He goes on to observe
that most slave sales apart from estate divisions and bankruptcies involved teenagers and young adults. Slave parents hated slave owners

for making such sales. Specifically, Gutman comments, " 'Good' masters hesitated making such sales; 'bad' masters did not; all masters poisoned the relationship between slave parents and their children."[2] Undoubtedly, the black family lived with the threat of the potential sale of one or more of its members. Just as it did not recognize slave marriages, the law did not protect the black family. However, Gutman's work established that most blacks lived in nuclear families during slavery and that black men and women sought out marriage during nineteenth-century Reconstruction as a legal way to confirm and sanctify their unions and bolster the black family.[3] He notes that upon emancipation "most Virginia ex-slave families had two parents, and most older couples had lived together in long-lasting unions." Strongly disagreeing with Daniel Patrick Moynihan's influential work on the black family, Gutman argues that the post–World War II migration of blacks northward caused significant family breakup. Gutman attributed this breakup not to the "tangle of family pathology" rooted in slavery (Moynihan's argument) but to the chronically high unemployment and underemployment that greeted blacks displaced from the rapidly mechanizing system of southern agriculture. Put simply, blacks could not earn sufficient money to support family life in northern cities. The rise of global capitalism exacerbated this unemployment and underemployment, particularly from 1980 onward.

That blacks have had to fight to preserve, further extend, and develop their kinship systems in the face of pressures such as unemployment and underemployment reminds us of their deep commitment to family values. In their long and oppressive history, blacks really have put families first. This concern to protect family life is one of the roots of the deep compromise faced by black battered women in the housing projects of Nashville. It was only during the twentieth-century redemption (1980–2000) that domestic violence in black kinship systems appeared on the political radar. Such interest in extending police "protections" to the black community arose partly in response to the calls for police reform articulated by the Kerner Report. However, as my ethnography reveals, protecting black women from violent intimate partners does not simply turn upon the provision of more effective and proactive community policing services. Rather, the plight of black battered women exists alongside the disadvantaged position of black families in general and the ever weakening position of black men in the global economy. The assault on black kinship systems during the twentieth-century redemption actually renders black women more rather than less vulnerable to intimate violence.

Marcie, a black victim of domestic violence, told me it was difficult to report her abuser. After attending a domestic call at Marcie's home, a detective and I dropped her off at a friend's house in the Edgehill projects on a Saturday night around midnight. Marcie told us she wanted to go in quickly because people might label her a "snitch." Any association between a black battered woman and the police, including turning in a man who beats her, risks housing project residents' applying such labels. The battered woman is more vulnerable still if her abuser sells drugs or engages in street crime. As Marcie walked to her friend's house, a half dozen young black men stood within a few feet openly selling drugs in an Edgehill parking lot. They scrutinized the detective and me closely. We also drew stares from a group of five or six people standing in the front yard of a crack house. At that time of night in Edgehill our unmarked and rather run-down police vehicle did not provide us with what I perceived to be adequate protection. My fear was palpable, and I was glad to leave the scene. I could not help wondering how Marcie and others lived under such conditions.

Bessie talked of how black women feel compromised reporting black batterers because in so doing they must become accusers. These black battered women worry that in identifying their abusers to police they might perpetuate stereotypes of black men as "violent." Bessie believes that the women's movement neglects black battered women and is unable to see how its emphasis on the empowerment of individual women does not take into account black women's concern with the black community as a whole:[4]

> What we have learned is that it's anger about a lot of things. Not just him beating her. It's anger about what she doesn't have access to. It's anger about not having an education. It's anger about not having money. It's anger about not being able to take care of her children. It's anger about the stigmas, the stereotypes, and the system. It's anger about her own situation but also anger about his situation. The inner conflict about "I have to report him and he's a black man. When I report him, what does that do to him? Then I become part of the system." The whole issue of the disproportionate number of black men that are in prison. And the whole black man plight—just dealing

with that, is tough. It's tough. Very tough. So when sisters come
to our program, we are very respectful of them just for having
courage to pick up the phone. You see what I'm saying? She
becomes part of the accuser. And that's a lot to deal with.[5] But
at the same time, as a victim, I've got to make myself safe. So
it's a lot of emotions and a lot of feelings in there. And in terms
of fighting back, they say we fight back more, and sometimes
I really don't buy that because of our spirituality or our religi-
osity. And when you're part of a religion that says to you, "Forgive and forget," there's a part of you that you're denying, and
that's the anger. And it takes that last hit. Then you say, "I
can't do this anymore." Everybody reaches a place when they
say, "No more."

Some battered black women talked of their need to have a father
figure to help their sons negotiate masculinity and the streets.[6] These
women talked of putting up with domestic violence so that abusers
might help their sons survive the dangerous world of the housing projects. Living in safer neighborhoods, although not necessarily safer
homes, white women did not face the same kind of trade-off.

During my ethnographic research in Florida and Nashville, a number of black women told me that they see battering as more of a white
woman's problem that they, as black women, would not put up with.
Alison, a black battered woman from Florida who killed her abusive
husband, rendered an eloquent statement of this viewpoint: "White
girls are gullible. White girls will put up with centuries of abuse. They
will not fight back. It is just the way they've been brought up. They
are very soft. They are taught to be obedient. A lot of white girls even
let their kids run all over them. Black women are a little smarter."[7] If
this view that black women will not or should not put up with battering is pervasive, then black battered women may experience considerable shame. Perhaps this shame is of a different form, degree, and
intensity from that suffered by more affluent women of European ancestry.

Domestic homicide rates among blacks are higher than those
among whites and Latinos.[8] However, some research reveals that this
effect falls away dramatically when researchers control for socioeconomic status.[9] Studies of all persuasions suggest higher rates of
domestic violence among poor blacks than poor whites. Noel Cazenave

and Murray Straus report that at the lowest income levels "black and white respondents . . . have similar rates of severe spousal violence except at the $6,000–$11,999 income level where the rates are notably higher for blacks."[10] Bureau of Justice Statistics (BJS) (1998) show black women more vulnerable to nonlethal intimate violence than women of all other races.[11] The disproportionate victimization of black women could be the reason more black women commit domestic homicide. Between 1992 and 1996, 11.7 per 1,000 black women experienced intimate male violence, compared to 8.2 per 1,000 white women. Over the same period, 2.1 per 1,000 black men and 1.4 per 1,000 white men reported intimate female violence.[12] According to official sources, intimate partner homicide declined in the black community at a much faster rate than among other races or ethnic groups.[13] This faster reduction might be attributable to increased policing of black communities; the mass incarceration of young black men, who are no longer available to either kill or be killed; the more efficient provision of medical services that reduce the death rate from things like gunshot wounds during domestic disputes; or the fostering of a social climate more critical of domestic violence, a climate promoted by the anti–domestic violence movement and the growth of shelter for women.

One possible reason black women do not report their own interpersonal victimization or that of their neighbors is that they see too much domestic violence in their communities. Without further detailed ethnography it is difficult to know how deeply embedded this desensitization to domestic violence might be among residents in Nashville's housing projects. In a public forum in the James A. Cayce public housing projects, a young woman recently reminded Bessie of some people's complacency toward domestic violence. Bessie explained:

I was out in Cayce Homes about three weeks ago facilitating a discussion on domestic violence. There was a young lady there that challenged me like I had not been challenged before by a teen in I don't know when. She challenged in that she was so desensitized to a family member who was experiencing domestic violence. It was a lethal situation. She was saying to me, "So what, Bessie, I know exactly what you're talking about." I'm up here doing the power-control wheel and talking about the dynamics, the cycle, doing all that. She says, "I don't care. You can tell me that all you want to but she keeps going back to him and he keeps beating her, so we just leave it alone. We don't do anything about it." So we were going back and forth with one another. I was determined to keep her talking. I wanted to hear that attitude. When I finally presented to her, "What if there were lots of people in the community that feel the way you do about domestic violence and everybody just accepts it?" She said, "That's how it is." And then, right at that moment, I realized how important it is for us to continue to educate in those particular communities because now it's just normal behavior. What that says to me is, if this is normal behavior to a seventeen-, eighteen-, or nineteen-year-old child, the chances of her being a victim . . . are greater.

However, my conversations with Officer Ron Hawkins, a white officer who worked in Edgehill for two years as community policing took off there, had a more positive view of the willingness of black women to report domestic violence:

Once they found out there were officers at the Edgehill Enterprise Office that were dedicated to making sure that they were safe, they knew they could call us and ask for a specific officer and say, "Listen, he came over again last night. He was beating on my door at three o'clock in the morning, screaming and yelling, cussing me and threatening to kill me." She would know that I have some history with her as far as her past incidents with this boyfriend or husband or whatever. We would say, "Okay, come on over to the office. We will come get you and take you down to get an order of protection," or if the protection order was already there, we would get a warrant for violating that order. They got to the point that they were doing it. And then we would assist them, of course, through the entire process. When they would come into court, we would show up too because we would physically make the arrest or we had some contributing information. Women would come in and say, "Hey, Officer Hawkins." They would come over and sit down next to us and we would tell them what the process was, what was going to happen, this is what we're doing, this is how things are going to happen today in the courtroom process. It made them more comfortable with it. Has it influenced others to call and report domestic violence? I think so. I don't have hard numbers, but I think it has.

In a discussion about the decline in domestic homicides, Detective Bronson offered the following observations, concurring with Officer Hawkins that the rise in community policing has led to an increased call volume on domestics:

Bronson: I know that Vanderbilt's Medical Center, for instance, is an excellent trauma center. I've seen them, the EMTs, say, "They're not going to make it." And they would get them to Vanderbilt, and they make it. I think the medical services have had a great impact on reducing homicides. I believe community policing is building more trust. We get a lot more calls a lot quicker. Reporting has definitely gone up. Whereas somebody else would say, "I thought I heard a gunshot next door but I'm not going to call. I don't want to get involved."

Websdale: So it's neighbors reporting as opposed to, say, victims increasingly reporting because of community policing presence? It's not like you're getting into the families but . . .

Bronson: I would say that both have increased.

However, it remains clear from my ethnographic findings in both Nashville and Florida that there are a significant number of women who do not call the police.[14] In Florida, it was among the ranks of these highly entrapped women that the domestic homicides occurred, with either partner killing the other. My ethnography reveals something of how black battered women feel about calling the police, but we need to learn much more. Clearly, as in Florida, a significant portion of people killed in domestic disturbances came from families that have had little contact with the police. Detective Bronson, concurring with my research into domestic homicides in Florida, which showed domestic deaths to be mostly crimes of escalating violence, intimidation, and entrapment of women, said: "Most of the homicides that are related to domestic violence are victims that we have never dealt with. We have had a few that we have dealt with, but a lot of them we never had the first call. You have to wonder if their family ever knew about any of this violence, and if they did, why didn't they call? People had to know about this after seeing all these injuries; it had to be going on, because the probability of them just shooting or stabbing them to death for the first time is very low. Most likely there is an escalation of bruises or broken bones."

Battered women also talked of their fear of public space,[15] though some appeared tough and street savvy, and said they did not find their particular projects threatening; those women were in the minority. Battered women's fear of the social and physical spaces surrounding their homes makes it difficult to get to shelters or attend support group meetings concerning battering or drug-addiction problems. Regina, who works with battered women from the projects in Nashville, explained:

> One of the things that we have had to deal with is their level of concern for safety, even in terms of being picked up by a cab to get to our program. The cab driver does not come to that area after a certain . . . time on certain days. We used to have support group meetings on Friday. If we didn't call a taxi before twelve noon, the taxi driver would not go into the area. That, to me, said a lot. So if we didn't call to say "pick up this woman at a certain place that is outside of the housing area," then we would have to make other arrangements to pick her up. Not only is this woman in danger in her home, but once she steps outside that door, it's like a war zone that public transportation will not enter. I'm not hearing from women that we are serving from that area that they feel safe because police officers are there on bikes.

Much of what I have referred to above concerns battered women who live in the poorest sections of Nashville, namely the public housing projects. Most of these women are African American. Most are unmarried and do not need to seek formal legal dissolution of their violent relationships. A conversation with two legal advocates for battered women, Henrietta and Germane, reminded me of the extent to which poverty is a barrier for women who seek to leave their abusers. I had witnessed this phenomenon before in rural Kentucky, where women reported using permanent orders of protection as "makeshift divorces."[16] It was disconcerting to see a similar drama played out in

Nashville, where, in the Latino community especially, there is a strong patriarchal imperative against divorce.[17]

Websdale: I attended a "domestic" the other day where a woman was looking for a divorce and was looking to move out of her relationship, and she was telling me that she managed to find a cheap source of a divorce, which was $375. She said it would normally cost $500 to $700 to pick up a divorce.

Henrietta: That is pretty standard. I mean, that is uncontested divorce with no property and no children. Just a very simple divorce.

Germane: When you get into a custody battle . . . I have a friend who left her abusive husband and she spent over $5,000 divorcing him.

Henrietta: Yeah. That's very discouraging for poor women and children especially. Men always threaten to fight for custody whether they want it or not. So it can be very very expensive. If a woman calls an attorney and says, "I have children and I want a divorce and I think he's gonna fight for custody," she will be quoted $1,500 outright.

Websdale: Yeah. I've done some research in Kentucky, and there I heard that women would just not get married again. They will just move away and not get divorced because it so difficult, expensive, and time-consuming. Do you see a lot of that?

Germane: I do. Especially in the community that I work with, the Latino community. There is cultural and religious opposition to divorce to the extent that women will just separate and just never even bother to get a divorce.

Websdale: In a permanent state of separation, if you will, which in itself is somewhat dangerous.

Germane: It is. It is dangerous. They also limit themselves in terms of what they can actually obtain for things like child support. It becomes very difficult. In the Latino population, we're not known to just have one or two kids. Many have four or five, so it becomes very difficult to support a family that size. They don't want to further their state of danger by asking for child support or asking for a divorce. So many don't even bother with it.

The domestic violence case I initially referred to in my discussion with Germane and Henrietta warrants careful consideration. Andy

Baron had abused his wife, Nancy, on a number of occasions, was a drunk, and had problems keeping a job and supporting his family. Nancy was in the process of seeking legal advice regarding divorce and making moves to leave him. On a hot and humid afternoon in August, Andy used his vehicle to ram a car containing Nancy, Kirk (Nancy's brother), and Julie (Kirk's girlfriend). He had followed them to a back street and engaged in a verbal argument with Nancy, following which he rammed their car. Detective Eastwood and I arrived at the scene of what appeared to be a motor-vehicle accident. A patrol unit was already there talking with those at the scene. On our way to the scene we had passed under a bridge a hundred yards from the accident, situated near a truck stop in Nashville. There was large dent in the side of Nancy's vehicle and glass all over the road. Kirk told us that if he had not dived back into the vehicle (landing on the backseat) as Andy rammed them, "I would have been killed." While Detective Eastwood talked with Nancy, I chatted at length with Kirk. I asked him if he had engaged in a physical altercation with Andy that afternoon, to which he replied, "No, he knows better than that, I'd have kicked his butt." At one point Nancy told me that she had located a source for a cheap divorce who charged only $375.

Andy had driven away from the scene in his own car. A security guard from the nearby truck stop witnessed the confrontation and took off in pursuit of Andy. At one point Andy stopped his vehicle, drew a gun, and fired several shots at the security officer, who then gave up the chase. Eastwood and I learned of this shooting over the police radio. Eastwood directed the patrol officer at the scene to interview the security officer, who had returned to the relative tranquillity of the truck stop. I spent the next four hours or so with Nancy, Kirk, Julie, and other family members as Eastwood processed this case through the Domestic Violence Unit (DVU) of the Nashville Police Department, the Nashville night court, the emergency room, and the jail.

At the DVU Detective Eastwood filed four charges of aggravated assault against Andy, who, earlier that day, had also attempted to run down one of his own children. I thought to myself that Andy was not that good behind the wheel of a car, or that he was playing some kind of sinister game. We then proceeded to transport Nancy and Julie to night court to put these cases to the commissioner; Kirk followed in another vehicle. By the time we arrived at night court, it was dark. I glanced around to check out the scene, knowing that this is not always the most salubrious of places. There were twenty or so people milling around, some in tattered clothes, some in suits and nice dresses (attorneys?). As I continued the surveillance work of the wary and, by now, weary ethnographer, Detective Eastwood's radio blurted out a message: "Do you know of an Andy Baron who is now under medical treatment at the ER after receiving two gunshot wounds?" Eastwood wondered if there was any confusion over the name (Baron is a pseudonym for a very common last name), so he checked in with the dispatcher. Nancy was by now distraught in the back of the police vehicle. Julie was helping to calm her down. The dispatcher then confirmed that it was the Andy Baron who had reportedly rammed Nancy, Julie, and Kirk hours earlier and shot at the security guard who had pursued him. As if this was not bad enough, the tension built to fever pitch as the dispatcher told Eastwood that one of the nurses at the ER had described Andy Baron's injuries as serious and life-threatening. Nancy began to wail and throw herself around in the back of the police car, saying that Andy is the father of her three children, and that although he is an "asshole at times," she did not want to see Andy die. We slowly helped Nancy into one of the interview rooms at night court amid those charged with DUI, prostitution, and other offenses.

The patrol officer from the scene joined us. The situation had now changed significantly, because the patrol officer and the detective were not sure if Andy had shot himself or if Nancy had somehow shot him; the police learned that Andy had told the admitting medical personnel that his wife shot him (we heard then he had two gunshot wounds to the abdomen). The patrol officer entered the interview room, where Nancy was still sobbing. He told her to calm down and then asked her if she had erased any of the harassing calls she claimed Andy had made to her earlier that day threatening to hurt himself if she left him. She answered no, telling the officer that the calls were still on the answering machine. The officer, in a very serious tone, told Nancy, "Don't erase those messages; we'll need them as evidence." The patrol officer glanced at me, and we both knew why he needed them; so did Kirk, Julie, and Nancy, all of whom were now paying close attention.

The patrol officer disappeared, leaving me in the interview room with Julie, Nancy, and Kirk. Julie opened a container of pills. As natural as can be, Julie handed Nancy a tablet of Valium from her personal stash, saying, "That should calm you down." Having just witnessed a federal narcotics offense, I smiled rather wickedly to myself: the federal government was paying me as a consultant to work on this project. Being familiar with the effects of Valium, I knew that in approximately thirty minutes Nancy would relax significantly. Indeed, I sensed I had just experienced a rare and transcendent moment of "ethnographic empathy."

The police located Andy's vehicle, and Eastwood and I traveled to examine it. The crime scene analyst found no blood or gun, but did find a large knife under the driver's seat and a collection of empty beer cans. It seems Andy had gotten a ride from where he dumped the van to somewhere close to the hospital. We then visited the ER, where we learned the truth about Andy's medical status. He had two superficial gunshot wounds, seemingly caused by his pinching folds of fat on his stomach and shooting through them. Eastwood and I looked at each other and headed back to night court. By the time we arrived, the patrol officer had listened to Andy's recorded threats to take his own life if Nancy left him.

Behind a thick shield of bulletproof glass and looking down on the courtroom, the commissioner signed out the warrants to pick up Andy. I broke away from the group as we left night court to visit the restroom to urinate. This was clearly a mistake, and if I had not been with a police officer I would probably have been better off finding somewhere quiet at the back of the building to relieve myself. As I left a small, dirty room, that was liberally blessed with a mixture of vomit and fecal material, I ran into Kirk, who took me to one side. I had become quite fond of Kirk as the evening wore on. Indeed, I wondered to myself at the time, somewhat cynically, if this was the kind of male bonding the middle-class men's movement was bleating about. He said he was happy that things worked out right and that his sister was getting justice. It had been clear to Kirk all along that Andy was a game-playing manipulator who had shot himself to get attention. Perhaps at last his sister would see the light and move beyond "this loser." Kirk went on to say that he was due at work in the morning; it was late, and he wanted to get home. I asked what kind of work he did. He told me he delivered flowers and that his boss was already considering him for promotion. According to Kirk, the other drivers were not as quick or reliable as he was. He had been on the job only a month. He then made a strange face and said, "You know, I'm sorry I won't be delivering flowers to Andy at the morgue tomorrow." We smiled and shook hands. People discuss death easily and lightly on the streets.

Police arrested Andy a little while after he left the hospital. We got a call that we needed to book him into jail. As I left the court building and headed toward the jail, I wondered if it was the same jail where police used to beat black men in the elevator. I quickly reminded myself that it was not, that things had doubtless improved in Nashville, and felt a little easier as I rode up the elevator with Eastwood into the booking area. I mentioned the state of the restrooms at the night court to Eastwood, and he looked at me as police sometimes do at academics and said something like, "What do you expect with the prostitutes who work the area, the homeless men, and the drug addicts who sleep in there at all hours?" I reflected on the $375 that Nancy said would pay for her divorce, assuming, as Germane and Henrietta had reminded me, the divorce was straightforward. Eastwood and I went on to the next call.

Violent and Manipulative Black Women?

bell hooks traces the stereotypical image of young black women as "sapphires," or "evil, treacherous, bitchy, stubborn, and hateful," back to the ideologies of slavery.[18] Ideas that young women of color have become increasingly violent seem to derive more from the misogynist tendencies of the media rather than from a careful consideration of the empirical evidence on girls' and women's uses of violence.[19] As noted earlier, there is no debate about the disproportionate involvement of black women in violent acts such as domestic homicide. Neither is there any doubt about the rage existing among some black women over their miserable social conditions. What is missing from much of the media coverage of black women's crime is its political and historical underpinnings and its meaning to the perpetrators themselves. When viewed in these ways, what may appear to be reprehensible violence or manipulative behavior turns out to be largely a survival mechanism. In talking about the involvement of some black women in drug dealing and other forms of crime, Bessie commented: "It's a survival mechanism . . . because of the oppression. If you look at some of those guys and some of the female victims themselves they just want more. You gotta eat, you got to have somewhere to sleep, and you got babies to feed."

However, some police officers told me that they perceived some women to be using the domestic violence laws to manipulate more money out of the drug dealers with whom they were involved. Officer Barry Maul thought that a small number of women from the Edgehill projects sometimes manipulated the domestic violence laws to their own advantage. He noted women's increased willingness to call the Edgehill Community Policing substation once they heard officers would be more responsive:

> When they became aware that there were people that actually would say, "Okay, we'll listen to what you have to say and we will help you," when they became aware of that, they didn't hesitate to pick up that phone. We had a problem with them calling our substation office instead of calling 911. They were calling our office over here for emergencies and that would of course slow down our response time. Once they learned the laws were there to protect them, we had some manipulation of the DV laws right off the bat. Tennessee has very strict domestic violence laws concerning if there are any signs of injury. We have to make an arrest, according to state law. They've taken the discretion away from the officer. Women became comfortable enough that they would call us and say, "Hey, this has happened. . . ." The guys supported lots of girlfriends over here. The girlfriends would let [them] hide in their places, store drugs in their places, store guns in their places, but we would run into the domestic violence. A few of the women would say to the men, "Give me a coupla' hundred dollars cause I want to go to the club tonight." The drug dealer would say no. And the girl would go call 911, "Hey, he just beat me up. I want to get a warrant on him." The drug dealer would laugh as we were taking him to jail. They're going, like, "She ain't coming to court. I'll give her a few hundred bucks when I get out of here and she won't come to court." And she wouldn't show up in court to prosecute the domestic allegations.

I found no expression of this viewpoint among others with whom I talked. It seems likely that cases where women manipulate drug dealers like this are rare. It may be that Officer Maul was buying into the views of drug dealers who battered women rather than identifying any major trend in the policing of domestic disturbances in the projects. It seems unlikely to me, given the violence meted out by some dealers, that any more than a handful of women would try this kind of black-mail.

The links between battered women and drug dealers are much more pronounced among African American communities in the housing projects than they are elsewhere. Hispanic women I talked with from poor neighborhoods told me that authorities jailed them for their use of self-defense. Germane, who has considerable experience working with battered Hispanic women, summarized these problems: "We do have a lot of women who assault their offenders or get charged with it. It's so bogus. I've had a couple of my Latino clients who actually ended up in jail because they have assaulted their husbands, and when I speak to them, I'm like, 'Why were you arrested?' And it was because the police asked, 'Did you hit him?' and they said, 'Yes, I did.' But then the police don't get the whole story. Who was hit first? Patrol officers should be identifying the primary aggressor and asking those questions, but they are not."

In nearly all cases in which Latinas used defensive violence, police later dropped the charges. However, those women still have to go through the degradation of admission to the jail, loss of contact with their children, and attempting to make bond. Many of Germane's clients are not able to make bond, so they stay in jail until their hearings. This vulnerability to the degradation of jail stems directly from the poverty of these women and the tendency of some police to see women as violent and potentially manipulative. I do not mean to imply that women never initiate violence against men in interpersonal relationships, or that women cannot be primary aggressors in those relationships. However, it is unwise to use the word "battering" to describe these episodes of female violence. I concur with Ann Goetting, who reserves the word "battering" for "an obsessive campaign of coercion and intimidation designed by a man to dominate and control a woman, which occurs in the personal context of intimacy and thrives in the sociopolitical climate of patriarchy."[20]

Black Men, Battering, and the Housing Projects

In chapter 3 I discussed research showing that young black men are more likely to commit "violent" crimes than their Caucasian peers, especially offenses the general public fears, such as robbery and murder. It is an understatement to say this tendency contributes to the demonization of black men. Black men are overrepresented among perpetrators of domestic violence and domestic homicide, just as black women are overrepresented as victims of these offenses. Are black men biologically programmed to commit violent crime? No. Otherwise we would see much more crime in all-black communities, especially those communities where blacks enjoy a higher standard of living than they do in the housing projects of Nashville. Were biological explanations valid, we would also expect to see much higher rates of violent crime such as homicide in other countries with high black populations, and we do not.[21]

My focus is on domestic violence among the poor, those typically subjected to the most intense forms of community policing. I asked myself, "What do the black men who live in some of Nashville's public housing projects think about domestic violence and gender relations in today's society?"[22] In particular, I was keen to explore how our explanatory models, such as the power-control wheel designed by the Domestic Abuse Intervention Project in Duluth, Minnesota, might apply to black batterers. Interviews with European American battered women formed the basis for the construction of this wheel. The power-control wheel explains domestic violence as a means for men to control women and to exercise their power over them. It emphasizes men's use of coercion (including violence) and threats; intimidation (through looks, gestures, actions); emotional abuse (put downs and so on); isolation (stringent surveillance and regulation of what a woman does, who she sees, and so on); minimization and denial (making light of violence); the children as a tool to control the woman (e.g., threatening to take them away); male privilege (regarding decision making, being the master of the household, treating the woman as a subordinate); and economic abuse (preventing her from accessing or knowing about family income, making her ask for money, giving her an allowance).

We need to reconstruct this power-control wheel in the case of African American battered women. At some level, the domestic violence of black men parallels that of white men; they use similar techniques, similar forms of coercion, threat, and intimidation. However, we must ask, Can the black perpetrator of domestic violence engage in the same strategies of isolation and resort to the same forms of detailed surveillance of black women as European American men might? Black perpetrators I talked with typically did not live regularly with their intimate female partners. Many were themselves under the close scrutiny of the criminal justice system, especially by police and probation officers. Clearly, the impoverished black perpetrator of domestic violence, subject as he is to the occasional spell in jail and not able to move into and out of the housing projects with ease, cannot easily exert daily controls to the point where he isolates his partner within a family home. Similarly, with his access to children restricted, often by guidelines laid down by the courts and managed by people like probation officers, he will likely not be able to use them to control his partner in the way a European American man might. The impoverished black batterer cannot typically threaten to have the children taken away, fight for custody in the same way through the courts, and so on. Similarly, given his more detached physical presence, mandated by a combination of criminal justice system constraints, public housing rules, welfare policies, and the lack of available jobs in the inner city, the black perpetrator's "enjoyment" of traditional "male privilege" is either greatly attentuated or practically meaningless.[23] Clearly, social class and racial disadvantage rein in male privilege.

As we have seen, slavery involved a profound attenuation of black men's rights and privileges vis-à-vis black women, an attenuation that did not result in the emasculation of black men but rather subordinated their patriarchal privileges to European American planters, who ultimately owned and regulated the bodies of slaves. Likewise, the notion that black men are able to abuse women economically by preventing them from accessing or knowing about family income implies that there *is* a family income or, indeed, a family, to speak of. Most of the black women in the Nashville projects derive their miserable economic benefits from the state. At best, an impoverished black man from a ghetto supplements his female partner's welfare benefits and is therefore unable to engage in the kinds of economic maneuvers more readily available to employed men. All these observations about the limited ability of black men to exert their power and control over intimate female partners raises an important question: Does the narrower, abbreviated, and more frustrated patriarchal privileges of black men result in their using more violence, threats, and intimidation than their European American or Latino peers to regulate and dominate women? Is this the reason a number of studies show that among the lowest income groups, black men use more violence than their European American counterparts? Could this be one more reason why the domestic homicide rate among blacks is much higher than that among

Latinos, European Americans, and Asians? Put differently, does the compromised societal position of black men in a global economy promote their resorting to more-violent forms of patriarchal regulation in their intimate relationships with women?[24] These are important questions that warrant close attention. My entree into these matters is through conversations with people on the street, in their homes, and in various institutional settings.

In a conversation I had with Henry Oliver, a black man in his early twenties, the deeply compromised entitlements of black men vis-à-vis black women appeared embedded in a much wider set of social relations whereby many black people, men and women, feel they are not really "free." For some black men, being free may include the right to use violence to enforce patriarchal privileges. Henry had considerable experience with the police and criminal justice system in Nashville, and our conversation took place while he was on probation for a domestic violence offense. According to Henry, he shoved his girlfriend after she had assaulted him because he turned up late with some groceries and provisions for their children. The couple was living apart at the time of the offense. Henry was arrested. His girlfriend remained at home in the public housing projects with their children. I did not speak with her.

One of Henry's principal concerns was with what he saw as the frantic status competition between men in the projects over every conceivable issue, including sexual access to women. For Henry, going to jail left him to wonder who might be hitting on his intimate partner.

Henry: . . . and my kids, and my lady gonna get with somebody else . . . the next dealer? Or whoever? That's the man's worst fear in the projects, lady bein' with somebody else. . . . You hurtin', you can't get out of jail . . . you life still seem like it's fucked up, because, you know, you always bein' watched.

Websdale: Is that one of the roots of tension between black men in the projects? You know, going to jail, coming back, wondering what's going on, competition between men, between dealers?

Henry: The men . . . 'cause like I said, man, everybody's for 'emselves in the projects. That's why it's the way it is in the projects. Everybody's for 'imself and tryin' to make so much money. . . . In the projects it's just totally different. I mean, in the projects, it's who's the man, who has the shit, who has the most shit and wants to have so much shit to get out, you know, and you don't know when it's enough, when to stop—it's never enough. Money ain't never enough, you know, regardless, I don't care, you can have a normal job and money's never enough 'cause you always need money to spend. . . .

Henry made it clear to me that he disapproved of men beating up their partners. "It need to be equal between men an' women, you know, I'm not against that. If you have some crazy guy that just beat these women . . . that's wrong, and I'm all for Metro to step in an' do their job. I don't like seein' no woman get beat. . . ." Henry noted how "wicked and evil" some black women can be if men decide to exercise their male privilege and move on.

You have arguments, an' damn, some women can be wicked and evil and call Metro 'cause it seems like you wanna move on and be with somebody else. They do it out of spite and . . . Metro's not stupid—they oughtta see that other side of it too. Why come up here an' arrest me? I was arrested you know, and my, my kids seein' me bein' arrested, it's like, "Damn, do you even care, don't you got kids, how would you feel? . . . Only thing you doin' you doin' you're job, which you feel like you gotta do, and that's putting me in cuffs, shit, you're not even listenin." . . . This woman got a little control of my fuckin' life and now, you know, the male is even more angry because he, like I say, "Damn, I'm not even livin' free . . ." I'm not even livin' free.

The collective exposure of young black men to the criminal justice system has sensitized them deeply to being incarcerated for domestic violence. In my conversation with several black batterers, this manifested as a thinly disguised anger toward their partners for calling the police on them. Of course, black women know of the oppression and discrimination meted out by the criminal justice juggernaut. These women often delay calling police until the violence escalates to near-lethal levels. Again, this may be another reason why we see higher levels of domestic homicide among African Americans. This sensitization might be all the greater if the man perceives he has done no wrong and thinks he is being manipulated. Regardless of the facts of domestic cases, clearly men like Henry think about their plight and their lack of freedom, weighing it carefully against their love for their children and their deeply compromised needs to be fathers and providers. There are a number of paradoxes in Henry's words, and perhaps some implied threats about how he or other (hypothetical) incarcerated black men might get even with "their" women from behind bars:

Henry: I don't want to go to jail. I'm just tryin' to live. I love my boys dearly, man, an' it's like, I got to meet her on her terms. When I got out of jail, my probation officer sayin', "Just stay away from her . . ." And I don't want her to cry wolf again. . . . I can't see my kids till they fuckin' grow up, you know, and then if I come over it's like on her terms, you know. I'm so angry. I'm feelin' like a monster now, I feel like a monster because . . . you know, once I'm in jail, it changes the male image . . . with the woman, the relationship, and, especially, if you got the kids, man . . . I'm talkin 'bout the guys that do love their kids, wanna dress 'em like them, they love that type shit, man, you know, just keep their hair neat, and they just want the best for 'em, man, just give 'em all the shit that they never used to have. But once you go to jail, man, I'm tellin' you, then you get back with the woman, sometimes it might just be 'cause the male do right by her now. Some men can be doin' this. Others got a plan, they just wanna stay with her, lay over with her for a while, kiss her ass, do whatever. . . . He mad, you know, inside, but, you know, he got a plan. . . .

   Yeah, and then you got these guys puttin' hits out on these girls, you know, have somebody else come around, "Hell, if I can't do it, I'm a have somebody come and just catch ya out one night, fuck ya up, beat you up,'cause they feel like they can get away with it. Nine times outta ten they can get away with it at night. You can play the role like, "Damn baby, what happened?" you know like, "What happened?" But you really had her fucked up. . . .
Websdale: So you're saying that guys would actually hire somebody . . .
Henry: . . . to fuck her up. . . . Then you know they victims . . . even if they ain't with 'em no more . . . hire 'em to fuck 'em up.

   . . . You gotta pay child support and they wanna go downtown, just to keep draggin' you through the system. A black man hates gettin' dragged through the system. You can be in jail and have motherfuckers from the outside work for you.

   . . . So what makes you safe? 'Cause he behind bars?

Henry is clear about his frustration with the criminal justice system, his lack of freedom, and the fact that it is possible to exact revenge on women from behind the bars of a jail cell. He expresses deep dissatisfaction with his lot in life, not only his inability to see his children on his terms, but also his seeming inability to provide for them economically. A number of black men told me that once the criminal justice juggernaut labeled them a "criminal" or "ex-felon," it was more difficult for them to find and keep regular paid work. If the criminal justice juggernaut's close regulation of black men makes them more likely to use violence against their intimate female partners, then such close regulation constitutes yet another assault on the black family and contemporary black kinship systems.

It is not my suggestion that black men use violence to control women just because they have been oppressed by slavery and its many ugly legacies.[25] If this were the case, we would expect to see many more black domestic violence offenders. Neither do I want to run the risk of excusing black men's violence against women by framing it as a displacement or expression of their hostility toward the criminal justice system or other oppressive social arrangements. What I hope I have raised is the possibility that black men who exert power and control over women through violence have fewer manipulative, surveillance-based tactics at their disposal and, as a result, may resort to more-overt acts of violence and intimidation than their better-off peers of European ancestry. If it is the case that some black men are compelled by broader social forces to employ more violence and direct coercion to control their intimate partners, then I suggest that this patriarchal compulsion has been amplified during the twentieth-century redemption by the rise of the criminal justice juggernaut.

Policing, Battering, and Poverty

During the 1990s the city of Nashville supposedly became a national leader in the fight against domestic violence. In spring 1994 Mayor Bredesen led a $1.08-million initiative against family violence, creating the Domestic Violence Unit (DVU) at the Nashville Police Department,[26] adding more prosecutors and probation officers to the criminal justice system, and increasing services and assistance for victims. The institutional changes accompanied legislative developments that sought to strengthen laws against perpetrators of domestic violence. These new laws began to take effect on July 1, 1995, and included a simplification of Tennessee's stalking law that made it easier for police to press charges and for prosecutors to convict;[27] the adoption of a preferred arrest policy for police, encouraging them to arrest primary aggressors; the establishment of a domestic violence coordinating council to provide education and training to police and judicial agencies across the state; and provision for magistrates to impose conditions of release or bail upon defendants to protect alleged victims.

From its inception the Nashville DVU was the largest of its kind in the nation, with thirty-four specially trained investigators. Before the formation of the DVU, one detective followed up on the approximately eighteen thousand cases a year. This meant that only patrol officers handled the domestic cases, with the Homicide Unit handling the killings. Domestic violence homicides decreased significantly after the formation of the DVU.[28] Each year from 1990 to 1993, police recorded roughly twenty-five domestic homicides. In 1994 and 1995, annual reports reveal fifteen and twelve killings, respectively.[29] During the 1990s the Nashville Police Department pulled in millions of dollars in federal funds to augment the DVU initiatives. On a visit to Nashville in July 1996, Attorney General Reno made a point of praising the DVU and the way it works with the courts and prosecutors.[30] Not unexpectedly, as the DVU grew, so too did the number of domestic violence calls it handled.[31] Similarly, the number of protection orders issued against batterers increased from 700 in 1993 to 3,500 in 1995. The courts developed special dockets to handle domestic cases, and the jail developed a batterer's treatment program. Clearly, these developments translated into real criminal justice system protections for at least some battered women. Among the battered women I talked with, many spoke much more highly of DVU officers than they did of either regular patrol officers or more-specialized community police officers. For victims of domestic violence, the DVU officer is more likely to understand the dynamics of abusive relationships and less likely to accept or buy into the manipulative or minimizing behavior of violent men. Likewise, DVU officers are more knowledgeable about the services available to battered women. In certain cases with a perceived high risk of lethality, DVU officers engaged in what they called "stalking the stalker." Such policing included maintaining a close surveillance on batterers who stalked their victims, putting a trace on their phones, videotaping them, and working with the victim's employer to ensure workplace safety. Rudy Smith, director of the Madison domestic violence program in Nashville, explained, "For us, it's the difference between daylight and dark. . . . The change in procedures and attitudes have made a difficult situation for victims easier than it once was."[32]

The rise of the Nashville DVU as a national model happened during a period when violence against women became a hot issue in party politics. The passage of the Violence Against Women Act (1994), the establishment of the Violence Against Women Office in Washington, and the increased flow of federal funds to the states are all part of the broader contextual frame within which the Nashville DVU emerged. It was no small achievement for the DVU to rise to prominence as it did. Some of its fame derives from the work of individual officers at the Nashville DVU. Sergeant and, later, Lieutenant Mark Wynn's acknowledged expertise in the area contributed much to the unit's reputation and sterling work. However, amidst the hoopla and accolades, at the time of this writing the Nashville DVU is in disarray. Mark Wynn resigned because of political infighting; the long-term captain of the DVU, Shirley Davis, moved to another department; a recent $500,000 COPS grant awaits completion; and women of color in the housing projects continue to complain about their compromised plight as victims of domestic violence.[33]

Undoubtedly, the Nashville DVU does a lot of good work on behalf of victims of domestic violence and has probably saved the lives of a number of women. However, the stories of individual battered women and others remind us that battering is not primarily a criminal justice problem, it is a social problem. The presence or absence of police will typically not deter interpersonal victimization behind the closed doors of the family home. Domestic violence is socially patterned and patriarchally generated, and there are sharp limits on what the criminal justice system can do to prevent it.[34] Battered women and their advocates told me of marked improvements in services for victims of domestic violence. Doubtless, the establishment of the DVU and the use of advocates to train criminal justice professionals contributed these improvements. Angie, an advocate for battered women, said: "When I look back over the time period . . . yes, I have seen changes in how police respond to domestic violence. We have done a lot of training with the police department in terms of social service programs, shelter programs to help police officers understand the dynamics, because maybe seven or eight years ago the general attitude was, 'Oh, it's just another damn domestic . . . ' "

However, battered women and their advocates alike noted definite limits on the nature of that change. None of the women felt that community policing had or would make much difference to battered women. I asked Bessie if any of the women she worked with had reported a difference. She told me: "I'm not hearing from women that we are serving in Edgehill comment about feeling safe because police officers on bikes are there. I don't think victims of crime feel that the system has been improved because you place three, four, or five more police officers. The territory is so large and the issues are huge. You can have a police officer on the west side of the project, but what about the east side? Just because a police officer is outside her home, in the community, doesn't mean that it increases her safety level inside her home. There is a whole lot more change that is required to make victims of crime feel safe than to have a few more police officers available in the community."

Saturation community policing may not make black women feel safer, because those women have a deep suspicion of police. Andrea, who works with battered women in Nashville, told me that community memories of racial oppression died hard. The media coverage of the police's brutal treatment of blacks reenergizes these memories. "And you think of black families that have grown up here and what they have experienced, and that history gets shared. And so again, that fear and distrust will get shared. That still permeates," said Andrea. Bessie told me what the women at the prison told me; she could not, as a black woman, assume that police officers were going to protect her:

> I have had situations where I've walked right out of my office into a drug bust.[35] I have had situations where I'm going to my office and I'm stopped by the police and had fear of the police. When I'm interacting with a police officer, I cannot assume that the police officer understands my experience. I cannot assume that the police officer is there to protect me. And that is the experience of the residents of those project areas. You got a lot of things that you're dealing with there. For example, we approach this issue of domestic violence along with everything that is going in the world. Racism, the huge problem of the importing of drugs, drug culture—that it is a business, that it is a way to make a living, and that some of these women are

victims of that. So to just say that the presence of police officers has improved her safety—we can't make that blanket statement.

Some women at least implied that more saturation community policing might benefit women in the projects. Samantha, a battered black woman I met at an East Nashville support group, differentiated between the performance of the DVU and regular patrol. She then went on to say that round-the-clock intensive police presence combined with a detailed knowledge of domestic violence might have more of an impact than current community policing efforts.

Websdale: So the rise of community policing in the last three or four
    years really hasn't made that much difference to domestic violence?
    Maybe the DV Unit has made a difference?
Samantha: Yeah, but not the regular policing.
Websdale: Regular community policing?
Samantha: No, they need to be more educated. And if they're going to
    do it, do it twenty-four-seven, not just have it during the daytime
    when everybody is at work and everything is calm. But then at
    nighttime, and you call and they come out and they're acting nasty
    because they're coming into a low-income area, and the woman
    might be high, ya know, whatever, that woman is trying to get
    away from her pain for some reason or this man has gotten her
    strung out.

Indeed, research shows that many women victimized by violence often medicate their pain with drugs and alcohol.[36] Indeed, many women who use domestic violence shelters have substance abuse problems. To this group we can add a significant number of women who enter personal relationships with male drug users, addicts, or dealers. If he supplies her with drugs and he later begins to batter her, she must choose between her addiction and her victimization. According to some DVU officers I talked with who worked with women in these situations, women's addictions far outweighed their fear of occasional battery. Officer Peter Simon was one such DVU detective: "I know that we have had several battered women where the men were providing drugs for them. That was one of the things that was keeping her there. Cutting that drug link for them is not a choice. She would rather take the beating than give up the drugs. It seems that the women I have dealt with more or less knew that they were dealers in the beginning. They were not really afraid of them then, but they have had a problem with them and have become afraid of them."

Bessie saw a number of younger black women intimately involved with gang members or drug dealers. She feared for their safety and worried that their abusers would force them to use lethal defensive violence. Note how Bessie's words on the retributive powers of gang members and drug dealers echo those of Henry Oliver:

> One of the groups that I'm real concerned with is the age group of fifteen-plus through age twenty-five to thirty. Many of these younger women are in relationships with violent men who are gang members or drug dealers. Their sense of safety is definitely low, not only because of the violence they are exposed to in the relationship, but the violence that they are more likely to experience if they try to leave the relationship. If he doesn't harm her, somebody else will. So she's trapped. So when you think of a person who is trapped and they are in an environment where there's violence or drugs, they're going to fight back. They're trying to save themselves. I think most of the time black women are trying to defend ourselves; if it's not physically, it's socially. It's one way or the other being on the defense. And again, with that stigma and stereotype of "an angry black woman." Who can live under that? Who can survive that?

Relationships with men who work in the subterranean economy can end up backfiring on women if authorities know of the illicit association. In March 1996, President Clinton signed the Housing Opportunity Program Extension Act, an initiative designed to combat crime in public housing. Drug dealers, gang members, and so-called violent criminals were the principal target of the legislation. Building on the Cranston-Gonzalez National Affordable Housing Act of 1990, which permitted housing authorities to evict tenants for criminal activity, President Clinton made what became known as "One Strike and You're Out" official policy. Clinton's move allowed authorities to better scrutinize applicants and tenants for past and present criminal activity and to evict tenants whose actions on or off public housing premises threatens the safety or well-being of other residents. The housing authorities did not have to rely upon an arrest or conviction to prove the disruptive behavior of problem tenants. Neither did the offender have to be the person whose name appeared on the lease. "One Strike" holds the entire household responsible for the behavior of individuals or their associates. As President Clinton put it, "I challenge local housing authorities and tenant associations: Criminal gang members and drug dealers are destroying the lives of decent tenants. From now on, the rule for residents who commit crime and peddle drugs should be one strike and you're out."[37] The problem is that a battered woman whose name appears on the lease as a public housing tenant is subject to eviction if she cannot "control" the behavior of her abusive partner. As Claire Renzetti puts it, "One especially insidious aspect of One Strike with respect to battered women is the inherent assumption that the abuser is a person under the woman's control, when domestic violence research consistently shows the opposite to be the case."[38] The battered woman in public housing may not call police, take out a restraining order, or otherwise report abuse because she fears eviction. Likewise, she may hesitate to report her abuser's criminal behavior (e.g., drug dealing) not only because she fears retribution from him or because she relies on that criminal activity to feed her children, but also because she fears that the police attention will result in her eviction or limit her ability to apply for public housing in the future. As I heard from women in Nashville, some batterers coerce their victims into criminal activity, such as writing bad checks, selling drugs, storing weapons, driving getaway vehicles, and so on. If she attempts to leave him by applying for tenancy in public housing, it is possible that her involvement in those criminal activities will present grounds for housing authorities to deny her application.[39]

As we saw in chapter 2, a number of female housing project residents make perfectly rational choices about how to survive given the economic exigencies of their lives. If authorities catch women with offenders in and around their homes, or if women receive frequent visits from police, authorities might evict them.[40] According to Officer Simon, "I know that there have been several cases where the patrol officers have told us that if the guy comes back, she will be evicted. Women know that if they are linked to any kind of criminal activity, particularly drugs, they can pretty much be put out of the house."

Germane's understanding of the eviction of battered women from public housing for their association with either criminals or the criminal justice system is similar to Detective Simon's. Germane goes further and warns us of yet another compromise faced by battered women who have to weigh possible eviction against calling the police if their abuser breaches an order of protection. In Germane's words we again see the complex intersection of poverty and safety issues for battered women, particularly those of color, who disproportionately inhabit the lower echelons of the Nashville housing market.

Germane: A lot of women lost housing in the community and in different housing projects because of the number of police cars coming to their house. The housing authority think they are troublemakers and they lose their housing. These are police cars for their own protection from domestic violence. These women are skeptical about the orders of protection anyway because when abusers come around, the women can call the police; but after so many calls, they can be evicted because they are seen as causing a problem.

Websdale: Regardless of the nature of the call?

Germane: Regardless of you being the one who is assaulted and the man has been told by police to leave the place.

My conversation with Ramona at the Tennessee prison was also consistent with Germane's observations about the compromises faced by battered women. She noted, "If anyone in your house is caught in your house sellin' drugs then you get evicted."

Bessie acknowledged that many black women negotiate compromising relationships with black men. Given the combination of public housing rules that do not allow live-in men and the constant harassment of black men by the police, black women engage in intimate relationships cautiously and surreptitiously. This subterranean trafficking in intimacy in the public housing projects is reminiscent of the way some slaves used to arrange to see their intimate partners who lived on different plantations. As Gutman notes, "Such visits between kin with separate owners—and especially husbands and fathers separated from their wives and children—regularly dot the historical record documenting slave behavior. . . . Ethan Allen Andrews learned that drunken young white men chastised an Upper South slave husband whom they found in bed with his wife and without a pass."[41] Of course, many slaves also made these visits *with* passes, and some owners actively encouraged intimate relationships between slaves from different plantations. Bessie summarized the tense way in which the social conditions within the housing projects compromised intimate relationships among blacks:

> When you're dealing with that particular community, housing projects and welfare, there is a mentality. There is an expectation. There is a code that people live by, and you're not going to see many men visible because the women know they are not supposed to have men living there with them. One of the ways to supplement their lifestyle is to have a man available to them for finances or just because it is normal to have a mate. They have to compromise how they experience that because the man is not supposed to be there. That is just understood. To get into housing projects, you have to meet a certain index of eligibility, not only financial eligibility. There is a way to get the man there. . . . You are not going to see men. The visibility is going to be low until the evening.

The women I spoke to at the prison said that domestic violence was often hidden from police:

Beth: Community policing is only gonna affect outer appearances on the streets. Domestic violence is hidden a lot more.
Tabatha: Community policing doesn't really exist, and even if it did, you'd have the same officers on bikes and they're still going to have the same attitude! The attitude hasn't changed any, and that's the thing that I'm looking at. It's not so much the response time because I don't think that's it.

At the other end of the criminal justice conveyer belt, Officer Steve Samson, who worked the drug trade undercover for a number of years, concurred. Now, as a detective with the DVU, he told me, "I'll be honest; my personal experience is that community policing has very little, almost nothing, to do with domestic violence."

Most battered women seemed to agree that the life circumstances of poor women dictated how they escaped their interpersonal victimization. In other words, policing is a peripheral rather than a central concern. Brenda, another prisoner, explained the problem succinctly:

> Here's what I think the big problem is. With women and children, they can't leave 'cause they pay day care and their job

doesn't pay enough money for them to pay rent and take care of their families. They can't count on the perpetrator to be paying child support; the odds are that he's not gonna pay it. Nashville needs some transitional housing for victims of domestic violence. They have all this transitional housing for drug addicts and alcoholics, but I think the psychological effects on victims are so great that it does affect how they work in their jobs and how they function in society. They've been abused for so long. These women can go to shelter and get services, but can they take care of themselves after they have to leave the shelter? You know, a majority go back to their abuser because of the financial strain, and I think that problem has to be addressed here in Nashville.

Policing Black Kin

I opened this chapter with two stories of black women incarcerated for defending themselves against their violent intimate partners. Latinas and Caucasian women use much less preemptive, resistive, and defensive lethal violence. The reasons for the resort to homicide remain unclear, although the imprisonment of black women for offenses such as these suggest that the criminal justice system has determined for itself the root of these crimes: the illegal use of violence with the intent to kill or seriously injure.

To sum up, then, many black women in the projects find it difficult to speak about domestic violence. The reasons for this include a desire to preserve the privacy and sanctity of black kinship systems, a historical tendency dating back to slavery; women's involvement in criminal activities; religious pressures from the church to forgive and forget; mistrust of the criminal justice system, housing authorities, the welfare system, and other state agencies; seeing the reporting of abusers as a form of cultural/racial disloyalty or betrayal; and women being inured to violence because of its prevalence in their homes and on the streets surrounding their homes. Once again I emphasize the social and historical forces that compromise the personal safety of black battered women and the integrity of black kinship systems, including community policing. The regular patrol of black neighborhoods by police dates to the period after the twentieth-century reconstruction and particularly after the Kerner Report recommendations. The emergence of community policing initiatives intensified this police presence and surveillance, especially in the later half of the twentieth-century redemption. It also highlighted the profound disjuncture between the forces of the criminal justice juggernaut and the desire on the part of blacks to preserve the efficacy of black kinship systems already under attack during the redemption. Essentially, community policing purports to confront family violence. However, police officers and battered women alike suspect that such an initiative fails or is of limited worth. Community police feed black males and, to a lesser extent, black females, to the jails and prisons. Black women implicate community policing in the assault on the black race, a realization that makes it doubly difficult for those women to call the police if their intimate partners assault them.

Other themes emerged regarding the policing of domestic violence in the projects. Black women's rage was never far from the surface of my ethnography. Women expressed rage about being victimized but also a deep anger about their miserable social conditions, the treatment of black men, the diminished life chances of their children, their poor housing, their being subject to ridiculous welfare rules, and so on. Indeed, the policing of these unfortunate women far transcends the official incursions of the Nashville Police Department, extending into every nook and cranny of their lives. It was this combination of surveillance, regulation, and abject poverty that led some brutalized women to take their chances with criminal subcultures in the projects. I will return to this theme in the next chapter.

The intimate surveillance of black women's lives extended to their personal relationships with men. Women told me that they had to negotiate their intimate relationships carefully. They wanted lovers, fathers for their children, providers, and friends. On the other hand, they did not necessarily want them at any cost; including, for some, the cost of interpersonal violence. However, this was not always the case. I talked with several women who calculated that the cost of being occasionally assaulted did not outweigh the benefits of a male partner's financial support; such was their personal struggle with poverty. At still another level, the criminal justice juggernaut, the welfare system, and the housing authority all mediated black women's intimate relationships. In short, what we see in the projects is a strict regulation of women's sexuality in a manner that differs from the patriarchal measures employed by individual men in the bedrooms of Nashville's leafy suburbs. In projects like Sam Levy and Preston Taylor, black men have restricted access to women, running the gauntlet of police, drug dealers, acute unemployment and poverty, and the like. Women know too well the rules of the poverty game and how it affects and shapes their interpersonal relationships. They also know from the local crack whores, and those drug dealers who have polygamous relationships with women, what other "options" are available. Indeed, as we have seen, public space for battered women in the projects is not "free" space, a place of refuge from the violence behind closed doors. Rather, as some women described it, public space amid the crack pipes and gunfire is hostile terrain, in which an incarcerated batterer can still "pay her back." Community policing, insofar as it further regulates black heterosexuality and enrages black batterers, probably perpetuates this misery. In short, community policing, like global capitalism, is one more nail in the coffin of black kinship systems.

My ethnographic findings strongly suggest that poverty and racism exacerbate intimate violence against women. It may be that black male batterers feel compelled to use more overt violence, threats, and intimidation to exact some modicum of control over their partners. This overdependence on violence may be the reason we find disproportionately more domestic violence and domestic homicide among poor black communities. Indeed, it might be the case that their deeply compromised and highly mediated access to female partners and their generalized rage at their lot in life generates more intimate violence. Clearly, we need more research into this phenomenon.

Finally, intimate violence against women also occurs when men have jobs, a say in society, and a decent place to live. It is the case in these "better-off" families that this violence in often secretive, cumulative, and hidden from the gaze of the state. Herein lies the final limit of police intervention, be it community policing, the DVU, or regular patrol. Policing cannot compensate for the patriarchal generation of domestic violence. Indeed, we might view the policing of relatively powerless black communities as a mirror image of broader patriarchal controls. On the other hand, policing can save lives, connect some battered women with various support services, and perhaps prevent or delay homicides.

Poor black men and their street activities attract the disproportionate gaze of the criminal justice juggernaut. Does this gaze turn them into better fathers? Providers? Partners? Probably not. Rebecca, a black woman from the projects in East Nashville, expressed her concern: "There aren't any role models because they're all locked up in jail. When I tried to reach out for help for my son, ya know . . . I knew deep down inside that I needed some help with him, even when his father was with him. And his father was a drunk, and then when he came home he wasn't a father and he wasn't a husband. He was just a man in the house. It seems like in Nashville black people are just stuck."

That community policing has a difficult time penetrating families is as obvious to some police officers as it is to battered women. According to Officer Mike O'Reilly: "We've spent so much money and time on community policing, and my question is, 'How much money and time are we spending on family-oriented policing?' Because if you look at the community, it's families. If we can't police in the family, then everything else is just window dressing. The streets may be clean, the junk cars may be towed off, the graffiti may be cleaned off the bridge or the local barbershop wall, but that's just window dressing. We're getting the cart before the horse."

My ethnography demonstrates that policing domestic violence in the projects is one part of a battery of social controls regulating black kinship systems, public violence, the drug trade, prostitution, and, more broadly, the increasing "surplus" urban poor. Sociologists are too quick to examine these phenomena in isolation from each other and from history. The movement against domestic violence, laudable as it is, suffers from the same myopia. We must understand such violence not only as a product of black male power and control over women, but also as a reflection of the broader historical management of the black urban poor.

C H A P T E R

Crack and the Cracks in Neoliberal Democracies

■ The Nashville poor are well aware that they are subject to rigorous social quarantining, numerous social stigmas, and stringent surveillance. Many understand their misery in terms of the lack of meaningful labor and rampant racism. This racism eats away at their lives on the street and includes disproportionate amounts of police harassment and brutality. In the workplace, it translates into fewer supervisory jobs, lower pay, and greater difficulties getting hired. Because of these negative experiences, many blacks from the projects have mixed feelings about mainstream values that emphasize and celebrate individual achievement through hard work. Many among the very poor perceive that they have extremely limited access to the American Dream. Their elders have seen meaningful and/or relatively well-paid labor disappear, lamented police brutality and indifference, and lived through redlining and other forms of social exclusion. For the Nashville poor, the individual rights and freedoms of neoliberal democracies are racially exclusive and therefore hollow.

Most residents deeply resent the violence associated with the subterranean economy and its effects upon their families, even if they can understand why some younger black men engage in the drug trade. Many of those involved in that economy have incorporated or colonized ideological images of the demonized black male into their personas, creating resistive and highly idiosyncratic styles of dress, demeanor, and language. Some writers have labeled this "code of the street" an oppositional culture, forged out of a combination of economic marginality and a history of racism.[1]

Clearly, some of the tenets of the code of the street are oppositional insofar as they ridicule and ironically colonize legal norms, describing, for example, the decision to engage in the drug trade as "getting legal."[2] It is important to note the similarities between the subterranean economy and the mainstream capitalist economy. Both involve hierarchical organization, exploitation of lower-level workers, and a massive overconcentration of wealth among the "fortunate" few. Only a few drug dealers "make it," escape the projects and enjoy some of the accompanying status and trappings. We might best see those few dealers that make it big as entrepreneurs engaging in quite rational market behavior. The essential difference between the two economies is that the subterranean is illegal. The seeming indifference of some gun-toting drug dealers to life and community well-being is consistent with the anarchic ethos of global capitalism, an ethos that seeks out cheap labor at whatever social cost, precipitates environmental calamities, destroys local ways of life, and pockets politicians just as street dealers conceal vials of crack cocaine.

Mainstream criminology has contributed to the maintenance of this false dichotomy between the two ways of earning money and, in a small number of cases, accumulating considerable wealth. At times, the spoiled identities of the poor appear amidst ideologies that explain criminality in terms of bad personal choices, dysfunctional families, moral degeneracy, or other forms of turpitude. For conservative critics of crime, the solution is simple: "Wicked people exist. Nothing avails except to set them apart from innocent people."[3] Put simply, the best way to deal with these offenders is to incarcerate them, isolate them, and recognize that rehabilitation is unlikely. Constructing criminals as indecent, immoral, or degenerate conveniently avoids the ongoing legacies of slavery and the enormous costs of global capitalism. This "convenient avoidance" by politicians and corporate moguls represents the real indecency, immorality, and degeneracy of modern American life.

In this chapter I focus on the subterranean economy, particularly the crack cocaine trade in inner-city Nashville. I argue that saturation policing of the drug trade feeds black bodies to the criminal justice juggernaut and ignores the civil rights of surplus populations, particularly young black males. This selective targeting of the offenses of black males undermines the rule of law and renders civil rights racially exclusive. In a system of law that presents itself as universal, such a contradiction ultimately calls into question the credibility and legitimacy of the legal code and police practice.

The Panic about Crack Cocaine

Crack is inhalable cocaine made by heating powdered cocaine (cocaine hydrochloride) with water and bicarbonate of soda, producing a crystalline substance.[4] This process, originally known as freebasing, emerged first among the ranks of powdered cocaine users in the 1970s as a means of producing an intensified state of ecstasy. The active ingredient, cocaine, spreads through the crystalline substance. This substance is more easily vaporized than cocaine hydrochloride. When users inhale the vaporized cocaine, they absorb it over the entire surface of the richly vascularized lungs. It travels through the bloodstream, arriving at the brain in a surge, providing users with a powerful rush.[5] Users told me of the euphoric experience of inhaling cocaine from a crack pipe, emphasizing that they felt more confident, productive, and energized. As Stella, a black woman I talked with at the Tennessee prison, noted, "I felt relaxed and tranquil. I felt like I didn't have a care in the world."

The distribution of crack cocaine to the housing projects is a lesson in how sellers reach the most seemingly remote market niche, the urban poor. Before the appearance of crack, powdered cocaine was an expensive, upmarket commodity that was snorted to produce euphoric effects within fifteen to thirty minutes. In the form of crack, users had access to an immediate state of ecstasy, albeit fleeting, for a few dollars per "rock." However, the innovative deployment of cocaine in cheap inhalable forms such as crack would have meant little without unemployed and underemployed people who bought it. This army of marginalized and disenchanted young adults, bypassed or discarded by the dismissive logic of Reaganomics, readily prepared, marketed, and consumed crack. As Craig Reinarman and Harry Levine put it, "Smoking crack cocaine offered an intense but very brief intoxication. This inexpensive and dramatic 'high' better suited the finances of the inner-city poor and their need for 'instant escape' than the more subtle and expensive effect provided by powdered cocaine."[6]

The moral panic about crack began in 1986, inaccurately positing that crack was an epidemic, or, worse still, a plague upon the country.[7] However, according to Reinarman and Levine, most people who try crack or powdered cocaine do not continue to use it. This evidence is inconsistent with the widespread misperception that once people smoke crack, there is no going back.[8] Reinarman and Levine argue that it was not so much the pharmacological qualities of crack that influenced its depiction as an evil drug so much as the people who were using it. Crack users come from the poorest, most marginalized sectors of U.S. society, such as people living in public housing.[9] Unlike the wealthier users of cocaine, the urban poor had little or no stake in regular, well-paid work. In addition, they had no access to drug treatment facilities or other advantages that would have mediated and moderated their use of cocaine. The concentration of crack use among the urban poor provided political opportunities for Reaganite conservatives and many others to blame urban blight on crack and its depraved users. Put simply, crackheads became scapegoats, and the joblessness caused by global capitalism and the backlash against the civil rights gains of African Americans got lost in the ideological shuffle.

Federal drug laws impose extremely harsh mandatory sentences for those convicted of possession of crack cocaine. To draw a five-year sentence, a convicted offender needs to have possessed only five grams of crack cocaine. Under the same federal statute, it would take possession of five hundred grams of powdered cocaine to receive the same sentence. Politicians argued that crack cocaine, the mainstay of the subterranean economy in poor black neighborhoods, was more addictive than its powdered equivalent, produced a faster and more intense high, and was cheaper and therefore represented a greater threat to public health. In addition, there was much violence and street crime linked to the crack cocaine trade. This hook, the real "threat of violence" among the very poor, provided political leverage for the upgrading of the criminal justice system. Critics of federal drug laws argue that the physiological differences between the two forms of the drugs are not the real reason for the sentencing disparities. Rather, they point to racism and the differential targeting of drug use by blacks, especially the use of crack cocaine. These critics include the U.S. Sentencing Commission, which attacked the federal drug laws as the "primary cause of growing racial disparity between sentences for Black and White federal defendants."[10] Other critics simply see the crack cocaine statutes as new Jim Crow laws.

The underground crack economy in Nashville, as elsewhere, developed as a consequence of joblessness. Young black men began to sell crack as a means of making a living. Understandably, a significant number of alienated blacks used crack to numb the pain of postindustrial marginality and to provide a fleeting sense of euphoria. The decision of authorities to target the crack cocaine trade is as profoundly political as the decision of major corporations to take their operations overseas to exploit cheap labor markets, leaving urban blight in their wake. To put it bluntly, police agencies primarily confront the social malaise produced by postindustrial society. To be sure, police are not dupes in this process. Some officers believe in the law-and-order mission and the drug war, citing the violence and devastation associated with the subterranean marketplace as the justification for their increased presence. Many others also discern what goes on in the projects as a social and political problem rather than a law enforcement matter. Police work between a rock and a hard place. To secure their jobs in an economy increasingly short on meaningful, well-paid labor for working-class and lower-middle-class men, police must effect arrests, justify their existence, and ensure that their departments attract more federal funding. They must feed blacks and Hispanics into the growing prison system, itself staffed by corrections officers and others drawn from the same job market sector as police officers. Like the slave patrollers of old, working-class white men employed in the criminal justice system regulate still poorer men and women of color discarded by global capitalism. These moves toward what Nils Christie has called "gulags, Western style" accompanied the decreases in the state provision of affordable housing, welfare, and education.[11]

Vice as a Survival Strategy

I asked Byron Reed, a black man in his early thirties from the East Nashville projects, why crack dealing was commonplace in his community. He replied: "Selling crack pays money. It's a job. You get paid every day. You have to do what you have to do sometimes. You don't let your kids starve. You can't get a job. Some people been to jail and it's hard for them to get a job. . . . They probably went and try to get jobs, but won't nobody hire 'em 'cause of their backgrounds. So, well, they takin' it in their own hands, and well, you know, they might rob, just start robbing people. Or sell drugs, see how that works."

Jerome Stacey, another black man I talked with from the East Nashville projects, told a similar story. Jerome hated his job, hated the stereotypes attached to black men in the workplace, and clearly saw that he was going nowhere in regular employment. Jerome stressed that once one enters the cycle of drug dealing and incarceration, it is very difficult to return to regular wage labor. I heard stories like this numerous times on the streets of Nashville. Employers are not keen to hire ex-felons. For those individual men, the effects of such labeling force them back into the subterranean economy. Those who used to make money dealing drugs face a much more difficult time going "straight" because they quickly realize just how exploitative the job market is and how little money they make compared to when they were dealing: "You hate your job. So you quit the job and you feel like, 'Now I'm just workin' for the fuckin' government.' Then it's back to the dope. And you say, 'This is my money,' and you sell the dope, get out here, then you busted again. And it's like a damn circle, and, like, when you get of jail, and when you just went in there for dope, maybe you might lay low for a while, you know, three or four months, but then you back at it. . . . You know you bein' watched and shit like that, but you know you sellin' for you. . . . The shit is crazy. Bein' stopped and everythin'. 'Cause they know, man, with these cars and shit, man, they already know it's drug money. . . . You just can't have a car. . . . I gotta sell dope."

The fast money made dealing crack stands in stark contrast to the daily rhythms of working at a minimum-wage job. However, the fast money comes with a price tag in injuries, deaths, and fear. Robert O'Neill, a Sam Levy resident, put it like this, "If a little boy is, say, thirteen, his momma is struggling, and he goes out and makes money, about $1,200, she's not going to turn that money down. . . . But what looks good *to* you ain't always good *for* you."[12]

Henderson Kelly, manager of the McFerrin Community Center in Sam Levy, had worked in the projects for thirty years. He noted the instant riches possible as well as the short-term aspirations associated with such a lifestyle: "Kids just see one way, and they make the jump all the way from poverty to the big money, and the money that comes from drug dealing," Kelly told reporters of a recent conversation he had with a fifteen-year-old drug dealer who constantly looked over his shoulder. The dealer told Kelly, "If I can have a pocketful of money, two good cars, and some women, I don't mind dying at twenty-five."[13]

Street drug dealing and prostitution pervade other poor parts of Nashville as well. Officer John Bradbury told me of the case of a racially mixed trailer park in East Nashville. Several of the residents he dealt with suffered various forms of mental illness; some were on medication, others received some form of psychiatric counseling. While riding through the neighborhood, we talked about vice as a survival strategy:

Websdale: Do you think those folks see the drug dealing as just a way to survive? I mean, a lot of these folks have nothing else, right?

Bradbury: Right. A lot of these people are on disability and maybe on welfare or something like that. They can't legitimately make over so much money per year and maintain that status. "Why would I want to work at Burger King making this amount of money when I can do this for three hours and make triple that amount?" There was a gentleman that I arrested myself. I had three charges on him. He had a stolen vehicle and he was a known dope dealer in the area. He was sixty-seven or sixty-eight years old. He got his granddaughter hooked on the stuff. She's prostituting now and she's only fifteen or sixteen years old. The family structure has gone down the tubes.

Websdale: You have people working prostitution in here?

Bradbury: Not out here. It's too easy to spot. You'll find two or three over at the old man who I was telling you about who was a dope dealer. But you don't really realize that they're prostitutes because they walk from one house to another or just stand out at the edge of the driveway.

Detective John Wilson is an African American officer who worked undercover drugs for several years in various housing projects. We talked about stemming the tide of drug dealing through saturation or community policing. Like other officers, he was well aware of the magnitude of the problem and its political dimensions:

Websdale: And do you think you were successful? Or did you just displace the dealing?

Wilson: To be totally honest with you . . .

Websdale: We can go off the record any time you want.

Wilson: No. I don't have a problem telling you. To be totally honest, it's like standing under a waterfall, with the water running down, trying to plug it up at the bottom of the long fall. You have to go up to the top sometime [chuckle]. So, you know, we made arrests, but it was just a continuous thing. That's the drug problem. Until we stop the demand, it's going to be hard to stop it. Among the drug dealers, you don't snitch, and among the users, you don't snitch. Do not snitch. So that's another reason why it's so hard to stand there under this waterfall with a cup trying to stop this. Because you don't get as much cooperation as you might expect. Me and you may see dealing as a problem. Somebody else may see it as a solution.

Websdale: Yeah. I think that if I was living in these situations, I might use it myself, to be quite honest with you.

Wilson: Absolutely. You know, I've thought sometimes that maybe if I was in this same environment then I'd be a product of this environment. I guess that those who commit criminal acts have their agenda and what they see as their way of life, and for most people this is a way of life. To them it's not necessarily about being a criminal. It's about survival.

Resorting to vice as a means of survival extends to women who allow their houses to be used for illegal purposes such as selling drugs, providing prostitution services, fencing stolen property, storing weapons, and gambling. One late afternoon on the periphery of the Edgehill housing projects, Officer Olsen and I crested a hill: to the east was a playing field, to the west, some ramshackle houses. One of the houses used to be a crack house. Nashville police had executed a search warrant on the premises the previous year. A major drug dealer was using it for storage. The house was in his grandmother's name, and she allowed him to use it as a safe haven in return for significant amounts of cash. The dealer also paid her bills and allowed her to do what she pleased with the house. Had the grandmother, as owner of the house, moved beyond the poverty of those living nearby in the projects? Probably yes. Had she been hooked on the fast and ready cash to a degree that well exceeded her survival needs? Probably yes. Indeed, there were several instances where well-to-do dealers made enormous amounts of money, stashed it, and engaged in a variety of acts of conspicuous consumption. These successful dealers remind me in some ways of the salivating financiers one sees on CNN's *Moneyline*.

The women I talked with in Nashville who had worked or were working as prostitutes all told me that it was something they engaged in to pay the bills, feed their children, or, in some instances, feed their drug habits. Their drug habits typically took over after they began prostitution, coming, as they often did, into contact with street dealers or others who, for a price, would ply them with drugs. Poor women in Nashville are more inclined to enter prostitution than to engage in criminal activities such as the street dealing of drugs, burglaries, or robberies. However, I did meet several women who had dealt crack, usually in tandem with male dealers, or who had burglarized homes. In those few instances when women had burglarized, they worked alone to feed a drug habit. As Philippe Bourgois observes, the world of drug dealing is male-dominated, with few openings for women.[14]

Economic necessity was the reason Melanie, a white woman in her midthirties, worked as a prostitute. Melanie agreed to talk with me after I paid her twenty dollars, the price of oral sex on the street. She gave me about fifteen minutes of her time, the time it would take to get in a john's car, give him oral sex, and be dropped off again on Dickerson Road. Melanie told me that men who wanted just to talk with her were the "weirdest of all." I pondered this remark as we talked, keeping an eye on the black man nearby trying to fence what he said were genuine gold chains and the pimp who pulled up onto the forecourt as Melanie and I conversed. I also had my eye out for the white unmarked police vans that passed by, not wanting to be arrested for soliciting while consulting for the U.S. Justice Department. Melanie told me, "My kids was hungry, and I had to do somethin'."

Street prostitution is not the only way women provide sexual services to survive. One I interviewed at a homeless shelter in Nashville openly told me she had prostituted herself for a place to stay. The director of the facility told me of a survey they conducted that revealed that about one-fifth of their homeless clients had done the same. While not illegal, this kind of trading reminds us that the line between prostitution and other forms of sexual activity is not as clear-cut as it may first appear. Of the battered women I talked with, several mentioned that they stayed with husbands or intimate partners after having been raped because they feared the streets, the shelters, or other possible alternatives. Clearly, there are parallels between sex for money or crack cocaine, sex for a place to stay, and sex within the context of a patriarchal marriage. The differences between woman as homemaker and woman as destitute, crack-addicted prostitute are powerful patriarchal polarities, one reinforcing the other. However, the differences are not as pronounced as they may seem. Many women enter prostitution after unsatisfactory or abusive intimate relationships with men, or while still in such relationships. Melanie told me that she was married, and pointed to her husband in a nearby truck, who, according to her, "kept watch over her."

I talked about prostitutes with Officer Barbara Denton, who had worked vice for a number of years in Nashville and knew the Dickerson Road area well. "Some people think we're making progress. I don't think so," she said. I commented that women who are selling their bodies aren't doing it because they like it. "Yeah, you're right," she said. "People don't grow up thinking, 'I want to be a prostitute.' "

The Social Ecology of Vice

The distribution, sale, and use of illegal drugs often take place in and around public housing projects. Authorities in Nashville built the housing in rows, as opposed to the high-rise public housing in some cities such as Chicago. The placement of the Nashville public housing projects near the intersecting freeways makes them easily accessible to buyers of drugs from far afield, even neighboring states such as Kentucky. Indeed, a cursory glance at those arrested for the purchase of street drugs in the projects shows buyers coming from all parts of Nashville and beyond, as well as within the projects themselves. Those living within public housing who want to buy drugs are probably more likely to use crack houses and the less-visible street vendors. Buyers from farther away typically buy from their vehicles, fast-food style.

Most people living in the projects have a good idea of where the crack houses are:

Websdale: Do you have any sense of how many people are involved in the drug trade?
Wilson: I think it's very embedded. I would say maybe at least a third of the population of those particular areas. And then, the other two-thirds have knowledge of it.
Websdale: Everybody knows?
Wilson: Everybody knows.

With some humor, a key informant named Alex told me that though he may not know the individuals dealing drugs out of a crack house in the projects, he intuitively senses where those houses are from the nature of the activity around them: "If I'm riding around in the neighborhood and I see a lot of people going to the same house, you know, they ain't selling damn moon pies or dinners or nothin'. You know what I'm sayin'? You can tell from the look."

From my fieldwork it seems likely there are at least half a dozen crack houses in most of the projects; in some, many more. There appear to be fewer in Edgehill and Vinehill, where police presence has increased significantly since the introduction of community policing. It is impossible to know how many women in the projects casually sell drugs out of their homes without offering other services such as prostitution and gambling. It is also the case that various forms of drug use and drug dealing take place all over Nashville, although the crack cocaine trade appears to fade considerably as one moves beyond the housing projects and their vicinity.

I interviewed a battered woman named Denise at a homeless shelter in north Nashville. Denise was a recovering crack addict who had been at the shelter for six months and had completed a drug treatment program there. She had been in a relationship with Steve, a black drug dealer. The day before our interview, a street dealer killed Steve over money Steve owed him. The two had lived in a run-down neighborhood in north Nashville. Steve had spent much time away from the home, turning up at odd times with people whom Denise did not know. Denise had used crack frequently and spent her paychecks on the drug. She had several children, one of whom had Down's syndrome. Denise had worked a regular job and Steve had worked at a minimum-wage job at

Wendy's, supplementing his income by selling drugs. Denise and Steve had not run a crack house. Rather, they may have been typical of a number of people who subsist at the lower end of the job market, barely making ends meet, seeking solace as well as some extra income in crack, and paying a dear price in the process. Denise is a reminder that the subterranean economy radiates beyond the projects to other areas and lifestyles, where people may be gainfully employed but still in dire trouble. Denise told me:

> I had to get crack on the street, and all of sudden I'm gettin' high everyday. I was trying to leave Steve, but he kept on beating me. Sometimes he would beat me in front of our son, and sometimes when I was pregnant with my daughter, he'd try to kick me in my stomach. Sometimes he'd bring people over to my house I wouldn't even know. I'd wake up, people would be in my house, and then me and him would get into it, and he'd beat me up. I was just real tired of it. . . . But I feel real bad because, uh, we had his funeral yesterday. He got killed. He was shot out on North Seventh Street. What happened was he was trying to get his life together and a dope dealer confronted him about ten dollars he says Steve owes him. And Steve said somebody's gonna pay it for him. They got into a big fight, and then after the fight, the guy got a gun and shot Steve in the leg, and then shot him point-blank in the head.

At night, drug dealing of all kinds is much more evident in most of Nashville's public housing. On the periphery of most projects, users and small-time dealers conduct business on the streets and from parking lots in front of stores, bars, and other commercial sites. Many have prior convictions for drug offenses or other infractions such as disorderly conduct, burglary, theft, criminal trespass, and resisting arrest. In Edgehill, most of these fringe-area users and dealers do not carry guns. This may be because they encounter the police more often than dealers in other areas do and do not want to get caught carrying a weapon. Often these men know women in the projects, have friends there, or just pass through from elsewhere. On the fringes are often the most debilitated users of crack cocaine, people with drawn faces, thin bodies, and a weary demeanor. If police pat these men down, they sometimes find vials of crack, or crack wrapped in small plastic bags, hidden in various pouches or within clothing. One night an officer I was riding with patted a black man down in Edgehill and located crack in a small plastic bag in a hidden lining in the collar of his jacket.

The threat posed by small-time dealers on the fringes of Edgehill, subject as they are to more intensive community policing, may be more benign than it is around some of the other housing projects. In other projects, such as Sam Levy, John Henry Hale, and Preston Taylor, the drug-dealing scene seems tenser and the threat of violence more overt. For example, I visited John Henry Hale on several occasions at night and walked around the area extensively during the day. At night the area is alive with drug dealing.[15] Officer Paul Parks, whom I rode with one night in John Henry Hale, told me that some drug dealers terrified the workers in the neighborhood stores when they dodged in to avoid police. Parks told me that one of the stores was running numbers, rather like a similar grocery store on the fringes of Edgehill.[16] However, the new owner had not yet developed the kind of symbiotic relationship with street dealers that I witnessed in Edgehill.

Parks: That store right there is under new management. The buyer was heavily into numbers. During the day you'll have a lot of people hanging at the corner, dealing. When you come up, of course, they walk into the store. I'll be honest; the store clerks are terrified for their lives.

Websdale: So in Henry Hale they're gonna carry guns more?

Parks: You're gonna find more, yeah. And they're not likely to produce them on police. What they'll do is, you'll end up with foot pursuits, and during the foot pursuit you'll see a silver object fly through the air and end up in a field or something. But somebody they perceive as a threat from the community, they'll shoot 'em in a heartbeat.

As one moves closer to the projects, perhaps onto a main thoroughfare heading into the dense and depressing housing, the social ecology begins to change. Here are sellers who may come from elsewhere or who may have an intimate relationship with a woman living in the projects. These men hang out on their own or cluster in small groups, typically waiting for someone to pull up in a vehicle and buy drugs from them. They often carry significant amounts of cash and are more likely to carry weapons than those smaller-time dealers and users on the fringes. They may deal out of houses in the projects or bring in drugs from safe houses elsewhere. According to Byron, one of my key informants from East Nashville, the junior sellers from the houses might help the "main man" who runs the house. In return for their selling drugs on the street, they may earn a cut of the take, a rock or two of crack, or both. These are often prime selling sites, and there is a pecking order determined by street reputation and, particularly, the willingness or proven ability to use violence. Shootings around these locations are commonplace. It is risky to buy drugs from these sellers because the buyer has no real way of sampling the goods in the presence of the seller. Often buyers will make the purchase and take off to a safer, less visible location to use the drugs. Given the transient nature of life in the projects, the turnover of residents, and the vulnerability of street dealers to incarceration, the police, violence, and death, it is not easy, let alone safe, for the disgruntled buyer to request a refund. At this level the sale of fake drugs to unsuspecting buyers sometimes occurs. Sellers dispense fake drugs with care, for obvious reasons. Such sellers likely move quickly through an area. Sales of counterfeit drugs may increase when supplies of the real product are short. As Officer Denton put it, if dealers sell the fake stuff, which looks like dry wall or wax, "to the wrong person, the buyer can come back and shoot the seller." In March 1998 one unfortunate group sold fake cocaine to undercover police officers. The sting, which resulted in eighteen arrests at ten different street-corner locations, netted cash, several bags of fake cocaine, and a van.[17]

In the projects along a main thoroughfare, it is commonplace to see men at the ends of rows of houses that extend into the center of the projects. In Preston Taylor and John Henry Hale, I noticed men both in the daytime and at night, often in pairs, keeping watch at the head of the row. Several key informants advised me that these men carry firearms. They may sell drugs, but their function is more one of surveillance, or countersurveillance if they are keeping their eyes on the police.

It is from these entrance points to the housing rows in some of the more dangerous projects, such as John Henry Hale, Preston Taylor, Sam Levy, and Settle Court, that we see acute territoriality, sometimes violence and turf wars accompanied by gunfire. As one proceeds down the rows, which I did at night on only a handful of occasions, one sees the occasional crack house, often watched by other men closer to the house. This complicated system of protection and surveillance serves to warn interlopers, the police, and other would-be dealers. Some police officers I rode with simply would not venture into those rows at night in places such as Sam Levy or Settle Court, citing the danger and risk involved. Police raids and saturation patrols or service responses within these areas involve a show of coordinated force, and even then violence between police and residents, rock throwing, the overturning of police vehicles, and the firing of weapons at the police occur.

A number of key informants told me of the activities inside crack houses. The drugs available in these houses are generally of superior quality to those sold by street vendors, if only because the buyers often come from the community and sample the goods on the premises. Dealers rely upon community residents for the houses, lookouts, runners, smaller dealers, and so on, and it makes for poor business if they provide substandard crack there. Dealers come in all shapes and sizes. Some will work out of one house, others will distribute to a variety of street sellers, and others will operate a number of houses located throughout the city. Those who work out of one house within a set territory will have women in that house who perform a variety of tasks, from providing sexual services to those visiting the house to selling drugs. Many of these women use crack cocaine, some to the point of extreme addiction. The men who visit these houses mercilessly exploit and abuse these women. In the crack houses, HIV infection rates run very high. According to Byron, the men who run these houses operate locally and see the women who work in them as disposable: "The dealers in certain areas, certain parts of town, they stay in their own part of town, and have their own drug house, you know, and the women in the house is not their spouses, not their girlfriends, it's not nobody to 'em, you know, they just really using 'em."

Authorities sometimes remove the children of these exploited, diseased, and drug-addicted women who cannot provide proper parental care. In 1995 Mary Walker, the Nashville juvenile court referee who adjudicates cases of child abuse and neglect, told the *Tennessean* that the number of crack cocaine–addicted mothers had quadrupled from 1992 to 1995. Walker noted that in one six-month period, 825 children passed through the dependency court. Of these, 620 had mothers addicted to crack. She told the press, "We hear 40 neglect dependent petitions each week with an average of three children per family. . . . 70–80 percent of those children come from homes where crack cocaine is a problem."[18] Whatever the criminal justice juggernaut, the welfare system, and the housing authorities do to the black family, we must not lose sight of the fact that crack cocaine also devastates black kinship systems.

The norm seems to be that dealers will remain within a certain territory, often defined by the boundaries of a particular housing project. Only a small number of big dealers use several women at different houses around the city. The big-time dealer often has intimate relationships with each of the women who manage his houses. As we talked at the Tennessee State Penitentiary, Jewel told me of her relationship with one such dealer, who owned several crack houses in Nashville.

Websdale: So, the dope man can have more than one woman?

Jewel: Oh, yeah.

Websdale: How many women might we be talking about roughly?

Jewel: It all depends on how much money he makes. He may have five houses.

Websdale: And there are women in each house? And he'll control the houses?

Jewel: Yes. They'll work for him in the houses. He may have a house in north, south, east, and west Nashville. So just in case the police . . . bust one house, he still have more that they don't know nothin' about . . . so he still goin' on an' takin' care of business while they done cracked into this one.

I had this guy that I was dating, and he was, he was like, like the head. I stayed, I stayed with him, okay, and he had, you know, girlfriends here and here and here, and I remember one time he was talkin' about 'em. I knew he was messin' with these other women, okay, but I didn't care, as long as he took care of what I asked him to take care of. I'd say, "I want you to give me what I say I need, I expect you to give it to me . . ."

. . . One day, he wanted to go on out to the lake. I mean, this man owned boats, jet skis, everything. He wanted to go out to the lake, and he was never abusive, at least not with me, because he knew I'd fight back. I'd fight a no-win situation. He wanted to go out to the lake and have a cookout. A lot of us loaded up the cars, an' when we was at the lake I looked around and I'm seein' all these girls, flirtin' [laughter] and floatin' around, you know, an' I'm knowin' that these are the one that he's seein'. We all went out to the picnic, unloaded everything, all of us cookin' together, listenin' to music, I mean just like we one big happy family . . . you know, an' some of 'em have it like that. And then, you got some, that the women are like, "I hate that bitch," they gonna slash them tires, break your windows . . . But I was at the point that where I didn't care 'cause I was gettin' what I wanted, and when I wanted to go somewhere, I went, you know? He was the funder, he funded me. So I pretty much gave him his room to do what he wanted to . . . and I had my room to do what I wanted to. There are some dealers who are big enough to do that.

Assessing the precise extent of drug dealing in the housing projects is impossible. The inmates in the focus group at the prison told me of their involvement and pointed to the pervasiveness of dealing. All the women had at some point lived in the Nashville projects, and a number of them had sold drugs there or "worked" in crack houses. Given their complete immersion in this subculture, they may have overstated the prevalence of drug dealing. However, their views are worth noting.

Websdale: So how many folks would you say in your projects were involved in drug dealing?
[laughter]
Eloise: I know what you sayin'. The whole community there is involved. I go to the back door, it was like every other apartment. And all ages. . . . You've got people standin' on the corner sellin', then you got people in the house sellin'.
Websdale: How many houses? . . . Half the houses, or a third of them?
Bertha: When night falls, hell, its kinda wide open. Basically, most of the women who live in the projects either have a boyfriend that's dealin' drugs so they get mixed up in it that way . . .
Websdale: Most of the women?
Bertha: . . . most of the women, yeah . . .
Romona: . . . I know out in east Nashville a lot of people that hang around out there don't live there, you know, and during the day it's kind of subtle. You have your office people there and your maintenance people walkin' around, and then you got police too. . . . Most of the dealers are asleep durin' them hours because they've been up all night. . . .
Bertha: A lot of people that stay in the projects . . . if they're not sellin' it, they're addicts.

Most of the women in the prison focus group lived in projects much less accessible than others to police. There were no women in the group who had lived in Edgehill since the arrival of saturation community policing in 1996. The presence of daytime police surveillance seems to have cut down on open drug markets in Edgehill. Some residents have taken to calling the police to cut down on dealing activities. Those who come from the outside to buy have learned that if they want to avoid apprehension by police, they had better buy inside a house rather than on the street. Based on reports gathered from community members and others, the community policing in Edgehill expedited the process of obtaining search warrants for suspected crack houses. Instead of the traditional months of intelligence work, police now move within weeks to search possible houses. All this police activity affects the social ecology of drug dealing in Edgehill, probably displacing it to other locations. Officer Olsen explained as we rode through Edgehill one night:

Olsen: The young guys walking into the house there, we've had reports they're dealing out of there, but they all live there too. They went around the fence real quick when they saw the patrol car. That's one of our hardest ones around here . . . when they deal out of the house. No matter how often you stop 'em on the street, they're not going to have anything on them, and after a while, after you keep stopping 'em like that, they're gonna say, "Oh, harassment, harassment, harassment." We try to build somewhat of a case, help out our unmarked units to go over there and make drug buys and then hit 'em with a search warrant. But it annoys me the time it takes to lead up to that.

Websdale: How many drug houses do you have in Edgehill?

Olsen: Oh, not many. Not many. Maybe a half a dozen. In the three years that we have been doing this, we have established so many contacts in here that these people now will call over to our police station and say, "Hey, they're doing this out of that apartment." We will get an undercover officer to come over and make a buy, and we will bring search warrants in. I'm talking, we do that stuff within weeks, not months like it normally takes to get a search warrant. We get it done within weeks, which shuts them down.

What we have noticed in Edgehill is that the open-air drug markets have closed. If you come to Edgehill to buy drugs, you had better buy inside. Everybody knows that. The drug users know that you can't come to Edgehill and find a drug dealer standing on the street corner. You have to know what apartment to go to, and then you have to go physically inside that apartment to purchase the narcotic. That is because of the presence of the bicycle officers and the patrol officers that have focused so much on this area. In the second year that we were here, it became known statewide, Edgehill was a free market. We had drug dealers from Memphis coming in trying to set up shop. We had drug dealers coming from east Nashville coming over here. We arrested one right in this little area right over here, wearing a bulletproof vest, and he had a forty-five caliber semiautomatic pistol and a pocket full of cocaine. We rolled up on him on bikes. There was no place for him to go, and we saw the bulge and had him at gun point, so he did not even think about drawing the pistol. We asked him where he was from, and he said he was from over on Settle Court, which is east Nashville. We asked him, What was he doing over here? That in itself is usually a death sentence for drug dealers, to go into different territories. And we said, "What are you doing here? Are you out of your tree? Have you gone mad?" He said, "Man, everybody knows that Edgehill is a free market." And then we arrested him. Around that time there was a quadruple homicide just outside of the Edgehill boundary. They were all from Memphis, and they were known as the Memphis Boys. We speculate that they were in town to try and set up shop here. And people in Nashville apparently didn't want to have anything to do with that. But Edgehill became known statewide as a free market 'cause there was no open-air drug dealing anymore.

Websdale: So you know where the houses are now?

Olsen: Oh, yeah. If somebody starts dealing out of one of these houses, it won't take us long at all. It won't take us but a week or two to identify where it's coming from. Then after that, setting up the reverse stings to establish probable cause for search warrants, it won't take us long at all. And, like I said, that's not just because of great police work, as far as us being Sherlock Holmes. It's because these people in here will call our office right over there and say, "Hey, they're setting up shop right next to me. They're selling right out of the apartment next door to me."

Byron provided further information about life inside the crack houses of Nashville:

Websdale: Are they selling sex out of there too—prostitution?
Byron: They doin' anything they want to do, whatever the dealer says to 'em. Whatever he say goes. It don't matter. All times of night. . . . They can sit in there and smoke crack, they can have sex in this room, they can . . . do whatever they want to, right there in front of everybody.

On the rare occasions I watched the comings and goings outside a crack house, the activity was frenetic. Holly, one of the women in the prison focus group, told me:

Holly: The dope dealers, they in and out. The crack houses are just crowded with people that smoke it, sell it also.
Websdale: . . . Is there anything else going on in the house as well?
Holly: Sex, everything. You would be surprised. You would be surprised.

Citizens of Nashville learned about events in crack houses from a much-celebrated local case. In February 1998 two brothers, Darrell McQuiddy, aged twenty-six, and Sean McQuiddy, aged thirty, pleaded guilty to federal drug-trafficking charges and money laundering. Authorities indicted the McQuiddys, along with Timothy Hall, Victor Tyson, and John A. Gooch, for "knowingly and intentionally" distributing cocaine and crack cocaine. Darrell McQuiddy was a ninth-grade dropout who became a millionaire drug dealer by the time he was twenty-five. He had been dealing drugs since he was in high school. From April 1995 to February 1997, Darrell ran a crack house on sixteenth Avenue North in Nashville. To say Darrell indulged in conspicuous consumption is an understatement. He bought new Cadillacs and Mercedes Benzes, spent $9,000 on a diamond watch, and owned and operated a nightclub in north Nashville called McQuiddy City. He allegedly buried $100,000 in cash in his mother's backyard in case lean times struck. Darrell had a string of intimate female partners who bore him a total of seven children. He bought those women houses. In addition, he bought his own mother a new house when the violence from the drug trade impinged upon her old dwelling. Police arrested two dozen dealers supplied by McQuiddy's operation. The operation allegedly brought eighty kilograms of cocaine into Nashville each month. A contact of Sean McQuiddy's in Florida originally supplied the drug ring. Unfortunately for the McQuiddys, someone gunned down their Florida supplier outside a Nashville nightclub, and they had to replace him. Their new supplier had a business in Las Vegas. Darrell McQuiddy sold the drugs to other dealers in Nashville as well as in his own crack house, located at 1509 Tenth Avenue North, and in Sean McQuiddy's crack house in a triplex at 1744-A Sixteenth Avenue North. Police caught up with Darrell McQuiddy's moneyman as he pulled out of Darrell's driveway carrying $487,000.[19]

With the McQuiddys of this world hauling out nearly half a million dollars in drug proceeds to launder, it is no wonder that there are acute competition, territoriality, and violence in the drug trade. This territoriality and violence stand at the intersection of a number of forces. First, for many young men, drug dealing seems the only rational solution to the entrapment of the housing projects, the dearth of jobs, and the grind of menial labor. The choice to pursue illegitimate opportunities inevitably runs the risk of attracting heat from the criminal justice juggernaut. Second, because the drug markets are illegal, antagonists do not resolve disputes through the courts. Competitors in the subterranean economy must defend their territory, use their resources to expand and colonize new space or they will shrivel up and die. The constant flux of men in and out of the projects, either into the jails or the cemeteries, creates new spaces, opportunities, tensions, and antagonisms. Third, the consumptive practices of the clients of dealers also contribute to the volatility. The postuse depression and paranoia of the client addicted to crack create a tremendous urge for more. The buyer experiences a physiological need for the drug, which at times causes the neglect of children and the committing of property crimes and acts of violence.

At the time I was riding with the community police in Edgehill, officers were working a drug-related homicide involving rival drug-dealing factions in Preston Taylor and John Henry Hale. Officer Olsen explained: "It's very territorial. We've got a homicide we're working right now between Preston Taylor and John Henry Hale. Someone from Preston Taylor came over and shot a kid in John Henry Hale. We are just waiting for the retaliation. The threats have been obvious. They ride around in their cars with signs in their cars saying, 'A life has been taken and a life will be taken.' Sometimes there is nothing we can do."

The tense competition for drug money lies at the heart of drug-related shootings in and around the Nashville projects. As noted in chapter 3, approximately two-thirds of the homicides that occur within a one-mile radius of the center of public housing projects stem from turf issues between drug dealers and/or users. Clearly, these shootings reveal tense turf competition and the refusal of some young men to back down. However, the ultimate root of the tension is competition over scarce material resources. The status trappings appear secondary to the basic drive to make money. Breanna, a battered black woman from the housing projects whom I interviewed after a support group meeting, said: "Most of the shooting and fights in the projects are between drug dealers or drug users. Somebody's trying to get over on somebody about their money. That's usually what it is. Or one drug dealer got more drugs than the next one, and he's trying to get it." Heavy drug users engage in theft, burglary, and robbery to acquire money to buy drugs. The public particularly fears the street stickup, which combines for the perpetrator the procurement of fast money with the power rush of a fleeting but nevertheless ascendant masculinity.

One night around midnight in Edgehill, Officer Denton and I observed a black man, Ralph Elliot, walking out of the projects. He hid when he saw us. Denton got out of the patrol vehicle and confronted Ralph about what he was doing. Ralph told Denton he was visiting a woman named Cathy. Denton quizzed Ralph on where Cathy lived and how he knew her. Although Ralph told Denton he had known Cathy since high school, he could not remember Cathy's last name or where in the projects she lived. Denton then asked Ralph if he had a criminal history; Ralph noted a number of offenses, including armed robbery and burglary. Denton patted Ralph down and found what looked like crack cocaine in a hidden lining in his collar. She then cuffed Ralph and arrested him for criminal trespass. The three of us traveled back to the community policing center in Edgehill, where Denton tested Ralph's suspicious substance using a simple chemical test. Denton told me the crack was "high-quality stuff." Since Ralph had no money on him, Denton deduced that Ralph was more likely a user than a seller. Denton ran Ralph's rap sheet while Ralph and I sat side by side. A newspaper was open on the table, and I saw Ralph straining to look at it. I rearranged the newspaper and placed it in front of him so he could see it. He glanced at me and thanked me for doing this, then proceeded to read the front-page story, which just happened to be the account of police brutality directed at Hispanic migrants that I documented in chapter 3. Denton then called me over to the computer screen, where we read Ralph's criminal history. Denton spoke into my tape recorder:

> He's got a record that's a mile and a half long. That's a parole violation. Drug paraphernalia. Possession of cocaine, possession to sell, probation violation, vehicle theft, receiving stolen property, public order crimes, disorderly conduct, robbery in '81. He must have spent time on these because it jumped to '93 all the way from '81. He spent some time. Robbery, agg[ravated] assaults; he obviously used a gun. Concealing stolen property, public order crimes, disorderly conduct again. Here's where things get real fun: burglary, burglary, burglary, robbery again with a gun, burglary, burglary, burglary, burglary, burglary, burglary, burglary, burglary, forgery of checks, concealing stolen property.

Having made her point about Ralph's criminal proclivities, Denton noted somewhat sadly that she had seen Ralph on a number of occasions over the years. Ralph's face had become lined and drawn during that time. Denton thought this was due to Ralph's increased use of crack cocaine. This pattern, Denton noted, was commonplace in the projects, and as Denton released Ralph into the darkness and rain with his paperwork for his court date, Denton surmised that Ralph would return to Edgehill and find a place to crash for the night.

I met several women who had committed crimes to feed their drug habits. In an interview at the homeless shelter, Amelia, a pregnant white woman who was an "ex–crack addict," told me that she had burglarized people's homes to feed her need for the euphoria of cocaine. She had been on crack for seven or eight years. Her husband was incarcerated at the time we talked, and Amelia was waiting to secure a place in low-income housing to have a home for her new baby. "I was doing real bad stuff whenever I got on it. I was taking people's money and stuff to get my drugs. I was lyin', manipulatin' 'em . . . to get in their homes . . . and I would go in and steal their money. . . . That's the reason they got me for five counts of aggravated burglary. I'd go out panhandling at people's homes . . . and manipulate 'em."

It is not enough to talk of the violence between dealers, sellers, and those who jostle for a better market niche on the streets. Intimidation is also used to further the goals of dealers, even if community members are not directly involved in the street economy and have no apparent desire to become involved. As I showed in chapter 2, a number of women in the housing projects and other poor neighborhoods live in what they describe as a state of siege, afraid for themselves and their children. Those who openly snub drug dealers or refuse to cooperate with their demands can face intense intimidation. Officer Olsen recalled the situation of a woman and her three children who were living in Edgehill. Dealers approached the woman about the possibility of using her house to store guns. The police did a good job of reading the woman's level of fear and her basic reluctance to cooperate with dealers; note how they gave her a chance to "correct herself" in this account from Olsen:

> We worked with a young lady who was being intimidated by the drug dealers. They were threatening her and her children if she did not hold these guns for them. Well, she was afraid to tell us, and we all knew she was afraid. This girl was genuinely afraid for her children's lives and her own because these drug dealers had told her what they were going to do if she did not cooperate. Yeah, we found drugs in her apartment and illegal weapons, but was it truly her fault? We didn't think so. The housing manager did not think so either, so we gave her the opportunity to correct herself, and she did. But we had to go to the lengths of moving her completely to another housing development because she was no longer safe here in Edgehill. The drug dealers that had been intimidating her had of course found out that she wasn't playing by their rules anymore and was playing by our rules. She needed a place for her three children to live. She was in fear of losing her subsidy checks, so she was not going to play by their rules anymore. Well then, of course, they said, "We are going to kill you." So we had to physically move her to another housing development, and that solved the problem. As far as I know . . . I saw her in a grocery store and asked her how she was doing, and this was two years past. She

said she was doing great and she had not had any problems with them. These drug dealers over here won't go over into east Nashville.

Once this woman had confided in police about the intimidation of dealers, there was no way she could remain in Edgehill, even with its more intense police presence. As another officer explained it as we rode through the John Henry Hale projects, "If you get branded as talking to the police around here, at the least you'll be shunned, at the most you'll be killed."

The social ecology of prostitution in Nashville is intimately interwoven with that of drug use and drug dealing. Like the drug trade, the sale of bodies occurs on the streets, in crack houses, in motels, in the homes of johns, in higher-class hotels, and in sex clubs. The women who exchange sexual services for money, drugs, a place to stay, or other commodities appear ravaged by the rigors of the street and at a distinct disadvantage in relation to their johns and men in general. The relative power of men does not stem simply from their economic privileges over women but also from a more generalized patriarchal domination. Prostitution is unlicensed, and prostitutes are unprotected from the violence of johns and other men and from the various sexually transmitted diseases and other health hazards commonly associated with sex work.

For a price, drug dealers and prostitutes provide buyers with a fleeting euphoria and sense of power. Both pleasures are, of course, illegal. However, the former is policed much more closely than the latter, a fact that has a direct effect on the social ecology of prostitution. In what follows, I map the social distribution of prostitution, paying attention to its various forms and its links with other types of criminal behavior.

Street prostitutes who walk the periphery of housing projects such as John Henry Hale usually work on their own, without pimps. Many are addicted to crack cocaine, some test positive for HIV and other sexually communicable diseases, and every one of them runs the gauntlet of violence that may come from johns, street criminals, or both. There are a number of similarities between these women and those who give of their bodies in crack houses or simply trade sex for drugs in general. One man, Kevin Jackson, who had experience with these kinds of trades, shared his sense of the desperate lifestyles of these deeply oppressed women:

Jackson: The power of drugs is so bad . . . it can turn you so you have sex with anybody. . . . She don't care, she wants the dope.

Websdale: She just wants the dope?

Jackson: She wants the dope, so, you know, you gonna get it . . . you know, but you taking chances, gettin' whatever she might got . . . HIV . . . The woman, man, it's like, that shit gross, man. . . . It's gross. You know she go days without baths . . . an' it's just, aw, man, you just know that's somebody's child, you know, even if she ain't got no child, but somebody had her—her momma. . . .

Around John Henry Hale street prostitutes work in the relative seclusion of freeway underpasses, abandoned buildings, obscure alleyways, and, of course, johns' cars. Officer Evan Kaplan, who knows the area well, explained:

Kaplan: Well, they're down and out. They're at the very bottom. Their class of johns tends to be lower-class, and a lot of times they're doing tricks for drugs or beer, or just to make it through the night.

Websdale: This is a dangerous area, though, for doing this stuff.

Kaplan: Yes it is.

Websdale: So what kind of guys you gonna get coming down here doing it? Black guys from the community? Are they gonna be regulars?

Kaplan: There'll be regulars. They tend to be low- to no-income people. People who get a welfare check and they don't have a significant other, or whatever, and they'll come down here and just try to get a quick one.

It is hard to tell whether these streetwalkers in places like John Henry Hale are worse off than the women who work the crack houses inside the projects. Both groups of women are impoverished, disease-ridden, and brutalized, and most are addicted to crack cocaine.[20] Other locations in Nashville attract a more varied population of johns than those associated primarily with women working the projects and their immediate vicinity. Here the johns are office workers, laborers, businessmen, drivers, lawyers, shopkeepers, ministers, police officers, and others.[21] As noted in chapter 2, Dickerson Road and Murfreesboro Road are the main thoroughfares where prostitutes ply their trade, which is carried out on the streets, in parking lots, in the cars of johns, in motels, and in a few massage parlors. Here sex workers operate in daylight hours as well as under cover of darkness, with business climaxing with the early flow of traffic into the city and the afternoon outflow, as men leave their workplaces and head for the serenity of the family home.

Picking up prostitutes on the street is much more visible than arranging to meet one in a motel room. Like drug use and drug dealing, commercial sex frequently occurs behind closed doors. Clearly, a number of hotel proprietors turn a blind eye to such activities, take a more active role by adding a small, informal surcharge to rooms used for prostitution, or warn occupants if police show up. These hotels are typically situated near informal prostitution zones around Dickerson and Murfreesboro Roads. In these settings, which typically rent at the lower end of the market, drug dealing often occurs in concert with prostitution. At times dealers occupy different floors from prostitutes, or different sets of rooms, again with the expressed or implied consent of management. In some rooms drug manufacture may also take place, ensuring, perhaps, the freshest possible euphoria for clients.

Before being closed by police in May 1998, rooms at the Esquire Inn sold for forty dollars per night, with a five- to ten-dollar surcharge for sex rooms. Drug dealers sold cocaine to a steady stream of johns in the rooms. Doubtless, prostitutes themselves indulged in this extra service, thereby offering an array of vice services comparable to those offered in crack houses. Like crack houses, motels such as the Esquire Inn were subject to frequent disturbances, loud noise, and occasional shootings. In 1997 alone, Nashville police were summoned to the Esquire Inn 222 times, on calls ranging from disorderly conduct to shootings. A similar "nuisance problem" arose at the Oxford Inns at 1516 Hampton Street in the East Trinity Lane area of Nashville. The Oxford was even cheaper than the Esquire Inn; residents paid a mere twenty-three dollars a night to reside in what police described as nothing but a crack house and brothel.[22] The first floor of the Oxford Inns was for legitimate guests. Drug dealers and prostitutes used the second and third floors, respectively. Lookouts with binoculars posted on motel stairs kept watch for police, while drug makers kept the air-conditioners on high with the windows open to avoid smoke alarms' being set off by smoke from pipes and cookers. According to police documents, dealers sold crack cocaine from second-floor rooms, and criminals approached guests with the option of purchasing what turned out to be stolen property. The same criminals also offered the services of prostitutes.

The social significance of vice joints like the Esquire Inn and the Oxford Inns cannot be read simply from the long list of infractions. Rather, these varied forms of vice must also be situated in the context of the surrounding neighborhood, with respect to the degree to which the illicit activities are visible. In the projects the crack houses are known to residents, but these residents have little political clout, they do not vote in large numbers, and authorities appear to acquiesce to the illegalities as long as they remain confined both physically and socially within the walls of the projects. However, off Dickerson Road the issue of the visibility of vice takes on new meaning, because it spills over into more racially mixed neighborhoods, often predominantly poor white communities. Here residents have more political clout than do those in the projects. It is also the case that prostitution on Dickerson Road has become visible to schoolchildren in the better-off neighborhood, raising the rather hypocritical specter of the moral contamination of this group of young people. For example, some children from the Shwab Elementary School passed the Esquire Inn on their way to school. The playground of the school was sometimes littered with condoms and syringes. This differential concern for the unseemly by-products of vice contaminating children who attend schools in predominantly white neighborhoods (rather than schools fed by children from the housing projects) has a long history in Nashville and in other major U.S. urban centers. Once again, such a double standard reflects the lack of social concern for the plight of poor blacks.

Philanthropy and the Subterranean Economy

In the aftermath of the 1960s demonstrations to desegregate lunch counters and movie theaters in Nashville, a number of young Nashvillians, members of the Southern Christian Leadership Council (SCLC), sought to join the freedom rides heading south to Birmingham, Alabama, Jackson, Mississippi, and New Orleans, Louisiana. The older clergy in this social movement resisted such involvement and warned the younger members of the dangers. At one point an older minister, Kelly Miller Smith, who was from Mississippi and aware of the dangers posed by angry whites resistant to desegregation, told them, "I understand the importance of what you want to do. I think some of you are going to die if you go ahead. This is not something to rush into. I want you to think about it more."[23] Frustrated, the younger would-be freedom riders decided to proceed anyway. However, they needed financial backing and were unable to cash a check for nine hundred dollars made out to them by the SCLC to cover the cost of tickets for the twenty or so riders. They approached a big numbers man, a gambler who usually had plenty of cash. David Halberstam described the interaction: "They found him, and the numbers man had looked at the check, and he had smiled, a small private smile all his own which went back to an age-old war within the black community between the good blacks, who went to church, and the bad blacks, who worked the night at different gambling joints. Then he had reached in his pocket and taken out a huge bankroll, and peeled off a few large bills. With that the money was available, the check processed by the two faces of the black community, the daytime face and the nighttime face."[24]

I draw upon this example for good reason. It is easy, especially given the way the modern media dramatize the evil of certain offenders, to think that those who sometimes engage in criminal acts are evil people. Put differently, it is tempting to think that there are profound character differences between criminals and noncriminals. However, contrary to what our current passion for crime statistics might suggest, it is hard to sustain distinctions between so-called criminals and noncriminals. The labels reflect the legislative priorities of political authorities and the enforcement foci of police agencies. Once labels are attached, people begin to live up to them and deviancy is amplified, hardened, and concentrated. Other, perhaps conflicting, identities are crowded out. As Frank Tannenbaum once put it, "The attitude of the community hardens definitely into a demand for suppression. There is a gradual shift from the definition of the specific acts as evil to a definition of the individual as evil, so that all his acts come to be looked upon with suspicion. . . . From the community's point of view, the individual who used to do bad and mischievous things has now become a bad and unredeemable human being."[25]

I have already discussed the way those who run the subterranean economy engage in perfectly rational economic behavior given the hand dealt them. There is a danger in seeing the code of the streets as an entirely oppositional culture. Such a conceptualization masks the many similarities between street criminals and the so-called noncriminal members of their communities. It also denies the similarities between these different factions among the urban poor—similarities in thought, loyalties, acts of kindness, rage, violence, and illicit behavior.

It is with these observations in mind that I mention the themes in my ethnography that speak to the similarities between "criminals" and the communities they live in and sometimes terrorize.

On a very drab rainy afternoon in March 2000, I met a young black man named Abel Hazard at the Foundry, located at the edge of John Henry Hale public housing. He was a member of a Christian group that provides spiritual support in the inner city and also offers material provisions for the poor. The Foundry is a huge, unused warehouse that is slowly filling up with the everyday items the poor need to survive. In addition to food and religious sustenance, the Foundry supplies the poor with clothing, furniture, pots and pans, and at times a place to stay. From one of the rooms on the second floor it is possible to watch the drug dealers in nearby Watkins Park. Abel told me that drug dealers in the community provide money for the Foundry, although he would not go into detail. I suspect this provision is through charitable donations. He also told me that the pastor of the church affiliated with the Foundry freely walked around John Henry Hale and was not bothered by the dealers. In fact, Abel told me that dealers curbed their language around the pastor and did not deal drugs in his presence. We found evidence of similar "scrupulous" behavior on the part of drug dealers in the McQuiddy case. Darrell McQuiddy told the federal judge who heard his case that he would not sell crack cocaine to minors or pregnant women. In addition, McQuiddy noted that his crack house observed the Sabbath, closing to honor God.[26]

Two black women in their midforties, both grandmothers living in the projects, told me of their experiences with drug dealers. Chiandra Tipton, who had lived in Sam Levy for thirteen years, told me that there had been a change in the character of the drug dealers in those projects. She told me, "A lot of the big drug dealers are locked up. Some of them used to help the community, you know, July Fourth and all that. But now, those guys are just out for themselves, their cars, you know. No good, disrespectful, selfish." It might be that in Sam Levy so many of the older dealers have been incarcerated that a shift occurred, and newer, younger dealers are less connected to the people in the projects, or that, given the rigors of the crack cocaine war, many community members have become more detached from community life and no longer know individual dealers. This may be peculiar to Sam Levy, which is subject to heavy policing and surveillance, especially in the wake of the Dollar General burning.

Glenna Jacobs, a grandmother of three whose own daughter "had problems with drugs, hence I'm looking after the kids," told me that dealers in Preston Taylor had often been kind to her and her grandchildren. Even though at one point she had been shot by a stray bullet from street gunfire and subsequently hospitalized, she reported having no fear of individual dealers. Glenna, who suffered a number of health problems including epilepsy, told me:

> I am not scared of the dealers. I am scared for my grandchildren being out there and having to listen to their language, talking the slang 'an all. The dealers have respect for me. I've known them since they were kids. They grew up with my daughters. They encourage my grandkids to do well. One of my grandchildren received thirty dollars from a dealer who knew my daughter. He gave her thirty dollars after my granddaughter got three A grades on her report card. This granddaughter is eight years old. The dealer told her, "You'll be a great young lady one day." And in other things they support the community. They give the most to the church and provide money for things like Easter Egg hunts for the kids. You know, a lot of those dealers, they don't do drugs.

Glenna told me that after the stray bullet shot her: "Those boys were good to me. They'd say, 'You want somethin' mama?' Now I don't like them pushing drugs in our community because it attracts other people in from the outside. But they give me cigarettes. One night when I was having seizures from my epilepsy, one of them dealers came into my house and rocked me to sleep."

Even some of the police officers I talked with acknowledged the popularity of some the dealers with women in the projects. Officer Olsen told me as we rode around Edgehill that when police arrested one of the dealers, a number of women broke down and cried.

Olsen: When we first started over here in 1996, there was one drug dealer, he was so popular that when we arrested him there were women falling down in the street, wailing and crying. He was going to jail for a long time. They were actually crying.
Websdale: Were they supplied by him?
Olsen: No, they didn't use drugs. They were used to his drug money.

He took care of all these girls with money. These were boyfriend-girlfriend relationships. And he had fathered several children with these girls. But he was their role model. He was a muscular man. As a matter of fact, he lay on top of that cement overhang right there and shot into a police car in 1995. He didn't hit the officer, he just shot into the car. But he was the role model. He was what these people looked up to. These kids over here looked up to him. The women admired him 'cause he had money, and that was what was important to them.

At least some dealers appear to exercise considerable caution around young children, refusing to deal around them. Part of this reluctance may come from the fact that community members would be outraged if dealers sold openly to the young. Glenna said, "If you are gonna deal to young kids round here, you'd better believe you're gonna have a posse on you." It seems that some dealers, if not the majority, are respectful of children. Byron explained: "The dealers try to show the children respect, and not be doin' it in front of 'em. They might hand out a whole lot of money to all the kids. So, and they see kids maybe looking bad, might need a haircut, and they'll say, 'Go on and get your hair cut, there's ten dollars.' The kids look up to the dealers, and all the dealers are like, you know, 'Don't nobody mess with the kids, don't nobody do nothin' to the kids in the projects.' Nothin' really too much happen to the kids in the projects. Now, some kids bein' neglected, you know, by their parents because their parents on drugs. That's bad. But they don't even know their kids being neglected. Probably on drugs all day."

The Politics of Vice in Nashville

The principal forms of vice in Nashville are crack cocaine dealing and prostitution. Police actively pursue the former but not the latter. There are clear political reasons for these different and long-standing enforcement styles. Nashville police largely wink at prostitution, a sacred rite of men, even though it is linked to violence against women. Most police officers I talked with saw it as a minor offense; some told me it was consensual and that they had problems with enforcing the law against it. Occasionally, the city of Nashville engages in high-profile campaigns against the crime. Convicted prostitutes may serve

a little time, flirt briefly with the pitiful offering of state support services, then usually go right back to their only way of surviving or feeding
their drug habit and/or their children.

Katrina, who worked as a volunteer at a shelter for battered women,
explained the relative indifference of police to prostitution:

Websdale: The police obviously know and see this prostitution going
   on.
Katrina: No offense to you as a man . . .
Websdale: No, go ahead.
Katrina: The justice system is run by men for men, with a man's way
   of dealing with problems. They don't consider prostitution or gambling a big problem. It's a personal choice kind of thing. And I think
   a lot of them just don't want to fool with 'em.

One of the prison focus groups turned up information on the half-
hearted and largely ineffectual policing of prostitution:

Gloria: They patrol an area . . . one certain area. . . . A prostitute just
   moves to another part of the projects. Then when they come patrol
   that area, then they move back down to the same area that they
   came from.
Rebecca: I've been there, done that. I mean, I know. Them officers
   know them working girls, and I'm gonna tell you the truth. They're
   not quick to put you in jail; they're not.

Candace went even further. She told me, as other heads nodded
affirmatively in the focus group, that the working girls somehow knew
when the police were going to target a certain zone of prostitution, a
motel, a part of the projects, and so on:

Candace: There's somebody always knows when this house is gonna
   get raided. . . . They get everything out. Somehow they know.
   Everybody clears out.
Websdale: When you say everybody clears out, you mean working
   women or dope dealers or what?
Gloria: All of 'em. They all go somewhere to a motel that's not known
   for prostitution, it's not known for drugs. Yeah. And you can guarantee that the crime underworld, I guess you can call it that, the

crime underworld has connections with the police. I'm a firm believer in that. Yeah. There's too many people that I would say shoulda got busted that didn't.

Priscilla: By some leak of information, they didn't.

Candace: It's not only with the policing though. It has to be with the court too, you know, because that's a lot of it too; they let a lot of 'em go.

I heard stories of the occasional police officer on the take getting paid, for example, to tip off motels before police raids. However, probably as many police officers play fast with the rules as do college professors and politicians. Officially, Nashville police report not confronting prostitution aggressively because they have too few female officers trained to work as decoys. According to Sergeant Melvin Brown, the city is too busy with the drug problem to train its limited resources on prostitution. As I noted earlier, in 1997 Nashville police responded to 222 calls of disturbances at the Esquire Inn. According to the district attorney general, Torry Johnson, the Esquire had "been repeatedly warned by police officers to stop the illegal activity and clean up its act, yet those warnings obviously were not heeded."[27] This example alone conveys a sense of police and criminal justice system acquiescence to prostitution. It also tells us that police, in marked contrast to their interest in drug dealing in the housing projects, sometimes find it difficult to make arrests for drug manufacture and sale out of these motels.

Police attack the drug trade with constitutionally questionable tactics. Their actions over the last ten years has accompanied the disappearance of drug and alcohol treatment services for the poor in Tennessee.[28] This disappearance and the concomitant arrest strategies reflect a broader shift away from treatment and rehabilitation of addicts toward a less caring and more dismissive warehousing of them in jails and prisons. Byron, like a number of other black men I talked with, explained how he felt about harassment from police:

Byron: Well, in my opinion, I feel like I'm harassed for no reason at all. You know, it's like . . . you walk down the street, uh, you could be trying to visit a friend from the housing projects, and I get off the city bus on one side of the street and the police is on the other side. I'm coming across the street. But before I get to where I'm going, you know, they, like, asking me questions. "Let me see your ID." "Why?" I'm askin', "Why?" He says, " 'Cause I want to. Is you on the lease?" I say, "No, but I'm visiting my mother, my sister, some of them, they on the lease. They got their car and their own project house and I'm a family member. Why can't I come see 'em without being questioned?"

Websdale: So they're stopping you for no reason?

Byron: For no reason. I mean, I get off one bus and come across the street and I got jewelry on or if I got a beeper on, and they say, you doin' something. They think everybody's dealing drugs. Everybody. It's a few people doing it, you know what I'm sayin? A lot of people go through there to buy drugs, and there's a lot of people go through there to sell drugs, and there's just a lot of people just walk through just to be walking though. I mean, it's just, I guess, "Whatcha you doin? Whatcha been up to? Where you work at? Do you work? Why you over here?" Just questioning me all the time. If you come out of the store with a sack of something in your hand, they want to look all in the sack—"What's in there—empty your pockets, put everything on the car," . . . and all for what?

Sometimes these tensions between police and the citizenry in the projects escalate to street altercations that create resentment. On occasion, the *Tennessean* reports these altercations.[29] In January 1999, near J. C. Napier Homes, police became involved in an altercation with local residents over an undercover drug bust. Katie Sharber told reporters that police exited an unmarked police car wearing black ski masks and approached her two grandchildren as they walked near the Napier Community Center. The children ran back to her house. Police claimed that one of the grandchildren was standing near a person arrested in the bust and that they were not sure of the relationship between the grandchild and the arrestee. Since both grandchildren ran to Katie Sharber's house after police had apparently asked them to stop, police pursued them. Shawnta Sharber, aged nineteen, told reporters she tried to leave her grandmother's house to inform the mother of one of the two boys that police had arrested him. Shawnta accused police of tearing off her jacket and handcuffing her. Police claimed Shawnta was belligerent and that she lost her jacket trying to pull away from them. They eventually arrested Shawnta for disorderly conduct. Her mother, Hattie Sharber, then arrived at the scene and allegedly started shouting profanities as police arrested her daughter. Hattie's boyfriend, Howard Bonner, witnessed the arrest, and when he tried to ask questions about it, Bonner told reporters that police put a gun to his head.

This case and so many like it serve as examples of what Jerome Miller calls "iatrogenesis" in the criminal justice system. Deriving from the field of medicine, the word "iatrogenesis" refers to the deterioration of the patient owing to the inadvertent but nevertheless problematic intervention of a physician. Miller also uses the term "iatrogenic punishment" to describe the exacerbation of criminality and the encouragement of recidivism among young offenders through incarceration. Numerous studies show that officially processing and confining young offenders increases rather than decreases their likelihood of reoffending.[30]

The targeting of young black males by police in Nashville has filled the local jail to the bursting point, swelled the ranks of the state penitentiary, and created a generation of black men of whom many have criminal records. With the negative stigma of a criminal record, it is more difficult to find regular paid employment and easier to be targeted by police. It is hardly surprising, then, that men like Rob Whittaker, whom I introduced in chapter 3, feel as if "a lot of young African Americans, especially the males . . . feel that they're walking around with a bull's-eye drawn on their head."

Black males are most likely to be the targets of the saturation policing of the housing projects. The differential policing of black males in part reflects the more visible circumstances in which blacks trade, sell, and use crack cocaine, a visibility obviously related to the miserable housing conditions in the projects and the unemployment and underemployment that generate the need to possess, use, and sell in plain view. However, this is not just a question of the police targeting blacks because it is easier to develop probable cause against them, make arrests, secure convictions, and keep the American prison gulags in business. Neither is this differential targeting a simple reflection of the racist tendencies of individual police officers, although, as I noted in chapter 3, racial profiling clearly goes on, and police do arrest black suspects more than white, often doing so on flimsier evidence.[31] Black men in the projects of Nashville lack access to good legal representation, a disadvantage that makes it more likely that they will accept a plea bargain. Over time, a spiral of negative interactions develops between police and young urban black males, ever amplifying the offending of those young men, constantly pushing them toward adversarial relations with police, increasing the likelihood that police will arrest them for offenses eventually labeled and processed as "violent." At another level, genuine and understandable rage develops that bleeds over into the commission of occasional acts of violence, making interactions with other dealers bloody, high-stakes affairs. As relations with police deteriorate and young black offenders read the writing on the walls of the criminal justice juggernaut, they come to increasingly fear and resent the police, which makes them tend to flee officers. If apprehended, these offenders are more likely to be charged with resisting arrest or resisting arrest with violence.

From time to time authorities reveal these differential arrest and incarceration rates to the public, just as they disclose the differential commission rates of "violent crimes" by black males. Politicians mercilessly exploit these stereotypical images of the black male as "threat," greedily feeding into the anger reflex of the nation. Willie Horton was one famous example of the cynical use of black men as a symbol of violent threat, but there have been many others.[32] The media constantly reinforce these stereotypical images of "dangerous" black offenders. The point that gets lost when the cameras pan to another bloody black corpse is that the vast majority of black men arrested and incarcerated for their involvement in the drug trade are arrested for possession and do not present a "menace to society." In his study of Duval County (where Jacksonville is), Florida, Jerome Miller learned that blacks constituted 12 percent of the population, more than half of those processed through the jail on a daily basis, and, because of their poverty and consequent inability to make bail, three-quarters of the average daily jail census. Just as happens in Nashville and across urban America, "the criminal justice system had penetrated the black community of this predominantly white county deeply and widely."[33] Such penetration by its very nature collects more black bodies to feed into the criminal justice conveyer belt.

None of this information is meant to deny the fact that some black offenders, like white offenders, are dangerous and vicious criminals from whom society needs to be protected. Indeed, given that black men do commit more crimes of violence such as robbery and homicide, it makes sense that there would be some overrepresentation of them in the criminal justice system. However, the key point emerging from my ethnography and the work of other researchers is that many black men who use violence do so to adapt to criminal justice surveillance and harassment, political marginalization, and the economic devastation of their communities. Even much of the violence between black men derives from the competitive pressures of the subterranean economy, the lack of respect between impoverished, low-status men, and the acute need to survive. As we have seen in my interviews, the endless and humiliating procession of these young men through the jails and prisons hardens them and exposes them to violence, machismo, danger, and the derision of correctional staff. Such experiences nurture hostility, amplify resentment, and further cut young men off from positive community influences, rendering them more likely to be violent in the future. There is plenty of evidence to support this contention, which forms the philosophical basis for the juvenile justice system, which at least at one point in its hundred-year history preached the parsimonious resort to incarceration because of the negative impact of labeling young offenders. Tagging someone with a criminal label also increases the likelihood that police will stop and question him or her in the future, further amplifying resentment and perhaps adding to the perception among police that a juvenile is drifting toward a life of crime and violence. As my ethnography shows, resentment builds because once the criminal justice juggernaut labels young black men as felons, it becomes increasingly difficult for them to find and keep regular jobs.

In Nashville, the *Tennessean* has occasionally highlighted the disproportionate targeting of black men in the crack cocaine war. In one article, reporter Laura Frank noted that of the three thousand people convicted for possession of crack cocaine in 1993, 90 percent were black. Facts such as these reflect the implementation of laws designed to confront the offenses of blacks as opposed to whites. Henry Martin, the chief federal defender in Middle Tennessee, put it as follows: "The drug of choice for whites doesn't carry as severe a sentence as the drug of choice for blacks. . . . Crack cases are just easier to make and there's no motive to change that. The prosecution has focused on the least powerful section of society. They're not going out to Belle Meade to arrest folks." The same article noted that roughly 40 percent of all drug dealers convicted by federal prosecutors are at the lower end of the drug-dealing food chain and do not attract the five- and ten-year mandatory sentences.[34] This is further evidence that many of those processed for these offenses are not menaces to society.

The innocuousness of some crack dealers was evident in one incident in Edgehill. Officer Olsen pulled into a forecourt where a dwarf crack dealer was "loitering." Olsen called out to him, asking him what he was doing on the property. The dealer told Olsen he was cutting through, and Olsen warned him that he was trespassing. He then turned to me and explained why he would not be patting him down for drugs and how handling this dealer became something of a rite of passage for rookie officers:

> He is a drug dealer. He never takes a bath and he absolutely will cause your stomach to churn if you take off one of those shoes. I am not kidding. I saw grown men vomit at the stench. He will not take a bath. He puts his crack cocaine in his shoes. When you get close to him, it is the nastiest thing you'll ever experience [groaning]. That's why we just warned him. . . . It will turn your stomach [chuckling]. He got to be a joke for a while. We would pick him up and pawn him off on newer officers, somebody who didn't know him. We would let them handle him. They would say, like, "Oh my God, what have you given me?"

Nashville police, like those in other urban areas, sometimes play fast and loose with the Bill of Rights. They clearly profile men in the housing projects and use the criminal trespass laws as a vehicle to do so. These constitutionally dubious practices provide an opportunity to search individuals for drugs. Police employ other dubious tactics to search automobiles. African American males confronted by a strong police presence cannot easily refuse to allow police to search their persons or their vehicles.[35]

In spite of questionable law enforcement practices, we must not assume that the criminal justice system is a monolithic entity and that the law always works against the poor. To appear credible, the law cannot consistently ride roughshod over the Bill of Rights; to do so would be to open the very institutions of so-called representative democracy to challenge. As Lenin once put it, "Democracy is the one best shell for capitalism," and to leave too many cracks in the shell by rolling back those popular and clearly beneficial aspects of democratic societies is to lay bare the exploitation, oppression, and disadvantage that lie beneath and infest public housing in cities such as Nashville.

In many ways, however, the drug war has created cracks in this shell and exposed the canker beneath. Even Republicans and some critics seen as conservative spokespersons on criminal justice issues are questioning the appropriateness of the drug war.[36] Neither are the courts and the judiciary blind to the erosion of constitutional guarantees. Recently courts overturned a number of significant cases that further extended police powers. Examples include the recent decision of the U.S. Supreme Court to uphold the *Miranda* warning to inform those arrested of their rights.[37] At the state level in Tennessee courts, we see a similar trend toward clipping the wings of law enforcement officers in drug cases. In January 1998, the Tennessee Supreme Court explained the liberties of police when patting down a suspect for weapons. The court dismissed a cocaine conviction after police found the illegal substance in a pill bottle located in the suspect's jacket pocket. While the court deemed it appropriate for the officer to search the suspect for weapons, it was not obvious by the "plain feel" of the object in the pocket that it contained cocaine. As a consequence, the court deemed the search inadmissible.[38]

As I discussed in chapter 1, Randall Kennedy has observed that slave codes operated within a legal tradition pervaded by notions of honor, duty, and appropriate application of the law. In particular, I want to reemphasize that courts reversed the convictions of blacks in 136 of 238 appellate decisions in southern states between 1830 and 1860 because of the failure to constitute juries correctly.[39] Indeed, E. P. Thompson, in his pioneering work on the Black Acts prior to the rise of industrial capitalism, notes the contradictory qualities of the rule of law: "The rhetoric and rules of a society are something a great deal more than sham. In the same moment they may modify, in profound ways, the behavior of the powerful, and mystify the powerless. They may disguise the true realities of power, but, at the same time, they may curb that power and check its intrusions. And it is often from within that very rhetoric that a radical critique of the practice of the society is developed."[40]

However, we must ask what potential the rule of law holds for addressing the plight of African Americans. Clearly, the policing of the crack cocaine trade, with its questionable tactics of surveillance, harassment, profiling, illegal stop and search, and so on, tells us that civil rights are racially exclusive. As Paul Gilroy observes, recent ideologies of crime sharpen the association between blacks and criminality. The police disseminate and reproduce these ideologies. "They have elevated it to sociological credibility . . . and mobilized it not only in the struggle to police the blacks themselves, but also as part of securing the consent of white citizens to police practices which they might otherwise find unacceptable."[41] Put simply, if we permit the erosion of constitutional guarantees to feed young blacks to the criminal justice juggernaut, then we step onto a slippery slope with negative implications for the civil rights of all.

6

From Elmina to Edgehill: Policing the Black Underclass

■ Historically, the modern state polices the very poor more closely than other groups because in many ways the poor have the most to gain and least to lose from not following the rules and laws of society. The first formal U.S. police systems emerged in the South to manage slave populations. Later systems of bureaucratic police regulated discontented workers, especially during the period of rapid industrialization from 1877 to 1937. Until rather recently, all police systems left the control of women's behavior to their intimate male partners, or, in the case of slave women, to their masters, followed by the black "head" of household. These observations ought not surprise us. It comes as no surprise, either, that my ethnography places community policing at the fulcrum of hostilities between the black underclass and political authorities, recalling the historical correspondences between the Door of

No Return at Elmina and the bars of the postindustrial prison. Tracing an unbroken line from the work of community police in Edgehill to the European slave trade speaks poorly but accurately of postindustrial America. Almost forty years ago, Franz Fanon observed angrily: "When I search for Man in the technique and the style of Europe, I see only a succession of negations of man, and an avalanche of murders. . . . Two centuries ago, a former European colony decided to catch up with Europe. It succeeded so well that the United States of America became a monster, in which the taints, the sickness and the inhumanity of Europe have grown to appalling dimensions."[1]

Community Policing

The constipated analyses of community policing do little more than waffle on the issues of police-community relations, styles of patrol, flattening the command hierarchy, producing a new generation of officers who are "problem solvers," setting up neighborhood watches, and educating the public to prevent crime. This blinkered literature is technical and administrative in nature, dull to read, and largely silent on all the major social and historical roots of crime, violence, and urban blight. It fails abysmally to ask those who do not participate in the "new neighborhood camaraderie" with law enforcement what they think of the new saturation-police presence. This dismissal of the opinions of all but the most compliant and optimistic members of the ghetto implies that we have little to learn from poor people's voices or that their reasons for not getting involved derive from their criminality, cynicism, or hostility. It is of limited worth to ask neighborhood politicians, heads of neighborhood watches, the few blacks in Nashville who serve on various crime commissions, and other neighborhood busybodies about community policing. We need to augment their opinions with those of crack dealers, drug runners, crack house employees, street prostitutes, and all those "branded" by the criminal justice juggernaut. These people burn under the iron of the juggernaut and are much more likely to help us understand the meaning of the erosion of rights, intense surveillance, loss of jobs, and the demise of black kinship systems. My ethnography is a tiny attempt to counter some of the totalitarian themes in the literature on community policing and the rhetoric of the U.S. Department of Justice on these matters.

Nevertheless, all this talk of community policing helps us understand social control mechanisms in postindustrial inner cities. The Clinton administration's push to put 100,000 new police officers on the street was as political as George H. W. Bush's use of Willie Horton. Likewise, the political construction of heavy penalties for possession of crack as opposed to powdered cocaine provided the "legal" rationale to justify saturating some neighborhoods with community police. To its shame, the U.S. Justice Department promoted the punitive handling of the "crack epidemic." The U.S. Sentencing Commission sought to lower the penalties for crack-related offenses. Attorney General Reno stood behind existing policies in Nashville, saying, "I strongly oppose measures that fail to reflect the harsh and terrible impact of crack on communities across America."[2]

Community policing allegedly brings law enforcement officers closer to the public, allowing them to assess neighborhood problems from the ground up and more carefully infiltrate communities to gather information related to crime and disorder. In theory, community policing is more proactive than traditional (professional paramilitary) law enforcement styles based on reactive patrol and responding to citizen complaints. Experiments in community policing appeared in the early 1980s in cities such as Houston and New York. Recent federally funded initiatives began to emerge in 1993 under the Clinton-Gore regime.

For some researchers, the rise of community policing constitutes a systematic response to the growing detachment of police from neighborhoods, with the pursuit of "serious offenders" taking precedence over minor problems associated with urban decay. These researchers partly attribute this growing detachment to motorized patrol and the scaling back of the more personal foot patrol. Vehicles can obviously patrol more quickly than officers on foot, covering more of a beat, particularly potential trouble spots. For some, the consequence of this increased efficiency was a failure to heed those symptoms of urban decay that invited colonization by criminals.[3] James Q. Wilson and George Kelling's seminal article "Broken Windows" used the broken window as a metaphor for urban decay. When police do not address such decay, the message goes out that the neighborhood is ripe for exploitation by criminals. These authors called for a return to "watchman" policing, with officers more visibly present in communities, on foot patrol, interacting with citizens, and confronting minor forms of disorder. According to Wilson and Kelling, municipal police had lost touch with their communities and needed to restore this connectedness to be more effective. Others disagree, arguing that such an interpretation of police history is inaccurate and overly romantic. For example, Samuel Walker argues that Wilson and Kelling overstate the degree of legitimacy municipal police enjoyed before the rise of the professionalization movement in the 1930s.[4] Whatever the pros and cons of these academic positions, the fact remains that municipal police did not serve and protect black communities during the time this loss of confidence supposedly took place. Indeed, as I have shown, the hunger to patrol black communities dates to the aftermath of the Kerner Report and especially the dictates of the twentieth-century redemption.

Criminologists have always asked what strategies might deter crime and enable communities to feel safer. Indeed, their need to purify society would be laudable if it were not so misplaced. The Kansas City Preventive Patrol Experiment showed that increasing traditional patrol intensities beyond a certain threshold made little difference in crime, citizen fear of crime, community attitudes toward the police regarding the delivery of police services, police response time, and traffic accidents.[5] The findings established a need to look closely at more proactive styles of policing, styles that were perhaps more probative of certain individuals and hot spots for crime, thus nipping criminality in the bud.[6] Subsequent research went further by suggesting that "rotating crackdowns" at certain troublesome sites or against certain groups of individuals might increase deterrence, at least in the short term.[7]

One scholar claims that "community policing is the new orthodoxy of American policing. It has become a flourishing alternative to what many police administrators view as the failure of professional policing to deal effectively with crime and quality-of-life issues."[8] In 1993 Robert Trojanowicz reported a national survey of police administrators that revealed 50 percent who had implemented community policing, with another 20 percent who were bringing it on board in the next year.[9] The Clinton administration formalized and extended the earlier and more experimental community policing models in cities such as New York and Houston, making available $150 million in fiscal year 1993 for the hiring of new police officers.[10] The goal of the U.S. Justice Department's Community Oriented Policing Services (COPS) program, which commenced in 1994, was to provide federal funding for 100,000 new police officers across the country by 2000. In a similar vein, in 1990 the Bureau of Justice Assistance made available grant money to fund eight innovative neighborhood-oriented policing programs. The delivery of more formalized federal backing for community policing initiatives fed into and reinforced the already burgeoning criminal justice juggernaut.

Community policing means different things in different jurisdictions. Usually, there is an emphasis on officers being trained as "problem solvers" and the community having some input into the nature of police practices. In Nashville, the entire police department has adopted the ethos of community policing, articulating, at least in theory, a desire for citizen input about law enforcement and related issues. However, as we have seen, the more intensified and federally funded community policing programs were concentrated in the city's southern sector and public housing projects like Edgehill. By 1996 Charles Miller, the press secretary for the Justice Department's COPS program, told the *Tennessean*, "Nashville has obviously shown that they have a good community policing program."[11] Coincidentally, perhaps, it was in the wake of the Dollar General Store burning (August 10, 1997) that the move toward formal community policing initiatives in Nashville really took off. This move received a shot in the arm as Vice-President Al Gore held a town hall meeting to talk about the subject. As *Tennessean* reporter Jon Yates informed readers, the COPS program had provided $11 million and one hundred new police officers for Nashville between 1994 and 1997.[12] At the "invitation-only" town hall meeting on community policing, sixty new police recruits flanked Vice-President Gore, who announced to the audience of hand-picked law enforcement officials and community leaders that the Clinton administration's policies had reduced crime dramatically in the preceding five years, with crime hitting a twenty-five-year low in the United States. Gore also reminded the audience that Nashville had received $18.6 million in federal grants since 1994, which enabled the hiring of 147 new police officers as part of the drive toward community policing. Cohosting the meeting was Police Chief Emmett Turner, who, exhibiting amnesia regarding the burning of the Dollar General Store, where presumably neither he nor Gore shopped, told reporters: "Our whole philosophy is community policing and I think it's working well. . . . I think we've built some bridges in various places all over the city. Obviously, there's a lot more to do and a lot more work but, overall, I think we've seen some good things."[13]

Gore's euphoria over the crime figures, his backing of community policing, and Chief Turner's statement that the entire philosophy of the department had shifted to community policing were, of course, politics par excellence. At the time of that town hall meeting, many of the Nashville housing projects were essentially no-go areas at night. Police continue to enter them with great caution and trepidation. To suggest that there is anything approaching "consent" for policing, or that the police and communities in these projects truly work together, is ludicrous. Unlike Vice-President Gore or Chief Turner, Stephanie Munger from James Cayce housing projects knew well the limits of police penetration: "In Cayce Homes, you might see a bike patrolman out there during the day, but when it gets nighttime, no way. They're not gonna be out there on that bike. There's guys out there with machine guns and stuff, walking around. It's a war zone."

Nashville police I spoke with disclosed mixed feelings about how community policing deterred crime, improved community safety, and repaired police-community relations. Most citizens I talked with who lived in the housing projects and had lived through the transition to a more "community-oriented" form of policing did not think the ethos made much difference to their lives. Even if community policing offered a formal public apology for past police excesses, residents might rightly view it with suspicion. A few people in Edgehill thought there were some visible differences in the street drug trade during the day, but at night dealing and other criminal activities still took place. Reverend Spohl told me that ten years ago, when the issue of community policing was first raised, there was more genuine community interest in law enforcement in Edgehill. He added that once the move toward community policing in Edgehill became institutionalized and Nashville received grant money to implement the initiatives, community involvement, interest, and commitment began to wane. It was as if once the "real" purpose, focus, and consequences of community policing began to emerge, it began to lose some of its appeal. From his experience in Nashville, Officer Bob Gladstone had this to say:

> The ideal and the idea of community policing was the police and the community coming together, working together. But in the projects there is always the problem of "snitching"; people just don't want to talk about certain things. You know, some people, they're part of this criminal activity, so they don't want others involved in community policing. And I work that area. You get discouraged because you go in there and you have these

expectations at the beginning. You talk about communication and all this kind of thing. You have expectations in the beginning about working together, trying to solve problems in the community, but the problems just keep coming and coming and coming. Then the community seems not to be as accepting of you as you thought they would be or you expected them to be, and so it breaks down and both sides kind of say, "Well, it ain't working right."

Clearly, some people in the projects, particularly older women, desire more police protection and welcome a greater police presence. Officer Olsen, among others, told me of a woman in Edgehill who was supportive of the community policing initiative.

There are very few old men who live here. It's mostly older women. These older women were sometimes influential. Janice Renton [pseudonym] was a huge impact on the community. She would come out of her door and yell at people who were talking bad about the police. She started cussing people that were talking bad about the police. "They're your friends." And we would come over and she would cook dinner for us. And whenever she was out grilling, she would always say, "Come on over and have a burger." She has been here that long. When you're a survivor, I guess you become a respected member and people listen to you. Because she really did some good things for us as far as breaking the initial barrier for people to open up and talk to us.

Even if community policing programs do overcome the problems Gladstone mentioned, police work itself militates against the building of trust between police and the public. The classic research by Arthur Niederhoffer on the New York City Police Department found that the cynicism of police officers peaked during the first seven to ten years of their careers, eventually tapering off but always remaining above the level of cynicism exhibited upon entry.[14] Several of the officers I talked with who worked the projects in Nashville displayed considerable cynicism about crime and the internal management of the police department. Given that the department was understaffed by roughly one hundred officers, some laughed at the very mention of the term "community policing." One officer raised his eyes toward the roof of his vehicle and sneered as we talked about the understaffing of the Nashville Police Department, community policing, and the nearly $300 million spent on the new football stadium. Officer Alan Jensen told me that he was cynical, that he took his work-related problems home, and that he did not want to have much to do with "humanity" once off the job. Jensen said his growing cynicism, and that of other officers, worked against developing trusting liaisons with the public, regardless of what the party line was on community policing. As William Westley once put it, many police officers perceive the public to be their enemy.[15] This caused them to develop an internal code that gave first priority to protecting each other and creating a highly homogenized police subculture.[16] Officer Jensen noted: "The worst part is it comes home with you. After a while you quit trusting people and you don't talk to your neighbors as much. I'll be honest—it now takes me a long time before I'll even talk to them and open up to them. It's hard making new friends after a while. And the killer part is, in a community like this [John Henry Hale Homes], especially with the community policing, you're supposed to go out there, talk to them, see what their problems are!"

Not all community police officers feel this way. Officer Ralph Olsen, who turned in a fellow officer for planting evidence on a suspect, told me that the police subculture in Nashville is not as tight as it used to be and that the "code of silence" is not as quiet as some think. To him, this meant that officers were more open to community comments and less cynical and defensive. However, Officer Olsen struck me as the exception rather than the rule among officers who policed the projects of Nashville:

> I hear people talk about the thin blue line and the code of silence. It ain't as silent as it used to be. I've had personal experience with officers who have done things that were against the law. And I just flat out told them, "I ain't going to jail for you. Bye." And I have exposed them. Now, at a great personal risk, yes. There are some people in the police department who can't stand me because I turned in a fellow officer for planting drugs on somebody. But I'm not going to go to jail for that man. I have a wife and am planning a family, and I've got a house. I'm not going to risk that for this overzealous officer who thinks he's going to fight the war on drugs by planting dope on people.

It's not going to happen while I'm present. There are some officers that thought I should not have turned him in. But there are also other officers that walk up and say, "Hey, you know, we're proud that you did that. You made us look good."

People sometimes assume that community policing is "softer" than traditional paramilitary styles of law enforcement. Police do provide more services for Edgehill citizens than do police in other projects. Such provisions may create the impression that police engage in social work. This is not my impression of community policing in Nashville. Though community policing in Nashville may purport to build cooperation, share power, solicit citizen comments, and the like, police authorities did not flatten existing command hierarchies, and community policing can still be extremely punitive. Incidents like the ritualized beating of suspects in the old jail elevator may have disappeared, but community policing is not soft. The illusion of softness at the Edgehill alert center is about as close as the criminal justice juggernaut gets to placative social welfare approaches that are more characteristic of European attempts to manage unemployment and poverty.

Community police officers saturate the southern sector of Nashville, at least during the day. In the immediate aftermath of the Dollar General burning and during the initial rise of community policing, authorities enhanced this saturation effect through the formation and introduction of FLEX units. The thirty-three-officer FLEX unit, so named because of its flexibility in responding quickly to "trouble spots" and "problem areas," formed in early 1998 and closely polices inner-city Nashville. Do intense surveillance, mass arrest, and increasing incarceration really reduce violent crime?

Crime statistics reveal the Nashville homicide rate at the turn of the millennium was down by more than one-third, and killings related to the drug trade were down by more than half from their peak in 1997. These changes parallel those in other urban areas.[17] The reasons for these declines remain unclear, although Chief Turner was quick to credit the incarceration of the city's most menacing criminals through saturation policing as one cause.[18] Police managers effected this saturation through a combination of community policing and FLEX units. FLEX units, as one resident of Sam Levy told me, "work like armies of occupation," roving from the periphery to the center of various housing projects, apprehending and arresting offenders as they go. Angela Rimsa told me, "To have the police right there is kind of stifling for the people that are there, in the sense that they feel that they're under siege by the police as much as under siege by the criminals." In August 1998, just one year after the killing of Leon Fisher, Chief Turner announced the introduction of multiagency roadblocks in and around the housing projects. As Sergeant Todd Henry told the *Tennessean*, "The message is out. . . . If you're going to be out there carrying guns and carrying drugs, police will be out there looking for ya." By all accounts, they were not only "looking for ya" but also "apprehending ya." According to Lieutenant Gordon Howey, in the first six months of 1999, FLEX officers confiscated 91 guns, 25 other weapons, made 4,201 arrests, and served 963 outstanding warrants.[19] In the central sector, officers revived a program called "Operation Safe Streets," whereby police engaged in hypersaturation, talking to everyone they encountered. As Lieutenant Jim Stephens put it, "We're basically trying to keep the bad guys off balance."[20] In 1998 the city reported its lowest crime rate since 1994, with decreased reports of robbery, rape, aggravated assault, burglary, auto thefts, and larceny.

Chief Turner openly acknowledged that he modeled his get-tough-on-crime stance on the New York City approach touted by Mayor Giuliani. The Giuliani administration did not back off its intense policing in spite of numerous complaints of harassment, violation of civil rights, the issuing of summonses for minor offenses, and police shootings of unarmed civilians. For example, the most violent precinct in Brooklyn, the Seventy-fifth, witnessed an increase of 27.7 percent in the arrest rate for the first half of the year 2000 compared with 1999. At the same time, major crimes in the area reportedly decreased 11.3 percent. According to Timothy Egan, New York police made 900,000 drug arrests during the 1990s, during which time the allocation of police services to narcotics enforcement increased sixfold. Authorities made almost one-third of those arrests for using and selling crack.[21] The *New York Times* reported the findings from interviews with about two hundred people from all five boroughs who come into regular contact with police. In the roughest neighborhoods in New York, residents reported "intense scrutiny from undercover officers . . . continuing to be ticketed and arrested for minor offenses . . . officers sweeping through housing projects and parks, asking for identification and patting down pockets."[22]

It may be tempting to draw the conclusion that saturation and get-tough community policing, mass arrest, and incarceration reduce violent crime. The crime statistics in Nashville and New York do point to a correlation between these tactics and lowered crime rates. On the other hand, it may be that the group most prone to commit common street crime, males of eighteen to twenty-four years, constituted a lower proportion of the population than they did in 1994. Evidence from New York suggests that the crack "problem" faded not because of increased enforcement and incarceration but because a new generation came to see crack users as "losers." Timothy Egan notes, "In New York, the use of crack stopped growing as its addicts became known as the biggest losers on the street. . . . There was a generational revulsion against the drug."[23] I did not detect this kind of "generational revulsion" in Nashville, although I met younger dealers who neither liked nor used crack, citing some of the street people whose addiction had apparently taken over their lives. Egan argues that, significantly, nearly every major city affected by crack cocaine followed New York's rise and decline in crack use, "regardless of how law enforcement responded." He quotes Selena Jones, a Harlem mother whose own mother was a crack addict: "If you were raised in a house where somebody was a crack addict, you wanted to get as far away from that drug as you could. . . . People look down on them so much that even crackheads don't want to be crackheads anymore."[24] Surveys of drug use among people arrested in New York showed that 35.7 percent of males over thirty-six years old had used crack recently, compared with barely 4 percent of fifteen- to twenty-year-olds. These results mirror survey findings across the United States that younger people are rejecting crack use. A 1997 survey asked crack users why they had given up the drug. Only 5 percent cited arrests or jail, compared with nearly 19 percent who said "they grew tired of the drug life." Dr. Lynn Zimmer studied the effects of police sweeps on drug use in New York in the 1980s, concluding that mandatory prison terms and hundreds of thousands of arrests "appeared to have no major deterrent effect."[25]

Evidence from other cities suggests that crime rates fell without saturation and coercive policing.[26] Fox Butterfield notes that cities such as San Diego and Boston recorded comparable if not more substantial reductions in crime than New York by engaging less in saturation policing and more in open conversations between police and citizens.[27] San Diego introduced community policing based on problem solving and community comments. Boston sought help from local ministers and selectively targeted hard-core criminals. They developed a multi-agency team that included representatives from the district attorney's office, the U.S. attorney's office, the Federal Bureau of Investigation, the Drug Enforcement Administration, and the Bureau of Alcohol, Tobacco, and Firearms. This team traced guns to particular street criminals. They approached black ministers "to win their cooperation in going after the ringleaders." The team invited known criminals, drug dealers, and young gang members to meetings where "they were warned the violence had to stop or there would be federal prosecutions. The few who did not heed the warnings have been arrested and are now facing long federal sentences." According to David Kennedy, a senior researcher at Harvard who also worked with the team, "The number of arrests and confrontations on the street with the police were minimal."[28]

One can hardly call either the New York or Boston models examples of "consensus building" with the community. In both cases the approach is punitive, involving the intensification of policing either through saturating the streets and neighborhoods (New York), or by orchestrating federal agencies, gathering information, and issuing heavy threats about long-term sentencing if gun violence does not stop (Boston). In New York, Boston, and Nashville, there was little recognition of the deeper historical and economic generation of violence. As my ethnography shows, numerous black men and women object to saturation policing. The head of the ACLU in Nashville called roadblocks "troubling" and "politically driven." The Reverend James Thomas of the Jefferson Street Baptist Church commented: "We want them to arrest criminals, but the way they go about it can cause problems. . . . What's developing is hostility, and no one seems to care, neither the police nor the black community. . . . We want police in the inner city. We want that. We want law and order. But we also want some respect."[29]

Over a quick meal, Officer Chuck told me that community policing in Nashville displaces or drives crime underground but does not eliminate it: "As far as cutting down crime, its not gonna happen. As far as making some in the community feel a little better and being able to talk to police, it's helping there. It's a feel-good program, and it's a starting place. Like in Edgehill, it may not be stopping crime, but by putting the officers in there, we're at least moving the serious crimes out of those projects. I mean, we have our small problem pockets, but we're always going to have them. The idea is to keep them to a bare minimum and keep fighting. We didn't stop any crime, we just displaced it is all."

All these conversations about lowering violent crime assume that "violent crime" means that offenders use violence. But we must ask carefully what we mean by the term "violent crime." Most so-called violent criminals do not use actual violence. Jerome Miller estimates that in 68 percent of crimes defined as "violent," there is "no physical injury of any kind to the victim." Among those injured, only around 8 percent use hospital emergency rooms for treatment. Miller comments, "Of the victims of all crime classified as 'violent' nationally in 1991, slightly over 1 percent required a hospital stay of one day or more."[30] Offenders classified as "violent" may threaten violence or imply its possible use, but most do not deploy it against their victims. Most "violent" street criminals do not injure or assault their victims, especially if those victims turn over what the offender wants.

Miller backs up his contention that the label of "violent criminal" is misleading by reference to the huge difference between arrest and conviction data. For example, of "399,277 arrests for aggravated assault reported by the FBI in 1990, only 53,861 (13.5 percent) resulted in felony convictions."[31] In a survey of the seventy-five largest counties in the country, Miller notes that among defendants charged with assault, "half the charges were dismissed outright and most of the remainder were reduced to a misdemeanor."[32] Conservatives interpret this attrition rate between arrest and prosecution as the courts being "soft" on violent offenders. However, Miller argues the huge disparity reflects overcharging by police agencies. He goes on to conclude, "The fact that police and prosecutors cannot always accomplish their agenda of arrest and imprisonment is less a measure of permissiveness in the courts than an indication that some vestiges of due process have managed to survive the hysteria of the times."[33]

Research by Patrick Langan and Clive Innes using National Crime Survey data tells us that fully one-third of misdemeanor domestic violence assaults would rise to the level of a felony offense if perpetrated against a stranger.[34] It is sadly ironic that saturation community policing in Nashville not only alienates the black community, but also does little if anything to improve the safety of women in their own homes. If there was ever a need to confront violence and tyranny systematically, it is in the case of woman battering. Community policing, with its intensive penetration of communities, not only sweeps many men into the criminal justice juggernaut, but also likely increases the social rage of these men, rendering them more, not less, likely to assault their own intimate partners.

Making Sense of Community Policing in Postindustrial America

The Backlash to Nineteenth- and Twentieth-Century Reconstructions

There is much violence associated with the subterranean economy. Clearly, incarceration is one way of taking some violent offenders out of circulation. Indeed, if authorities removed these individuals, we might expect a temporary diminution of street violence. Removing certain individuals may temporarily lower certain crime rates, but it does nothing to alter the social milieu from which crime emerges. Unless we address the historical and socioeconomic generation of violence in the inner city, any "gains" of incarceration will be temporary. New blood will flood in to fill the spaces left on the street by the incarceration of dealers. This strikes me as inevitable unless authorities improve the lot of inner-city black youth, support the black family, provide meaningful, well-paid labor, and do something to break the negative spiral of interaction between young black males and the criminal justice juggernaut.

The twentieth-century redemption witnessed the mass criminalization of young blacks through the drug laws. Such mass criminalization also occurred during nineteenth-century redemption, when political elites in the South rolled back the substantial gains made during Reconstruction. These gains warrant discussion. In 1869, blacks voted in two Negro members to the U.S. Senate, Hiram Revels and Blanche Bruce from Mississippi, and twenty congressmen. As Howard Zinn notes, this list dwindled "rapidly after 1876; the last black left Congress in 1901."[35] Black freedmen began to set up their own churches, educate their own children, and assert their independence from whites. In 1873 the new legislature of South Carolina introduced free public schools. By 1876 seventy thousand black children attended school where none had attended before. The backlash against the new empowerment of blacks was stunning and brutal. The Ku Klux Klan, among others, began its reign of terror just after the Civil War. The Klan articulated the hatred of many whites toward blacks. David Oshinsky notes that the ex-slave "became a scapegoat for the South's humiliating defeat. . . . Others saw the freedman as a symbol of all that had changed. For the planter, emancipation meant the loss of human property and the disruption of his labor supply. For the poor white farmer, it meant even more. Emancipation had not only crushed his passionate dreams of slave-holding; it had also erased one of the two 'great distinctions' between himself and the Negro. The farmer was white and free; the Negro was black—but also free."[36]

Whites in the South reasserted their temporarily compromised dominance over blacks without reintroducing slavery. They lynched blacks in alarming numbers. If authorities found blacks guilty of minor offenses such as vagrancy, drunkenness, or petty larceny, they imposed substantial fines. Unable to pay these fines, blacks faced jail time. Eventually the courts leased convicted blacks out to employers who paid the fine for them and received in return the labor of the "freedman." Convict leasing was a common practice in the South and was a means for landlords and merchants, the old slave-owning class, to benefit again from free labor. Lawrence Friedman details the brutality directed at the chain gangs and labor gangs in the South. He describes the mortality rates on these gangs as "staggering." For example, between 1877 and 1880, 285 convicts built the Greenwood and Augusta Railroad; of these, nearly 45 percent died. He comments, "You can imagine what it would take, what cruelty, what conditions of work, to kill off almost half of these men."[37] As the criminalization of black men continued after the Civil War defeat of the South, the color of jail and prison inmates changed from almost totally white to almost totally black, an overrepresentation given their presence in the population. During slavery blacks endured punishments such as whippings, but because planters relied upon their labor, those whipped returned quickly to work in the fields. Under the post–Civil War peonage system, things changed, and the criminal justice system became a means for reestablishing the old working arrangements between planters and blacks, although those black laborers were formally free.

The early 1880s saw the introduction of Jim Crow laws, first in Tennessee and then elsewhere in the South. Readers will remember from chapter 1 that groups of whites lynched more than 100 blacks per year between 1889 and 1918 and at least 204 blacks in Tennessee between 1890 and 1950. Reconstruction elicited a powerful backlash from dominant white culture that punitively and effectively redrew in blood the old racial boundaries. In 1883 the U.S. Supreme Court declared the Civil Rights Act of 1875 unconstitutional, reasoning that it did not rule out the discriminatory or exclusionary acts of individuals; rather, the act addressed only state-perpetrated discrimination. Once inserted as a legal principle, this logic culminated in *Plessy v. Ferguson* (1896), which formally introduced the "separate but equal" doctrine into law and custom. By this juncture in history, southern elites could claim the redemption of their territory, minus the reintroduction of slavery.

Even if many small white farmers resented the "gains" made by blacks, the poorer members of the races still had interests in common. Indeed, at the same time as the lynchings and the introduction of the Jim Crow laws, southern Populism arose as a major political force to challenge those who ran the economy and political system. From its origins in the mid 1880s, Populism was a grass-roots political movement that sought to unify poor whites and blacks against capitalist control of both industry and farming. At the Populist Party convention in Topeka, Kansas, in 1890, the famous Populist orator Mary Ellen Lease told the crowd, "Wall Street owns the country. It is no longer a government of the people, by the people, and for the people, but a government of Wall Street, by Wall Street, and for Wall Street."[38] Southern Populism created interracial alliances among the poor, alliances perhaps not reconstituted again until the mass civil rights organizing during twentieth-century reconstruction. As C. Vann Woodward noted about southern Populism, "Never before or since have the two races in the South come so close together as they did during the Populist struggles."[39]

The Populist Party promoted the eight-hour workday, safety guidelines in factories and mines, labor legislation, and the municipal ownership of utilities. Drawing support from wage workers, the unemployed, small farmers, sharecroppers, and agricultural laborers, Populism represented a significant challenge to northern industrialists, railroad monopolists, and southern planters. Of the 1892 Populist delegation, roughly two-thirds of the members came from the ranks of farmers' organizations, similar to the politically successful Granges (Patrons of Husbandry), and just over a quarter were from trade unions. During the 1870s the Granges had formed in every state to successfully push through legislation to curb the powers of railroad monopolists who charged farmers exorbitant rates to transport their produce. At this point in U.S. history, the rising capitalist class was unable to muster sufficient political support to prevent the Granges from prevailing in the courts. In *Munn v. Illinois* (1876) the U.S. Supreme Court upheld the constitutionality of a statute that regulated the charges of grain elevators and outlawed favoritism toward large-scale producers.[40] As corporations gathered strength during the 1880s, the Supreme Court was more yielding to their wishes and reversed the so-called Granger cases.[41]

The 1896 election was a watershed in U.S. party politics. From that moment in history, we can trace a decline in voter turnout and a growing disenchantment with formal voting. This election was significant because it was the first in which the forces of capital began to collectively organize on a mass scale to promote their own political interests. Marshaling huge financial resources, the Republicans triumphed over the Democratic Party and what had become its Populist wing.

It was around this time of the threat posed by Populism and rising labor organizations that a successful attempt to restrict the franchise of workers was made. In Mississippi a statute removed voting rights from those convicted of certain crimes, such as burglary, theft, arson, and obtaining money under false pretenses. According to Randall Kennedy, the legislature introduced this law "specifically to exclude blacks; the authors of the legislation believed that Negroes were especially likely to commit the designated offenses."[42] Kennedy also notes that the U.S. Supreme Court affirmed the constitutionality of such practices in *Williams v. Mississippi* (1898), even though it was clear to the Court "that the purpose behind the law was to racially bar blacks from the voting booth."[43] It was not until 1985 that the Supreme Court invalidated a similar statute in *Hunter v. Underwood*, an Alabama case.[44]

With the demise of Populism, the disenfranchisement of blacks quickened. Literacy tests, poll taxes, and raw intimidation by organizations such as the Ku Klux Klan excluded enormous numbers of black men from the voting booths. Some southern states constitutions permitted those who failed literacy tests to vote provided their ancestors (essentially, grandfathers) had been able to vote on January 1, 1860; an escape clause that no black in the South was able to take advantage of. In Louisiana, registered black voters declined from 130,344 in 1896 to 5,320 in 1900. In Alabama before 1900, 100,000 blacks registered to vote. After 1900 this number dwindled to 3,700.[45] Howard Zinn observes, "The laws that took the vote away from blacks . . . also often ensured that poor whites would not vote. And the political leaders of the South knew this. At the constitutional convention in Alabama, one of the leaders said he wanted to take away the vote from all those who are unfit and unqualified and if the rule strikes a white man as well as a Negro let him go."[46] Similar trends toward the effective disenfranchisement of blacks occurred across the South, and black enfranchisement did not reemerge until the twentieth-century reconstruction and the passage of the 1965 Voting Rights Act.

With large numbers of inner-city black men facing unemployment, postindustrial social control strategies have not used vagrancy laws or loitering and disorderly conduct ordinances to provide employers with cheap sources of labor. On the lower rungs of the postindustrial economy, there is little need for anything but the cheapest and most degraded labor in the inner city. The cybertech revolution, which took off in the early 1980s, added to the long-term displacement of labor and to the closer surveillance and control of employees in the workplace.[47] Indeed, employer replacement of human labor with machine labor underpins capitalist development. Machines do not get sick, go on strike, organize among themselves, or become disenchanted. In some ways, the cybertech revolution in workplace surveillance and control mirrors the growing surveillance capabilities of community policing.

Today, the criminal justice processing of those who use, deal, possess, manufacture, and distribute crack cocaine recalls the post–Civil War targeting of offenses that southern authorities thought blacks committed more often than whites. What became known as the "Mississippi Pig Law" warrants attention. In 1876 the Mississippi legislature passed a crime bill that targeted Negroes. Under this legislation, authorities redefined grand larceny, an offense punishable by up to five years in prison, to include the stealing of farm animals or any property worth ten dollars or more. As David Oshinsky notes, the Pig Law did little to deter the theft of farm animals, but it did feed large numbers of blacks into the prison system.[48] That system promptly leased those convicts out to Mississippi employers. The leasing applied mainly to blacks, because no inmate was leased if sentenced to longer than ten years. Given that authorities imprisoned whites only for the most serious of offenses, employers leased only black convicts.

In a manner similar to modern prisons being filled with drug offenders, the population of the Mississippi state penitentiary grew quickly from 272 in 1874 to 1,072 by 1877. We have seen that many people in the projects understand contemporary drug offenses as crimes of survival. Likewise, interviews with ex-slaves reveal that blacks simply had to steal from their masters to live. Mississippi legislators knew that hunger was at the root of most black theft of farm animals and, like their postindustrial counterparts, exploited it to the fullest. Sarah Fitzpatrick, a house slave born in 1847 in Alabama, explained: "Mos' all de 'Niggers' use 'ta steal in Slav'ry time, co'se 'bout all dey stole f'om dey Marster 'n Mistrus wuz sum'in t'eat, steal hogs 'n kill'um an' clean'um at nigh den dey dig a pit an' ut'um 'way in de woods, den dy go back dere an' git some uv'it when dy want it, an' cook it. . . . Any 'Nigger' would steal when he didn't git 'nuff t'eat. Ya' fam'ly didn't git but three an' haf' pounds uv meat, one an'er haf' pecks uv meal a week, dat wont e'nuff, so 'niggers' jes' had'ta steal."[49]

The sly and constitutionally questionable apprehension of young black men for criminal trespass, "profile" vehicular stops for minor infractions, and other invasions of privacy recall the Pig Law of Mississippi. The contemporary prison population expanded dramatically from 316,000 in 1980 to 846,000 in 1992. The rate of incarceration grew quickly from 139 per 100,000 in 1980 to 330 per 100,000 in 1992.[50] The average time served had increased significantly, from twenty months in 1990 to twenty-eight in 1998, reflecting the effects of tougher sentencing mandates. The American criminal justice juggernaut continues to incarcerate offenders, many of them people of color, in spite of the well-documented declines in crime. According to Raymond Michalowski and Susan Carlson, the rate of imprisonment grew by 46 percent from 1993 to 1998, giving weight to the argument that the writing of prison construction bonds is a huge business, making it very difficult for politicians to confront the trend.[51]

Not only are more prisoners doing more time; inmates are increasingly used as cheap sources of labor. During the 1930s Congress and the states outlawed the sale of open-market prison-made products because of protests by both labor unions and competing industries. However, with the globalization of capital, this practice has returned with a vengeance. Authorities offer prisoners reduced sentences if they work. In spite of protests that these prison industries exploit inmates by paying them well below market rates, provide few job skills, and pit inmate labor against nonincarcerated labor, the practice has grown dramatically since the late 1970s, the period corresponding to the rise of global capital, deregulation, and privatization. Between 1980 and 1994, the number of federal and state prisoners increased by 221 percent.

During the same period, the number of inmates working in prison industries increased 358 percent.

Convict leasing has assumed new forms in the last twenty years. We see inmates working in chain gangs in states such as Arizona and Alabama, recalling the post–Civil War South; we also see them making products for the open market. This shift, fed by the rise of private prisons run by corporations such as Wackenhut, makes inmates a potentially lucrative source of cheap labor. Indeed, the resort to convict labor is one way that jobs are kept in the United States. As Reese Erlich notes, "Some politicians and business people view inmates much as they see workers in the Third World." He goes on to quote Oregon State Representative Kevin Mannix, who argued that corporations should make deals with prisons in much the way that the Nike shoe company works with the Indonesian government. Erlich notes that Nike subcontractors pay their Indonesian workers $1.20 per day. He quotes Mannix as saying, "We propose that Nike take a look at their transportation costs and their labor costs. . . . We could offer competitive prison inmate labor in Oregon."[52]

Prison labor makes U.S. workers available to employers at a price well below market rate. Such availability makes convicts attractive employees again. Although the globalization of U.S. capital removes jobs to overseas markets with lower wage costs, the availability of prison labor counters this trend. U.S. workers who could not or would not work for a pittance now find themselves having to do so in order to reduce their prison sentences.

We must also note the racial and ethnic bias of the prison industry, with men of color overwhelmingly represented behind bars and supervised by poorly paid and disenchanted mostly white counterparts. Historically, the shift in the racial makeup of the incarcerated has changed dramatically since before the Civil War, when, as I noted, whites made up the majority of those in jail. From 1930 to 1992, the proportion of blacks in the prison population changed from less than a quarter (22 percent) to more than half (51 percent).[53]

Regardless of the intent behind the recent history of arresting and incarcerating young men of color, one cannot help being struck by the correspondence between the nineteenth- and twentieth-century redemptions. I refer not only to the similarities between the Pig Law and drugs laws. During the last fifteen years, black male voting rights diminished greatly as the criminal justice juggernaut took over their lives. Today, in seven southern states, one in four black men is permanently disenfranchised.[54] In Florida and Alabama the ratio is one to three. In 1998 across the United States, a total of 1.4 million black men (13 percent of the total) could not vote because they were ex-offenders, then incarcerated, on probation, or on parole. Altogether, the disenfranchised number 3.9 million. Significantly, those states that permanently disqualify a felon from voting are the same states that used literacy tests as a qualification for suffrage rights. Alabama disenfranchised 241,000 people because of felony convictions, 105,000 (44 percent) of them blacks. This means that nearly a third (31.5 percent) of black men in that state have forfeited the right to vote. To requalify requires a pardon from the governor. The state of Florida issued only 359 such pardons in 1996 and 1997. Florida has removed the right to vote from more people than has any other state. In total, 647,100 Floridians (5.9 percent of the state's population) forfeited the right to vote; of these, 204,600 (31.6 percent) are black. Of those disqualified, two-thirds are no longer in prison or have completed terms of probation or parole. Restoring their voting rights requires a special order from the governor and three members of the cabinet. People convicted of a state felony offense must wait a minimum of ten years after completing their sentences to reapply. Mississippi disenfranchised 145,600 people, of whom 81,700 (56 percent) are black. Convicted felons requalify through a pardon or executive order issued by the governor, or if the state legislature passes a bill and the governor signs it. As we saw in the 2000 presidential election, politicians win elections by the narrowest of margins; the loss of the black vote is of enormous party political significance.

I highlight a selection of these statistics because President Johnson's Voting Rights Act (1965) especially targeted Alabama, Louisiana, Georgia, Mississippi, South Carolina, Virginia, and part of North Carolina, automatically eliminating their voter qualification tests that included any requirement that people be able to read and write. As of 1997, 18,000 incarcerated black males in Tennessee forfeited their right to vote. Tennessee disenfranchised another 53,000 black males because of their previous felony convictions.[55] Article 4, Section 2, of the Tennessee constitution provides that the Tennessee legislature may deny the right to vote to persons convicted of "infamous" crimes. Crimes that qualify as infamous have become fewer and fewer over the years, rendering it less difficult for a convicted felon to reclaim the vote in Tennessee than Florida, Alabama, or Mississippi. David Bositis, senior political analyst with the Joint Center for Political and Economic Studies in Washington, told *Tennessean* reporter Dwight Lewis that this was because "Tennessee does not have a large black population," and that "Tennessee is a border state." In 1998 Bositis also told Lewis that "white states" such as Maine, Utah, Vermont, and Massachusetts allowed incarcerated felons to vote.[56] Of the four states mentioned by Bositis in 1998, three (Utah, Vermont, Maine) do not disenfranchise incarcerated offenders, probationers, parolees, or ex-felons. In the November 2000 elections in Massachusetts, voters elected to disenfranchise those offenders currently in prison.

Since the fall of the Berlin Wall and Soviet Bloc communism, capitalism now reigns with unfettered pride. However arduous, poorly paid, and racially segregated the work of black men and women might have been in the last century, the simple fact is that nowadays large sectors of the black urban poor are practically redundant in an economy that has passed them by. Although Nashville claims to have low unemployment rates and paid work for the majority, my ethnography suggests that for many of the very poor this work is not worth doing, not worth leaving one's children with a stranger for, not worth the hassle with an employer, and poorly paid compared with what the subterranean economy has to offer. Indeed, if we counted employees who work in the criminal justice juggernaut along with the growing army of jail and prison inmates, the unemployment figures would not look quite as rosy. Put simply, the rise of the criminal justice juggernaut and saturation community policing have contributed to the scapegoating of young, inner-city black men, diverted attention from the outflow of capital to markets where labor is cheaper, created a new, readily exploitable, and "captive" pool of cheap labor within the prisons, and artificially lowered the unemployment rate.

Economic Changes since 1980

In the year 2000 the electioneering rhetoric of the two front-runners would have had us believe that all is generally well with the economy. Vice-President Gore was anxious to associate himself with the apparent economic advances of the 1990s, while Governor Bush was keen to point out just how much further the nation can go. On the surface it may appear difficult to argue with the numbers. The Dow Jones Industrial Average leapt from 2,000 in 1990 to roughly 11,000 just before the

2000 election. Mutual funds such as Vanguard's moderate-risk Total Stock Market Index Portfolio returned nearly 20 percent a year throughout the 1990s. Even the most recent U.S. census data report that poverty rates are at their lowest in twenty-one years. In 1999, 32.2 million people (11.8 percent) lived below the federal poverty line, 2.2 million fewer than in 1998. This is the lowest proportion since 1979. In 1999 the census reported median household incomes at an all-time high. President Clinton boasted to the press, "This is a good day for America. ... We have proved that we can lift all boats in a modern, global, information-based economy."[57] However, these numbers obscure the increasing plight of rank-and-file workers, the unemployed, the underemployed, and the incarcerated. They also hide the fact that median household incomes have risen because more people in those households are working longer hours than ever; U.S. workers toil for longer than their European counterparts and receive less annual paid leave and fewer benefits.

The U.S. census also tells us that 23.6 percent of African Americans, 22.8 percent of Hispanics, and only 7.7 percent of non-Hispanic whites live below the poverty line. Put simply, the ratio of black to white poverty has changed little in a decade. The rhetoric of "economic success" ignores massive economic shifts in the world of work that do not bode well for most Americans. Many corporations downsized their workforces during the 1990s. The layoffs supposedly "streamlined" production, with many jobs being outsourced. In some industries these layoffs created acute shortages of skilled labor, eventually forcing employers to rehire former employees. The rehiring brought many workers back to their old companies without their former health and pension benefits, which created enormous resentment and deepened workers' insecurity. Edward Luttwak cites a Labor Department study that estimated that 17 percent of 5 million listed contract employees had resumed work for their former employers. He also notes an American management survey showing that among 720 newly downsized companies, 30 percent had rehired workers, usually without reinstating previous benefits such as health and pension plans.[58] As companies downsized and shed expensive labor, their stock prices often rose, at least temporarily. The real beneficiaries of this increase were major stockholders and corporate executives, whose wealth ballooned during the 1990s. From 1950 to 1975, the average hourly earnings of nonsupervisory employees in private, nonfarm employment, measured in constant

1982 dollars, rose from $5.34 to $8.12. Luttwak traces the rise of turbocapitalism to the late 1970s and the abolition of anticompetition laws and regulatory hangovers from the New Deal, the technological streamlining of the workplace made possible by these acts of abolition, the removal of import barriers, and the privatization of the economy. Significantly, from 1980 to 1997 the average hourly earnings, measured in constant 1982 dollars, fell from $7.78 to $7.66. Commenting cynically on the maldistribution of wealth in the American turbocapitalist regime, Luttwak observes, "In the greatly admired, long-booming American economy, in which four million people can now call themselves millionaires, and no fewer than 170 people have net worths in excess of $1 billion, sixty million or so rank-and-file employees have not done so well: in real dollars net of inflation, their hourly earnings were actually higher in the early 1970s, when the United States still had a heavily regulated economy. And more than seventeen million, fully employed 40 hours per week, 50 weeks a year, remain below the poverty line."[59] From the early 1970s, the earnings of corporate executives skyrocketed, from twenty to thirty times that of their employees to several hundred times more.

The growing polarization of wealth between the owners and controllers of capitalist production and those relegated to permanent underclass status is evident in the Nashville housing projects. Such growing disparities are also apparent between rich and poor nations in the increasingly globalized economy and between the rich and poor within those nations. Through its disproportionate influence on the World Trade Organization, the International Monetary Fund, and the World Bank, the United States spearheaded these invidious economic changes. It is not as if these increasing disparities have gone unnoticed. Protest against these sinister economic developments drew considerable police violence against demonstrators in the United States (especially in Seattle, but also in Washington, D.C., and Los Angeles) and, more recently, in Prague, Czechoslovakia.[60] Even the European Union recently balked at the rapidity and form of global economic development promoted by the United States, adopting a much more cautionary approach to issues such as genetically modified foods and hormone-fed cattle.[61] Within the ranks of the World Bank, some economists expressed concern. Economic analysts attacked a recent World Bank report on global poverty because it left out criticisms of free-market reforms that appeared in a draft posted on the Web in January 2000. The original author of the report, Professor Ravi Kanbur, resigned in June 2000 after disagreements with more-orthodox economists at the World Bank. Professor Kanbur had insisted "that redistributive taxation policies and social spending were vital in tackling global poverty."[62] Kanbur's critique challenged the free-market reforms promoted by the World Bank and the IMF and noted that such reforms "had harmed poor people in some countries." Duncan Green of Cafod, a Catholic aid agency, observed that the final report constituted "a comprehensive overhaul in which much of the draft's critique of conventional Bank thinking has been replaced by an apologia for business as usual."[63]

In the United States, the loss of skilled wage work and the rise of the poorly paying service sector accompanied a marked decline in labor union membership. The decline in the number of union jobs has been particularly acute for black men.[64] Comparing seventeen advanced industrial economies, Bruce Western and Katherine Beckett observe that collective-bargaining coverage and unionization are much lower in the United States.[65] These authors also note that even although the presence of unions has declined somewhat in European economies, the ethos of collective bargaining still directly affects wage agreements in nonunionized workplaces. In the United States, political authorities limit collective-bargaining rights, and most employers contract with individual employees.

The U.S. economy, with its relatively weak trade unions and its meager welfare provisions for the unemployed, most closely approximates the competitive market of free enterprise governed by the forces of supply and demand. However, the economy was much more stringently regulated before the 1980s. As Luttwak notes, a slew of intersecting federal, state, and local boards, commissions, bureaus, and the like had regulated numerous sectors, including the airlines; interstate trucking, bus lines, and railroads; telephones and other telecommunications; commercial banking and savings-and-loan companies; almost 90 percent of agriculture; natural gas; and nearly all electricity, gas, water, and sewage utilities.[66] The deregulation of the marketplace proceeded faster in the United States and Britain than in economies such as Japan's and Germany's. In the former economies, the state distanced itself from the marketplace, selling publicly owned companies to the private sector and replacing what came to been seen as inefficient government regulation with what Adam Smith once called the "invisible hand" of the market.

The Decline in Social Caring

As if the disappearance of meaningful skilled work through the privatization, deregulation, and globalization of U.S. capital is not insult enough for the working or unemployed poor, the United States has simply become a harsher, less caring society than it was even twenty years ago.[67] In earlier chapters I detailed the erosion of affordable housing; the rise of the new urban homeless, including increasing numbers of women and children among its ranks; and the welfare-to-work movement. The decline of social caring is evident at a number of other levels as well.

When I worked in a drug treatment facility during the 1980s, patients entered the program for at least twenty-eight days. Now it is difficult to receive drug treatment for a week, if at all. Even President Nixon's administration, for all its get-tough posturing regarding crime and its failure to implement the main recommendations of the Kerner Report, saw the need to have drug treatment as the centerpiece of its war on drugs. Treatment for those addicted to drugs has taken a backseat over the last twenty years to incarceration or worsening addiction.

One particularly cruel irony in the examples I touch upon is the use of disingenuous "promotional" language. In chapter 2 I showed how the selective upgrading of the "salvageable" poor happened alongside the relegation of those unqualified for an upgrade to superconcentrated ghettos. All this is couched in the language of the HOPE initiative. Offering utterly hopeless housing for those cast aside, authorities and politicians use the acronym HOPE (Housing Opportunities for People Everywhere). Politicians also market welfare-to-work programs as providing much-needed opportunities for "enterprising" behavior among the poor. Tennessee legislators market this welfare charade as the "Families First" program. The Families First program took off with the greatest energy in the southern sector of Nashville, known as the Metropolitan Enterprise Community. Authorities marketed the dramatic loss of drug treatment facilities as "managed care," a euphemism for cut-price care, or little care at all. What's next? Aerobics classes for vagrants? These disingenuous linguistic inversions reflect a profound cruelty and a failure to see the world through the eyes of those subject to these social policies. In part this reflects the lust of American policy makers for quantitative data they feel captures the truth about social conditions. Such empiricism also conveniently ignores the voices of those on the street, those targeted by the array of punitive programs, those unable to provide responses that fit neatly into the boxes on surveys. At still another level, the disingenuous language of "HOPE," "Families First," "managed care," and "Enterprise Communities" may reflect that uniquely American belief in individualism, that stalwart conviction that people can and should pull themselves up by their own bootstraps. American corporations reflect this lack of caring as they reap the benefits of the global economy. Indeed, the budget for social programs in the United States, compared even with the European capitalist powers, says it all. As Western and Beckett note, roughly one-quarter of the gross domestic product (GDP) of the large European economies is ploughed into social welfare programs.[68] The United States uses only 15 percent of its GDP in this manner.

Community Policing and the American Criminal Justice Juggernaut

In her original 1990 description of what she called the "justice juggernaut," Diana Gordon predicted that Americans would "probably" be "doomed to present levels of criminality for the foreseeable future." Referring to the period before 1990, she notes, "The impacts of the juggernaut are several, but . . . they do not include reduced street crime." She predicted that levels of street crime may be reduced owing to significant reductions in the proportion of eighteen- to twenty-four-year-old males in the population by the year 2000.[69] In the 1990s street crime levels continued to fall, probably at least in part because of demographic changes. It is possible that some of the reduction was due to the mass incarceration of large numbers of street criminals and the emergence of more extensive and penetrating forms of policing, probation, and parole. The trajectory identified by Gordon of a "broadening" and "deepening" of the justice juggernaut continues with a vengeance. By "broadening," Gordon was referring to the growth of panoptic state power. My ethnography reveals more intense forms of community policing and surveillance. Much research documents the more aggressive application of police tactics, the growth in the rate of incarceration, and the increasing time served by inmates.

The globalization, privatization, and deregulation of American capitalism provide one canvas for making sense of the rise of community policing and the criminal justice juggernaut. However, the U.S. economy is still regulated somewhat by the very activities of the juggernaut.

My ethnographic findings are entirely consistent with the macroeconomic analysis of Western and Beckett, who argue that the U.S. penal system acts as a regulatory mechanism to keep unemployment down. The black men I talked with told me just how difficult it was to enter or reenter wage labor after serving time. Western and Beckett find the same thing; the person labeled "felon" finds it more difficult to obtain and keep a job. They note that "large prison and jail populations conceal a high level of joblessness. If included in labor market statistics, the population of incarcerated men would contribute about two percentage points to the U.S. male unemployment rate by the mid-1990s. These effects are especially large for African Americans: labor inactivity is understated by about one third, or seven percentage points. . . . Our estimates of labor inactivity among U.S. men consistently exceed average European unemployment rates between 1975 and 1994."[70]

The rise of U.S. imprisonment rates since 1994 tends to lower unemployment. The criminal justice juggernaut and its community policing arm continually create a need for their own services, thereby increasing job opportunities for police officers, dispatchers, correctional officers, probation officers, parole officers, counselors of all kinds, and so on. Poor (increasingly minority) inmates are divided from juggernaut employees, both groups rendered increasingly vulnerable by the globalization of capital. At an ideological level, the penal "solution" also provides a scapegoat, an outlet for increasingly overworked, alienated, underpaid, and angry working people.

It is amidst these shifting historical and economic forces that we must situate the rise of community policing. Forget the red herrings about the historical erosion of community confidence in the police and the need to fix broken windows. The ideology of community policing fits sweetly with the spread of global capitalism and the joblessness, anomie, and despair left in its chaotic wake. Community policing and global capitalism pose as the forces of democratic progress without ever really asking subject populations what they want. In Nashville, community policing works on communities torn asunder by joblessness, the subterranean economy, familial breakdown, and violence. Overseas, capitalism continues to wreak havoc on local communities, replacing long-cherished mores and lifestyles with the seeming rationality of economic efficiency, destroying natural ecosystems in the pursuit of profit for the few, and corrupting local politicians.

The intense surveillance of the Nashville housing projects and the families who live in them is every bit about control, further stigmatization, and hiding the social harms of joblessness and urban despair. Community policing is the law enforcement equivalent of growing employer surveillance in the workplace, extending the ever-increasing presence and gaze of authorities into the lives of workers. At another level, community policing initiatives, with all their talk of consensus building and caring about community feedback, may constitute yet another example of the disingenuous language so characteristic of postindustrial America. We have witnessed how women in the projects reject community policing as protection from domestic violence. We have heard how black men see community policing as another form of harassment and intrusive surveillance, all the time eroding their sense of dignity, attacking their meager means of making a living when none other is available, and creating a situation where, as one man put it, black men feel as if they walk around with a bull's-eye on their foreheads.

Although the days of jail-elevator beatings appear long gone, we ought not mistake community policing for the softer side of law enforcement. Many residents in the Edgehill housing projects clearly appreciate increased police presence and the diminution of violence associated with the drug trade. However, what people would appreciate much more is gainful employment and the creation of safe, wholesome living conditions where their families can flourish. The presence or absence of community policing cannot furnish these conditions, cannot provide safety, and may serve to reassure only a few that things are better. In Nashville, community policing channeled large numbers of black men into the penal system, making it more difficult for them to find and keep wage work upon release. Community policing therefore contributes to a vicious cycle of incarceration, release, and reincarceration. Put simply, community policing, with all its intensive surveillance, creates a further need for its own services and that of allied branches of the criminal justice juggernaut. It achieves this by posing as a consensus-building form of social control yet thrives on and exploits the public's understandable need for safety. What community policing cannot do is rectify the social chaos created by broader economic and historical forces.

The criminal justice juggernaut now incarcerates black women at alarming rates for little more than associating with men who deal drugs to survive. Add this effect to the mass incarceration of black men and it is no exaggeration to argue that the juggernaut destroys black families. Welfare-to-work initiatives do little to alter this family malaise and may further accelerate the incarceration of black women. Indeed, the alternatives for black women who do not enter the wage workforce are the streets and the subterranean economy. There, a few women may be successful in eking out a living while constantly looking over their shoulders and negotiating the dangers associated with such a lifestyle. For those apprehended as prostitutes, drug dealers, and drug users, jail awaits alongside the prospect of losing their children.

The Door of No Return: Elmina Revisited

The findings of my urban ethnography do not paint a pretty picture of the multiple ways in which the very poor of Nashville are policed. Historically, poor populations have typically been policed most stringently at the very point of economic production, that site where social classes emerge. Disciplining the poor was mainly about ensuring their attendance and compliance in the socialized workplace. Put simply, people in industrial economies, detached as they have become from the land, had to go to work to survive. For slaves, the situation was different; they had to work because of their chattel status and did not earn wages. The story for women has been a little different in that those who did not work outside the home were often subject to varying degrees of patriarchal regulation within its confines. Women of color, particularly black women, were regulated by the master of the slave household and by males in their families.

Nowadays, in the postindustrial economy, a significant proportion of black men have become surplus to economic requirements. This surplus population presents new management problems since it is not subject to the regulatory mechanisms of the capitalist workplace. I do not doubt that young impoverished black males are disproportionately involved in street crimes such as crack cocaine dealing, robbery, aggravated assault, and homicide. What I doubt is the commonplace political wisdom that these are crimes of evil, deviant, and immoral people. Neither do I want to underestimate the tremendous pain and fear created by the criminogenic social conditions within which such crime and violence arise and flourish. But as globalization proceeds apace, we find ourselves at a critical juncture, where the very identity of nation-states is being tested and transcended by free-market forces. With the demise of the Berlin Wall and the communist challenge to capitalism, at least two strategies have emerged for coping with permanent underclasses. In the United States the underclass is increasingly fed into the criminal justice juggernaut, with community law enforcement and other forms of high-surveillance saturation policing acting as a principal conduit or method of initial apprehension. The American criminal justice juggernaut artificially lowers levels of unemployment, thereby giving false promise to the virtues of free-market capitalism. In Western European countries such as France, Germany, and Italy, welfare provisions are much more substantial and the punitive/incarcerative ethic much less prominent. These societies manage surplus populations with considerably more care and grace, although underclasses are still often ritually stigmatized as the principal sources of their own predicaments. In a country such as the United States, where government investment in public housing has principally manifested itself through the building of prisons and jails, it is high time to revisit urban chaos with a fresher, kinder mind-set. It is indeed a good thing that debtor nations, along with some European countries, are calling into question the virtues of unfettered free-market capitalism and its impact on poor populations. It is unlikely that most of these challenges will do anything more than propose the trimming back of the excesses of such unfettered corporate privilege and greed. The most prominent political choices currently offered concern the form and extent of redistributive intervention; weighing, for example, the degree of emphasis to be placed on social control strategies such as imprisonment or more placative social welfare programs.

These political choices seek out ways to best police the poor, not the rich. The violence of the rich assumes massive proportions and creates enormous social harm. Capitalism now not only transcends national borders, it also reinvents its own history of exploiting workers in the Third World economies into which it now insinuates itself. The crimes of corporations, numerous and far more destructive than any the poor can muster, will likely continue to evade the political radar of the polities that frame law, pass legislation, and fund its enforcement. Nevertheless, the policing of protestors in Seattle and Prague and the saturation policing of the Nashville housing projects are linked. Both manifestations of law enforcement seek to curb the response to the globalization of capital. In a country that ironically and rather disingenuously celebrates its constitutional rights and the rule of law, authorities recently turned parts of downtown Seattle into "no protest" zones. In Prague, jailed protestors were beaten in a manner reminiscent of those who used to be "taken for a ride" in the Nashville jail elevator.

In Nashville, the principal targets of policing are those populations rendered redundant by the very global process people in Seattle and Prague objected to. The protestors in Seattle and Prague may one day emerge from the history books as heroes. The drug dealers of John Henry Hale, Preston Taylor Homes, and Sam Levy will likely never grace a history book in the same way. However, it is these same dealers, those who hear their bullets, those who visit them in prison, and those who bury them who provide the substrate for ethnographers like me to purchase our bulletproof vests and write our litanies of complaint. It is also the black urban underclass that lives out the very evidence that protestors in different parts of the world use to attack the World Trade Organization, the World Bank, the IMF, and the invisible hand of the market.

It is not my argument that community policing works monolithically against the poor. Neither do I contend that saturation law enforcement works only against the black underclass. Clearly, community policing works in complex ways that sometimes benefit working people. However, in Nashville the black underclass constitutes the principal target of such surveillance and punitive measures. We cannot understand the intensity of such police pressure without recourse to the annals of history, laying it alongside the language of the street. We have re-created the Door of No Return in the housing projects of U.S. cities. That those who live there are the descendants of slaves is no accident. That the crack laws resemble the Pig Law is no accident. That blacks constitute the core of the discarded underclass is no accident.

Whether we ultimately reject capitalism, or embrace it in its milder, more regulated forms, the twentieth-century redemption is well under way. Leon Fisher passed through the Door of No Return, just as many others have. If they find a New World, let's hope it is better than the one they left behind.

NOTES

Notes to Introduction

1. I use pseudonyms throughout the book, unless quoted material comes from published sources.
2. See Trojanowicz, 1989: 6.
3. Gordon, 1990.
4. Irwin, 1985.
5. Clearly, there are more poor whites than blacks in the United States. In 1996 there were 36,529,000 people classified as poor. Of these, 24,650,000 (67 percent) were white, 16,267,000 (45 percent) were non-Hispanic whites, and 9,694,000 (27 percent) were black. However, 28.4 percent of blacks were poor in 1996, compared with only 11.2 percent of whites and 8.5 percent of non-Hispanic whites; see Luttwak, 1999: 94. My principal focus on blacks derives from my limited ethnography in Nashville and my observations beyond that city; it is largely black communities that have borne the brunt of recent saturation community law enforcement and get-tough policing initiatives.
6. See also Kennedy, 1998: 68–75.
7. Skolnick and Fyfe (1993) make a similar argument about the decline of police brutality in other parts of the country that have introduced community policing.
8. Gilroy, 1982: 149.
9. S. Miller, 1999: 7.
10. Foucault, 1980: 47–48.
11. Wrong, 1961.
12. Marx, 1969: 360.

Notes to Chapter 1

1. Walvin, 1992: 4
2. The slave trade among northern Europeans declined considerably by the early twelfth century, and was revived again in the context of colonizing the Americas. The relationship between the slave trade and the rise of industrial capitalism, particularly in England, is complex. Hugh Thomas (1997: 794) argues, "The slave trade should not be seen as the main, much less the sole, inspiration of any particular development in industry or manufacture in Europe or North America." He goes on to note, "The slave-trading entrepreneurs of Lisbon and Rio, or Seville and Cadiz, did not finance innovations in manufacture." Neither should we assume that it was

only white Europeans who somehow "benefited" from the slave trade. Although the slave trade was principally run by white Europeans, black tribal leaders and other blacks also worked for slavers, some amassing considerable fortunes.

3. See Bennett, 1968. Howard Zinn (1980: 24–25) notes, "The Virginians needed labor, to grow corn for subsistence, to grow tobacco for export. They had just figured out how to grow tobacco, and in 1617 they sent off the first cargo to England. . . . Black slaves were the answer. And it was natural to consider imported blacks as slaves, even if the institution of slavery would not be regularized and legalized for several decades. Because, by 1619, a million blacks had already been brought from Africa to South America and the Caribbean, to the Portuguese and Spanish colonies, to work as slaves."

4. The great majority of slaves lived in the South. It was only the twentieth century that saw a mass migration of blacks from rural to urban areas and from South to North and West. In 1910 there were 9.8 million blacks in the United States, 91 percent of whom lived in the South. From 1910 to 1966 the number of blacks living in urban areas increased fivefold, the number living outside the South elevenfold. See the Kerner Report, 1968: 12.

5. Giddens (1989: 254–255) considers notions of black and white as deeply embedded cultural symbols in Europe that doubtless informed the way Europeans perceived the darker-skinned people they encountered on the shores of Africa.

6. See Genovese, 1976: 4.

7. Slave traders and their backers used religion to justify the subjugation of Africans. Planters consulted the *Cotton Plantation Record and Account Book*, which instructed: "You will find that an hour devoted every Sabbath morning to their moral and religious instruction would prove a great aid to you in bringing about a better state of things amongst the Negroes" (see Zinn, 1980: 173).

8. Blassingame, 1972: 6–7. He estimates that 16 percent of these transported slaves died from undernourishment and disease.

9. Wish, 1937. He notes a court settlement of a slave insurrection insurance claim as early as 1785.

10. Thomas, 1997: 424. He notes most of the uprisings occurred off the African coast at the time of embarkation, although there were also insurrections on the open ocean.

11. Genovese, 1976: 7.

12. Kerner Report, 1968: 209.

13. Of the principal uprisings in the South, authorities crushed two before they gathered substantial steam: those led by Gabriel Prosser in 1800 and Denmark Vesey in 1822. Two others reached significant proportions by U. S. standards: the Louisiana Uprising of 1811 involved between three and five hundred slaves, thereby matching similar insurrections in parts of Brazil and the Caribbean. The Nat Turner rebellion of 1831 involved some seventy slaves. See Genovese, 1976: 587–597. As Genovese and others note, there was no major slave rebellion in the United States from 1831 to 1865, during which time notions of paternalism intensified, cruel treatment of slaves diminished, and planters increasingly emphasized the need to provide for slaves and to fulfill their obligations to them.

14. Genovese, 1976: 598.

15. Zinn, 1980: 167.

16. See Howard Zinn (1980: 127–128) for a discussion of the series of treaties with southern Indians. Between 1814 and 1824, whites acquired "over three-fourths of Alabama and Florida, one-third of Tennessee, one-fifth of Georgia and Mississippi, and parts of Kentucky and North Carolina. . . . These treaties, these land grabs, laid the basis for the cotton kingdom, the slave plantations."

17. Foucault, 1977. Kennedy (1998: 76–77) notes that blacks could receive the death penalty for many more offenses than whites. Virginia identified seventy-three capital offenses for slaves. In stark contrast, only one offense, first-degree murder, rendered whites eligible for the death penalty. Authorities used branding, maiming, ear cropping, whipping, castration, and other forms of physical punishment to discipline slaves long after these punishments had disappeared as a means of regulating whites.

18. Reported in the *Tennessean*, July 1, 1999: 13A, "What they found and found out about Hermitage slavery," by Larry McKee. President Jackson was writing to his son.

19. The courts did not recognize slave marriages.

20. Gutman, 1976: 137.

21. See Kennedy (1998, chapters 2 and 3) for a discussion of the legal rights of the races under slavery.

22. Kennedy, 1998: 78–79.

23. Massey and Denton, 1993.

24. Cited in Hawkins and Thomas, 1991: 67.

25. See Patterson, 1922, especially pp. 38–42.

26. See Henry, 1914. See also Wintersmith, 1974: 18–19.

27. Henry, 1914: 31.

28. Genovese, 1976: 22–23.

29. Wintersmith, 1974: 11.

30. Blassingame, 1972: 209.

31. Blassingame (1972: 210–211) notes that with improvements in roads and communications it became harder for these maroon communities to conceal themselves and stave off attacks from slave patrollers, militias, and concerned planters.

32. There is considerable evidence of much animosity between slaves and poor whites. For example, Genovese (1976: 22) refers to the recollections of ex-slaves who noted poor white neighbors as "one of our biggest troubles."

33. It lies beyond the scope of this book to explore the origins of these tensions in detail. However, for an interesting and detailed discussion, see Williams, 1961.

34. For example, in November 1865 a Mississippi statute penalized railroad officials for allowing blacks to travel in any first-class carriage used by whites. Florida passed a similar law the same year. Punishment included whipping or confinement to the pillory. See Friedman, 1993: 95.

35. Zinn, 1980: 198.

36. Lovett, 1999: 92–93.

37. See Kennedy (1998: 41) for a discussion of the factors associated with the demise of federal intervention in the South.

38. See Morison, Commager, and Leuchtenburg, 1983: 356. These authors quote

Henry Grady of the *Atlanta Constitution*: "The supremacy of the white race of the South must be maintained forever, and the domination of the Negro race resisted at all points and at all hazards, because the white race is superior."

39. Lovett notes that at least 204 blacks were lynched in Tennessee between 1890 and 1950.

40. Henry (1914: 48) notes authorities in South Carolina weakly enforced the ordinances dealing with minor offenses of racial etiquette. Fox Butterfield (1995: 57) notes less than one fifth of blacks lynched had been found "guilty" or been suspected of raping white women.

41. Wilbur Miller (1977) attaches great importance to nineteenth-century democracy in the United States, citing it as the main reason for the differences between U.S. and English policing styles. Miller's position is problematic since it ignores the fact that blacks and women could not vote in the United States in the mid-nineteenth century.

42. Luddism refers to the activities of a group of workers in England who smashed machines introduced to save labor in the textile industry from 1811 to 1816. Luddites protested reduced wages and unemployment. A major wave of Luddism affected the lace/hosiery trade in Nottingham, Leicester, and Derby in 1811 and 1812, and later spread to the cotton weavers in Yorkshire. The focus eventually shifted to Lancashire and Cheshire, the homes of the emerging and newly mechanized cotton factories. Food rioting and machine breaking occurred in Bolton, Stockport, and Manchester, all places where employers introduced new machines. Popular as the movement was with the local population and even the master stockingers whose frames they were breaking, authorities were indignant and passed the Frame Breaking Act in 1812, which made frame breaking a capital offense. In the summer of 1812, at the peak of the social disturbances, authorities stationed twelve thousand troops in Luddite districts between Leicester and York. In all, authorities hanged thirty Luddites. Luddism gained steam in these small towns, with scattered industries. As a political strategy, Luddism shared much with the reform movements of the day.

43. It is important to remember that the crowds who partook in these disturbances did not typically belong to what Marx once referred to as the *lumpenproletariat*: the social scum that are particularly vulnerable to reactionary ideologies and counterrevolutionary interests. See Marx, *The Eighteenth Brumaire of Louis Bonaparte* (Marx and Engels, 1970: 138), and Engels's preface to *The Peasant War in Germany* (Marx and Engels, 1970: 243). On the contrary, as George Rudé has indicated, these participants came from the ranks of local residents and respectable, employed people, not pauperized, unemployed malingerers, opportunists, and criminals. See Rudé, 1964; Hobsbawm, 1965.

44. The disturbance became known as the Peterloo Massacre. As George M. Trevelyan (1926: 623) put it, "It was called 'Peterloo' because it seemed to cancel the debt of the nation's gratitude for Waterloo. It had a great effect on the mind of the rising generation of all classes and of all parties."

45. See also Thompson, 1975.

46. Silver, 1967.

47. Hobsbawm and Rudé, 1985: 215.

48. Ibid.

49. Silver, 1967. As home secretary, Sir Robert Peel was one of the key politicians behind the passage of the Metropolitan Police Act of 1829. Peel's push for a rational-bureaucratic system of preventive policing was also consistent with moves away from harsh punishment toward Enlightenment philosophies of the rational, free-thinking man. In the arena of crime and social control, the work of Cesare Beccaria articulated so-called classicist principles, which dictated that punishments should be predictable, rational, impersonal, and proportional to the offense committed; see Beccaria, 1801. A modern, preventive police force was essential because criminals "chose" to commit crime and rationally weighed the possibilities of detection and apprehension. Thus, modern police presence and surveillance would ensure that the most rational choice was to obey the law.

50. See Silver, 1967; and Bunyan, 1976. From the earliest rise of capitalism, the city of London had always been the most adequately policed part of England. Bunyan cites a 1663 act that allowed for one thousand night watchmen to guard ships and warehouses in the docklands of London. Since that city was the largest port in the world at that time, half the world's produce moved in and out of London. The West Indian merchants who traded slave-produced sugar were the most prominent users of the docks then; see Bunyan, 1976: 60–61; see also Mintz, 1986.

51. Lane, 1967: 85. He suggests that the three major issues affecting social disorder at this time were abolition, prohibition, and immigration.

52. Lane, 1967: 30–34.

53. Cited in Richardson, 1970: 26.

54. Monkkonen, 1981: 55.

55. Ibid., 57. In contrast to Silver's argument that the London police arose in response to general calls for "order" in civil society, Monkkonen cites only a handful of cities where modern American bureaucratic police arose largely in response to rioting: Philadelphia, Baltimore, Washington, D.C., and perhaps Indianapolis, Boston, and Detroit. See Monkkonen, 1981: chapter 1.

56. See, for example, Harring, 1976, 1977, 1983; Harring and McMullin, 1975; Hoffman, 1979; Center for Research on Criminal Justice, 1975; Spitzer, 1981.

57. See, for example, Harring, 1983: 113–137; Cei, 1975: 161, 187–191, chapter 7; Hoffman, 1979: 105–110; C. Anderson, 1979: 285–335. Harring (1983: 125) writes, "The two great garment worker strikes of 1910 and 1915 demonstrated that the Chicago Police Department had degenerated into little more than the hired sluggers of the manufacturers." However, police did not universally act in favor of employers against workers. Harring cites examples in Columbus, Ohio (1910), and Indianapolis, Indiana (1913), where local police refused to break strikes. Hoffman (1979: 218) describes the prime function of the Red Squads in Portland, Oregon (circa 1914), and Seattle, Washington (circa 1918), as dealing with labor radicalism. Without resorting to Marxist explanations, Hoffman and Webb (1986: 384) note that the police in Portland, Oregon, used vagrancy arrests to control members of the unemployment leagues who agitated for jobs and relief during the 1913–1915 depression. I found similar targeting of transients in Eugene, Oregon, during the 1912–1915 period, during which time an unemployment league was run by the Industrial Workers of the World (IWW); see Websdale, 1994: 160–164.

58. Johnson, 1976. Even within the ranks of some Marxian scholars there is a reluctance to acknowledge notions of "crime" and "deviance" as legitimate areas of inquiry. See Hirst, 1975: 204.

59. Ibid., 91.

60. Ibid., 99.

61. Ibid., p. 97. See also Horan and Swiggert, 1951. For the rise of private policing in England, particularly around the docks in London from the 1740s, see Bowden, 1978, chapter 10. Patrick Colquhoun established a private police agency in London in 1745. John and Henry Fielding followed Colquhoun in this endeavor. Colquhoun's and the Fieldings' ventures into private policing in the form of regular patrol activities influenced Sir Robert Peel, who was instrumental in the formation of the London Metropolitan Police Force.

62. B. Hacker, 1969.

63. Preston, 1963. On January 2, 1920, Department of Justice agents raided communist and labor organizations, arresting some ten thousand people, many of whom were not radicals. Attorney General Palmer preceded the raids by an offensive against the Union of Russian Workers (November 1919), in which police arrested roughly three hundred members (Preston, chapter 8), and raids by federal agents on IWW headquarters in Chicago in September 1917 (Preston, 1963: 119). With the Bolshevik Revolution in Russia (1917) and socialist revolution in Mexico (1917), fears of Bolshevism and socialism ran rife, as did concerns about "foreigners." Indeed, the Palmer Raids relied upon a number of immigration acts that sought to limit entry of foreigners into the United States. The 1903 Immigration Act excluded certain immigrants because of their beliefs and associations; thirty-eight persons were excluded between 1903 and 1921 for holding anarchistic beliefs (Preston, 1963: 33). The 1917 Immigration Act allowed for the deportation of any alien found advocating or teaching either anarchy or the unlawful destruction of property. The Palmer Raids broke the back of the Communist Party in the United States. Federal agents illegally raided party headquarters in thirty-three cities in twenty-two states. Agents beat people and arrested them without warrants. For a discussion of the general decline of socialism in the U.S., see Weinstein, 1969.

64. Boyer and Morais, 1955: 262. Police agencies harassed, beat, and illegally arrested those from all walks of life who protested the social conditions of the Great Depression. For coverage of the policing of labor radicalism at the small-town level (Eugene, Oregon) during the Great Depression, see Websdale, 1993.

65. Terkel, 1970: 170–171, 172. Police had brutalized some picketers a couple of days earlier. On Memorial Day many of them turned up for a family picnic. Dr. Andreas noted a few rocks thrown at the police as the police opened fire, or perhaps a little before they opened fire. The crowd turned and ran from the police; this was when police shot them in the back.

66. Daniels, 1999: 9. Domestic violence laws had been in place since the time of first settlement of the American colonies. Pleck, 1987: 21–22, who notes that the Massachusetts Body of Liberties (1641) held that "Everie marryed woeman shall be free from bodilie correction or stripes by her husband, unlesse it be in his owne defence upon her assault."

67. Feminists tend to see the failure of the criminal justice system to intervene

in interpersonal violence against women as one way in which the patriarchal state has reproduced the domination of men over women (see Hanmer, 1978; Hanmer and Saunders, 1984; Hanmer, Radford, and Stanko, 1989; Edwards, 1989; and Walby, 1990).

68. Websdale, 1992. Using divorce case transcripts as a window into dissolving marriages, I argue that police intervened in less than 1 percent of domestic violence cases in Lane County, Oregon, between 1853 and 1960. Nowadays, in Oregon and across the United States, police know of roughly half of domestic violence incidents in their jurisdictions and intervene at much higher levels than was traditionally the case (Bureau of Justice Statistics, 1998).

69. Morris, 1999: 268

70. Fox-Genovese, 1988: 322.

71. Morris, 1999: 274.

72. Dorothy Roberts (1997: 29) points out that records reveal 10 percent of the slave population in 1860 classified as mulatto. She notes, "Most of these mixed-race children were the product of forced sex between slave women and white men." Roberts also cites the work of William Fogel and Stanley Engerman (1974: 133; see Roberts's footnote 23 on p. 316), who estimate that "the share of Negro children fathered by whites on slave plantations probably averaged between 1 and 2 percent."

73. Genovese, 1976: 371.

74. See, for example, Kennedy's discussion of the Mississippi High Court of Errors and Appeals in the 1859 case of *George (a slave) v. The State*; 37 Miss. Rep. 316, 318 (1859), 1998: 34–35.

75. Omolade, 1994: 73.

76. Ibid., 14.

77. Myrdal, 1944: 1189 n. 19. Myrdal notes, "Police service to Negro communities is limited largely to radio cruising cars. They do not go through the areas where most Negro homicides occur, but rather stay on the main thoroughfares which are given over largely to business purposes."

78. Sutherland, 1949.

79. Clinard, Yeager, Brisette, Petrashek, and Harries, 1979.

80. Carson, 1981.

81. For more on these matters see Reiman, 1990; Michalowski, 1985: 334–40.

82. See Hawkins and Thomas, 1991: 73; Rabinowicz, 1980.

83. Kennedy, 1998: 91. See also Hawkins and Thomas (1991: 76) for examples of this practice in Milwaukee from 1921 to 1923.

84. Gerber, 1976.

85. See Hawkins and Thomas (1991) for a summary of these incidents in places such as East St. Louis (1917), Houston (1917), Chicago (1919), Harlem (1935), Detroit (1942, 1943, 1967), Watts (1965), Newark (1967), and Miami (1980, 1989).

86. Kerner Report, 1968: v.

87. Ibid., x.

88. Ibid., 143–150.

89. Ibid., 17.

90. Ibid., 18.

91. See Skogan and Hartnett, 1997.

92. Critics do not call it community policing, preferring terms such as saturation policing.

93. New York City currently has 5 police officers per 1,000 residents, a level of saturation much higher than a city such as San Diego which also introduced a version of community policing in the 1990s; it has a ratio of 1.7 per 1000 residents. See *New York Times*, March 4, 2000, "Cities Reduce Crime and Conflict without New York-Style Hardball," by Fox Butterfield.

94. See Glazer, 1997; Sherman, 1997.

95. See Manning, 1997; Klockars, 1991.

96. Manning, 1997: 13.

97. Parks, Mastrofski, Dejong, and Gray, 1999: 515. Earlier research by Skogan in Houston, Texas, found that community policing initiatives reassured white homeowners and increased their feelings of well-being; however, for renters and blacks there was little discernible effect. Skogan (1990: 106) concludes, "In general, those at the bottom of the social ladder were not helped at all."

98. Popkin, Gwiasda, Rosenbaum, Amendolia, Johnson, and Olson, 1999; Popkin, Gwiasda, Olson, Rosenbaum, and Buron, 2000; Skogan and Hartnett, 1997.

Notes to Chapter 2

1. Kornblum (2000: 331) notes that in Africa, with an annual per capita income of $800, life expectancy is fifty-two years; in the U.S., with annual per capita income around $20,000, average life expectancy is seventy-five years.

2. See the *Guardian Weekly*, July 6–12, 2000: 3, "Rich live longer, poor die younger in divided world: UN report highlights growing gap between developed countries and those ravaged by war, poverty and Aids," by Victoria Brittain and Larry Elliott. In the thirty countries thought to have the highest level of human development, life expectancy at birth was more than 75 years. In sub-Saharan Africa it is 48.9 years, in Malawi it is 39.1 years, and in Sierra Leone it is 37.9 years.

3. Braudel (1979, 1: 83) notes at least two forms of plague: bubonic plague, the older form, in which buboes form in the groin area and become gangrenous; and pulmonary plague (the Black Death), which became evident with the pandemic of 1348 in Europe.

4. Pepys, 1985: 509, 513, 519.

5. Cited in Susser, Watson, and Hopper, 1985: 214.

6. Pepys, 1985: 518–519.

7. Braudel, 1979, 1: 87.

8. Ziegler, 1969: 131. Since the poor left few written records, there is little to document how they felt about the way the rich avoided the plague from the 1340s to the mid-seventeenth century. In later cholera epidemics in France (1832), Ziegler informs us, the "Parisian mob rioted through the smarter quarters, accusing nobles and bourgeois not only of suffering less seriously from the disease but of poisoning their impoverished fellow-citizens into the bargain."

9. Braudel, 1979, 1: 85.

10. Telephone interview, January 31, 2000.

11. See the *Tennessean*, January 1, 1997: 1A, "Murder in black and white: Be-

hind the statistics, many see Nashville's homicide rate as a symptom of lost hope," by Deborah Highland.

12. Braudel, 1979, 1: 85.

13. *Nashville Scene*, April 8, 1999, "Summit to focus on affordable housing," by Liz Murray Garrigan.

14. I interviewed many people from poor neighborhoods in Nashville. The interviews took place in shelters, at workplaces, in jail and prison, at the courthouse, in homes, in hospitals, on the street, in police precinct houses, over the telephone, in coffee shops and diners, and in other settings. In addition to these interviews, I observed social life in the housing projects of Nashville, talking with people on the street and conversing with a large number of people who work with the poor in various ways. What follows are ethnographic observations informed by analyses of police files, newspaper articles, census data, and other written sources.

15. Mayhew, 1968, 4: xi.

16. Giddens (1989: 221) identifies West Indians in Britain and Algerians in France as being members of the underclass.

17. Marx, 1970: 44.

18. Mann (1992) argues that Marx's use of terms such as "stagnant," "floating," "latent," and "lowest sediment" betrays an unsympathetic orientation to the so-called *lumpenproletariat*. Referring to Marx's approach, Mann notes that "when he asserts that certain sections of the reserve army of labour breed more rapidly . . . and 'succumb to their incapacity for adaptation,' while others are part of some criminal class, Marx reproduces the prejudices of the Victorian middle classes." Cited in Haralambos and Holborn, 1995: 91.

19. Marx argues that in bourgeois democratic republics characterized by universal suffrage, the rule of law, various political freedoms, and competition between formal political parties, exploited classes could clearly benefit and undermine the bourgeoisie. Karl Kautsky took up these observations, found in *Class Struggles in France, Part II*, and envisaged the possibility of socialism through the ballot box. In contrast, Lenin (1975) saw bourgeois democracy as the "one best shell for capitalism," and argued that democratic republics ultimately serve the interests of the bourgeoisie. For Lenin, the proletarian revolution would involve a "dictatorship of the proletariat."

20. See W. Wilson, 1987, 1993, 1996. For example, he notes (1996: 21) that "the proportion of men who 'permanently' dropped out of the labor force was more than twice as high in the late 1980s than it had been in the late 1960s." In his analysis of the "code of the street" in inner-city Philadelphia, Elijah Anderson (1999) distinguishes between the decent behavior of the working poor and the (presumably) indecent behavior of street families. He describes the street family in the following way: "So-called street parents, unlike decent ones, often show a lack of consideration for other people and have a rather superficial sense of family and community. . . . Members of these families, who are more fully invested in the code of the street than the decent people, may aggressively socialize their children into it in a normative way."

21. W. Wilson, 1996: xiii.

22. W. Wilson (1996: 15-16) takes issue with the work of Massey and Denton

(1993), who argue that the blend of a group's overall poverty rate with its degree of segregation leads inevitably to a greater geographical concentration of poverty. Wilson notes, "In the ten neighborhoods that make up Chicago's Black Belt, the poverty rate increased almost 20 percent between 1970 and 1990, despite the fact that the overall black poverty rate for the city of Chicago increased only 7.5 percent during this same period."

23. W. Wilson, 1996: 19.

24. For a detailed discussion of the relationship between race and class, see Solomos, Findlay, Jones, and Gilroy, 1982.

25. West, 1988: 22.

26. Jargowsky and Bane, 1991: 239, 245–246.

27. Although noting new levels of black suburbanization in some regions, Bartlet (1993) points out that levels of segregation have often increased within cities. See also Massey and Denton, 1993.

28. Luttwak, 1999: 95. However, he also comments (1999: 100) that these "famous underclass pathologies are not so pathological after all. It is surely less painful to be chronically unemployed if one is *not* sober, drug-free, and filled with a desire to work at a satisfying job." Citing a Rand Corporation study (1990) of drug dealing in Washington, D.C., Luttwak concludes that the average drug dealer is engaging in "perfectly rational" behavior given the dearth of other earning opportunities. He notes that "drug dealing at an average income of $12,500 per annum in 1987 was profitable enough to be the best career option for its universally uneducated participants."

29. See Model (1993: 185), who notes that by the 1970s in New York City, later-generation Italian Americans became increasingly uninterested in crime, particularly the drug trade. Their lack of interest and the growing flow of narcotics from the Caribbean and South America created openings for blacks and Hispanics to become involved. However, without a framework and history of subcultural norms to regulate their drug dealing activities, black and Hispanic dealers tended to "rely on personal acts of violence to establish and maintain their reputations as business people of consequence." Without cooperation within this newer cadre of dealers, Model concludes, it is unlikely that black and Hispanic drug merchants will create the market milieu required to foster long-term upward mobility for both the dealers and the law-abiding members of their communities.

30. U.S. Department of Justice, Bureau of Justice Statistics, Correction Statistics, 1997. For an analysis of the growth of incarceration and the rise of the criminal justice industry, see Chambliss, 1994; Christie, 1993; J. Miller, 1996; and Tonry, 1995. See reference to a U.S. Justice Department document on incarceration published in 2000 in the *New York Times*, August 20, 2000, "Number in Prison Population Grows Despite Crime Reduction," by Fox Butterfield. The report notes the total number of Americans in all jails and prisons to have been 2,026,596 at the end of 1999.

31. *Guardian Weekly*, February 17–23, vol. 162, no. 8: 1, "U.S. jails two millionth inmate," by Duncan Campbell. For more extensive analyses of the criminal justice complex as a lucrative industry, see Christie, 1993; and Chambliss, 1994.

32. Irwin, 1985.

33. Anderson, 1991.

34. See, for example, Carol Stack, 1974.

35. Anderson, 1991: 382. See also W. Wilson (1996: 61), who notes that in 1984, there were roughly 80 homicide deaths of black males aged fifteen to nineteen per 100,000; by 1992 this figure had increased to 180 per 100,000.

36. My discussion of housing issues draws upon the work of Quadagno, 1994: chapter 4; and Bartlet, 1993.

37. For a detailed discussion of how the FHA subsidized segregation in Philadelphia after World War II, see Bartlet, 1993. He notes that the FHA restricted loans to "black applicants seeking housing in white neighborhoods, on the grounds that this would disturb the social makeup of a community." Bartlet traces the current practice of redlining (assessing the creditworthiness of neighborhoods by their racial/ethnic composition) to these earlier FHA strategies. For a recent example of how race affects contemporary lending practices, see Coffey and Gocker, 1998.

38. Quadagno, 1994: 91.

39. Kerner Report, 1968: 467–468, 472.

40. Quadagno mentions tactics such as zoning and building codes designed to deter developers and refusing to install water and sewage facilities capable of supporting high-density housing.

41. Quadagno, 1994: 113.

42. Bartlet (1993: 152–153) describes this shift as "ideological."

43. Quadagno, 1994: 114.

44. Many see gentrification as a major plus insofar as it encourages people to reinvest in the inner city. However, gentrification often follows the mass incarceration of inner-city blacks. For example, in the U Street neighborhood of Washington, D.C., the subway system is running later, and an organic grocery store and a private jazz club with annual dues of $2,500 are due to open soon. What this does for the poor in these neighborhoods is not entirely clear. I assume the criminal justice juggernaut removed drug dealers, leaving fertile concrete for the middle classes tired of the commute from the suburbs or desiring a touch of inner-city risk! In Miami, specifically the Overtown and Liberty City areas, textile plants, production studios, and a food-processing plant are due to open. In New Orleans, the crack houses of the blighted Irish Channel neighborhood are apparently about to "benefit" from "avant-garde galleries, clothing shops and even a designer jewelry shop." One businesswoman, Patty Spinale, who opened a lingerie shop, was apparently relieved that the "neighborhood has really significantly cleaned up in the last two years, in terms of people investing in it. More tourists are comfortable with venturing in." Perhaps the nearby poor will be able to purchase new lingerie from this store to spice up their lives. See the *Chicago Tribune*, May 29, 2000, "In Neighborhoods Once Plagued by Crime, Residents Can 'Sit and Hear the Birds,' " by Pam Belluck.

45. See Scull (1984) for a stinging attack on decarceration policies in both the United States and Britain.

46. Rossi and Wright (1989) found that 76 percent of their sample of the homeless in Chicago were men. This contrasts sharply with the nearly all-male population recorded by Donald Bogue (1963) in mid-twentieth-century Chicago.

47. See Zorza, 1991.

48. Quadagno, 1994: 105.

49. Lovett, 1999: xv.

50. Citing the *Nashville Daily Union*, January 7, 1864, Lovett notes the Negro population at some 12,000 persons in 1864.

51. Gutman (1976: 226) notes that ex-slaves helped each other to a tremendous degree. This was seen especially in the case of orphaned black children whose parents had either died or been sold. This solidarity among blacks, steeped in African history and the long-term negotiation of slavery, meant that the Freedmen's Bureau provided relatively little material assistance for ex-slaves. This mutual-aid behavior among blacks during Emancipation occurred throughout the South and is "one important reason why over its full lifetime the Freedmen's Bureau materially assisted no more than 0.5 percent of the four million ex-slaves." (See also n. 35, pp. 582–583.)

52. Lovett, 1999: 73.

53. Ibid.

54. Ibid.

55. Ibid., 85.

56. Doyle, 1985: 48. He also notes that in 1930 the mortality rate for blacks was 170 percent that of whites.

57. Doyle (1985: 50) notes that the mother of Henry Emerson, a fourteen-year-old black boy, earned $9.50 for working seventy-five hours a week for wealthy white families in the suburbs of Nashville.

58. Halberstam, 1998: 107–108.

59. See Dicerson, 1977.

60. For a more detailed discussion of these matters, see Doyle, 1985: chapter 5.

61. Halberstam, 1998: 109.

62. Paul Willis (1990: 103) has written eloquently about the way in which young Englishmen feel about the threat posed by the streets. Note the parallels between his observations and those of the poor in Nashville: "Far from their threatening it, the street threatens them. This is a given for many young men. For them only social theorists and do-gooders have the safety and luxury to worry about how it comes to be like that."

63. The Napier/Sudekum development is discussed in the *Tennessean*, July 27, 1996: 1B, "Southside Enterprise Center opens doors to new business; Storefront part of new $3 million enterprise project." The article tells the story of Nella Frierson, who spent more than thirty years earning a living by braiding hair. She first worked out of her home in the Napier public housing project. She then worked out of a tiny building on Lewis Street. With the arrival of the Southside Enterprise Center, she was about to enter a new storefront.

64. Similar stories have appeared in the local press; see, for example, the *Tennessean*, January 1, 1997: 1A, "Murder in black and white: Behind the statistics, many see Nashville's homicide rate as a symptom of lost hope," by Deborah Highland. A forty-four-year-old black man, Johnny Wheeler, was returning to his home with his girlfriend just after she had cashed her government check. A gunman pushed his way into their apartment, killed Wheeler, and robbed his girlfriend.

65. Jargowsky (1994) notes that the majority of people living in urban ghettoes

are minorities. Indeed, the proportion of blacks living in urban ghettoes increased from 37 percent in 1980 to 45 percent in 1990 (W. Wilson, 1996: 14).

66. W. Wilson (1996: 12) defines ghetto poverty census tracts as those in which at least 40 percent of the residents are poor. By this measure, the projects in Nashville represent intense sites of poverty.

67. Readers should not read "nicest" to mean "crime-free." In July 1998 an eleven-year-old girl was raped in a vacant apartment after being accosted by an eighteen-year-old male who wanted her to smoke crack with him. See the *Tennessean*, September 15, 1998: 6B, "Rape suspect was on probation: Youth 'snatched' girl, 11, offered her crack, officer says," by Kirk Loggins. The offender, Shawn Johnson, admitted to having sex with the girl, although he said she consented. The girl claimed she was forced to have sex. According to her, Johnson dragged her into an empty apartment, went off to buy crack, and then returned to have sex with her. Johnson was on probation for assault at the time of the rape. It is significant that he did not have to go far to buy the crack.

68. *Tennessean*, November 1997: 1A, "Panel Gets Taste of Life in Inner City: Crime Commissioners find tour 'disturbing.' "

69. Average annual net incomes at Cheatham Place and Andrew Jackson are $7,092 and $6,614, respectively, significantly higher than those of residents in unimproved public housing such as Preston Taylor at $6,028, James A. Cayce at $4,789, Tony Sudekum at $5,427, John Henry Hale at $5,267, and Sam Levy at $5,085. Renzetti and Maier (1999: 9) report the average annual income of thirty-six female public housing residents they interviewed in Camden, New Jersey, as $7,733.

70. For a discussion of this issue, see, for example, the *Tennessean*, September 21, 1999: 1A, "Less room for poor in Hope's housing; Critics call program 'urban removal.' " See also the *Tennessean*, March 16, 1999, p. 1A, "VineHill Rebuilt as Suburb of Promise." Vinehill was a 1940s-style brick public housing complex that had fallen into acute disrepair. A HOPE VI grant program provided $13.5 million of the $18 million needed to raze the 280 old units and replace them with 76 duplexes on the same site. To be considered for the new Vinehill Homes, applicants had to agree to work or take job-training courses; the ultimate goal was that they would move out within five years and purchase their own homes.

71. "Less room for poor."

72. These selection criteria have already been applied to the upgraded Vinehill Homes. According to Jennifer Gilbert of the Metropolitan Development Housing Agency (MDHA), it will be difficult to get into the upgraded Vinehill duplexes. MDHA will carry out criminal background checks on all applicants, question previous landlords, and visit the current homes of applicants to make sure they are maintaining those homes properly. See the *Tennessean*, March 16, 1999, p. 1A, "Vine Hill Rebuilt as Suburb of Promise," In this same article, readers learn that the new Vinehill will be a fenced community with only one entry point, off Benton Avenue, which will have a security checkpoint.

73. "Less room for poor."

74. "Panel gets taste of life in inner city."

75. See Edin, 2000: 28. Her ethnography among 130 or so poor mothers scattered

through nine neighborhoods in Philadelphia revealed that "although mothers still aspire to marriage, they feel that it entails far more risks than rewards—at least marriage to the kind of men who fathered their children and live in their neighborhoods. . . . They say they are willing and even eager to wed if the marriage represents substantial economic upward mobility and their husband doesn't beat them, abuse their children, insist on making all the decisions, or 'fool around' with other women. If they cannot find such a man, most would rather remain single."

76. See Quadagno, 1994: 20–21.

77. Skocpol, 1991: 417. She notes (1991: 418) that "the number of female-headed families receiving welfare . . . rose from 635,000 in 1961 (or 29 percent of all such families) to almost 3 million by 1979 (or 50 percent of female-headed families)."

78. Quadagno, 1994: 119.

79. Kerner Report, 1968: 459.

80. Ibid., 462.

81. For a detailed discussion of the failure of FAP, see Quadagno, 1994: chapter 5.

82. Edin, 2000: 26. See also Edin and Jencks, 1990.

83. Research suggests that 20 to 30 percent of women enrolled in TANF live in violent relationships, and that roughly two-thirds report experiencing domestic violence during adulthood (Lein, Jacquet, Lewis, Cole, and Williams, 2001: 194; see also Honeycutt, Marshall, and Weston, 2001; and Pearson, Griswold, and Thoennes, 2001). Many other studies note that women on public assistance and others with low incomes are much more prone to violent interpersonal victimization. See E. L. Bassuk, L. Weinreb, J. Buckner, A. Browne, A. Salomon, and S. Bassuk, 1996; Raphael, 1996; and Hirsch, 2001.

84. This legislation passed into law as the 1996 Personal Responsibility and Work Opportunity Reconciliation Act. Readers will note the use of disingenuous language: women contract with the state and assume "personal responsibility" for taking up "work opportunities." One gets the misleading impression that there are real jobs to be had and real opportunities to be pursued, when most women will enter dead-end service sector work that will keep them poor. In addition, one might sense that women are somehow "responsible" personally for their ability to successfully enter paid employment and keep jobs. This type of language wholly ignores the massive structural forces at work in the global economy.

In some states, punitive and demeaning forms of surveillance accompany welfare reform. Michigan became the first state to require people to pass a drug test before applying for welfare. Authorities piloted the plan in five areas of the state in 1999. They hope to adopt it statewide in 2003. Under this law, if welfare recipients fail the drug test, they are subject to another. If they fail the second, authorities offer them treatment. If they refuse treatment, they can be denied welfare. As Kary Moss, executive director of the ACLU of Michigan, put it, "The state is starting from the assumption that the poor are criminals . . . saying that if you want money for food and shelter you have to give up the Fourth Amendment rights that others have." *New York Times*, May 30, 1999: Section 1:14, "Testing welfare applicants for drugs," by Robin Meredith. For more discussion of these issues see the *Detroit Free Press*, July 1, 1999, "Drug tests to be linked to welfare," by Wendy Wendland. In 1999 the

Michigan legislature also passed a finger-imaging requirement to monitor welfare recipients in order to weed out fraudulent claims.

85. Women head up 95 percent of welfare families in Nashville. Their average age is thirty-two, they have an average of two children, and most are unmarried. The typical welfare family of three in Nashville in 1996 received $185 per month. That increased to $226 per month with another child. See the *Tennessean*, January 23, 1996: 2A, "Keeping jobs major obstacles for welfare recipients." The article reports a study of 1,182 families receiving AFDC by Greg Harkenrider, who notes, "Although only one in five AFDC adults is working at any given time, 56.6 percent reported holding a job in the last year." This information is consistent with my interviewees' comments that jobs were scarcely worth having, few being conducive to good mothering. Harkenrider's study also dispelled the myth that welfare receipt becomes a deeply embedded dependence transmitted across generations. He found only three in ten second-generation welfare recipients, and one in fourteen third-generation recipients.

86. Any parents who were delinquent in support payments for more than ninety days or $500 behind in court-ordered payments would receive a warning letter giving them fifty days to pay up or face revocation of their licenses. This was a popular part of the Families First legislation; passing eighty-four to four in the house. Sundquist hoped to realize $13 million from these payments.

87. The actual breakdown was as follows: $44.7 million for day care for 15,877 welfare children (in 1995 Tennessee spent $58 million for child care); $10.5 million for transportation; $15 million for adult education, job training, life-skills classes, and other services; and $1.3 million for computer software to enable counselors to "manage" families.

88. *Tennessean*, April 7, 1996: 1B, "Welfare: Time limit or time bomb?"

89. Of all women admitted to the Tennessee Department of Corrections in the twelve months ending June 30, 1997, 24.7 percent were incarcerated for drug offenses; 20.5 percent for forgery, fraud, and embezzlement; 11.3 percent for robbery; 10.9 percent for homicide; 10 percent for burglary; 8.4 percent for theft and possession of stolen property; 3.8 percent for assault; 1.7 percent for escape; 1.3 percent for kidnapping; and 7.4 percent for "other offenses." See the *Tennessean*, September 28, 1997: 1A, "Statistics show prisons not just for men anymore."

90. "Welfare: Time limit."

91. Ibid.

92. Edin and Jencks, 1992.

93. Out of Hirsch's sample of twenty-six female felony drug offenders, twenty (77 percent) admitted being battered by a husband or boyfriend (Hirsch, 2001: 164).

94. Salon.com, July 20, 2000, "Swept away: Thousands of women, often guilty of little more than lousy judgment, are serving long prison sentences as drug 'conspirators,' " by Nell Bernstein. Copyright © 2000 Salon.com. See also Hirsch, 2001: 162. Her interviews with twenty-six female felony drug offenders revealed that courts convicted most for "possession with intent to deliver" very small amounts of drugs, with street values of five to ten dollars.

95. Bernstein, citing a 1997 survey of female state prison inmates.

96. *Tennessean*, April 10, 1996: 1A, "Employers need those on welfare; Job

growth predicted as time limits phase in." In a later article, Fox appeared quite gleeful about welfare reform: "We simply do not have enough workers to fill the jobs." Welfare reform "couldn't happen at a better time. It's excellent timing." *Tennessean*, September 25, 1996: 1B, "Job Market Awaits Many on Welfare," by Larry Daughtrey.

97. *Tennessean*, July 10, 1997: 4B, "Welfare-fraud sweep begins with 20 arrests," by Bill Carey.

98. See the *Tennessean*, December 11, 1997: 7B, "Give welfare moms more time to grow, advocates say," by Bonna DeLa Cruz.

99. *Tennessean*, December 16, 1997: 1A, "Food aid demand expanding," by Tanya Ballard.

100. *Tennessean*, December 18, 1997: 18A, "Welfare reform plan must stay flexible."

101. *Tennessean*, March 11, 1998: 1A, "Hunger problems growing: Minimum wage not filling the stomachs of working poor," by Jay Hamburg. In Nashville, demand for emergency food increased by 10 percent during 1997. In the greater Nashville area and the bordering counties, the demand for emergency food increased 20 percent.

102. *Tennessean*, April 19, 1998: 1A, "Welfare reserve a priority; Sundquist against 'raise' for Families First recipients," Bonna DeLa Cruz.

103. *Tennessean*, September 6, 1999: 4B, "Affordable quality day care harder for families to find."

104. *Tennessean*, December 22, 1995: 1B, "Honoring those who died: Memorial gives names, identities." by Jim East.

105. See the story of the arrest of Michael Hodges, who lived for thirteen years in a makeshift home under the Victory Memorial Bridge on land owned by the city. The homeless community that developed in this location was known as the "Cumberland River Trolls." Authorities cleared the land to make way for the construction of the new football stadium. Police charged Hodges with criminal trespass, a versatile tool for law enforcement. *Tennessean*, May 21, 1996: 1B, "Leaving city under the bridge; Metro reclaims land, man evicted, jailed," by Carrie Ferguson.

106. *Tennessean*, April 4, 1996: 14A, "An idea to help those who need us," by Rachel C. Wilson. The Room-at-the-Inn houses an average of 185 persons per night over the winter months in Nashville and, aside from the Union Rescue Mission, is the largest provider of beds for the homeless in Nashville.

107. See the *Tennessean*, June 11, 1996: 3B, "No cheap rooms available for homeless during Fan Fair."

108. See the *Tennessean*, February 7, 1997: 6B, "City plans battle against homelessness," by Carrie Ferguson. This article contains references to the exasperation of several business owners on Lafayette Street (close to the Union Rescue Mission) because of the way the homeless hang out on their premises.

109. "An idea to help those who need us," by R. Wilson.

110. *New York Times*, November 22, 1999. "A homeless man challenges New York City crackdowns," by Nina Bernstein. The article tells of the federal class-action suit brought by a group of homeless men arrested under a vague sanitation ordinance for sleeping in the street. One of the principal characters in the suit, Au-

gustine Betancourt, thirty-three, claimed he feared for his safety in the city's homeless shelters.

111. *Tennessean*, April 27, 1997: 1D, "Need work? Arena needs help, but . . ." by Mike Kilen.

Notes to Chapter 3

1. *Guardian Weekly*, August 10–16, 2000: 29, "Americans make pilgrimage to slaves' point of no return," by Douglas Farah.

2. Ibid.

3. See Fox Butterfield (1995). Biological explanations of crime reinforced such beliefs. Lombroso's 1876 work, published in the same year that Reconstruction ended in the South, was particularly important in providing a conceptual framework within which racist ideologies could flourish. These explanations paralleled the rise of evolutionary arguments in biology and the natural sciences. It was not a big jump in logic to posit the black offender as biologically prone to crime. It is no accident that Lombroso's work was more popular in the United States than in Europe.

4. Hobsbawm, 1965: 15; 1959: 16; 1972: 5–6.

5. In his discussion of the poaching and game laws on Cannock Chase in England, Douglas Hay (1975: 189) notes that according to the 1671 game laws, "a man had to be lord of a manor, or have a substantial income from landed property, even to kill a hare on his own land."

6. John Rule (1975: 169) notes that the term "wrecking" has no precise meaning but refers to "a range of activities varying from the casual pocketing of articles cast up by the sea to the deliberate luring of vessels ashore; from petty larceny to armed defiance of the law; from near beachcombing to open looting."

7. Styles, 1980. There was widespread local support for coining, including the support of men of property.

8. Rudé, 1973.

9. Winslow, 1975.

10. Doyle, 1985: 223.

11. The Supreme Court held that separate educational facilities are inherently unequal. This decision reversed *Plessy v. Ferguson* (1896).

12. *Kelley v. Board of Education of Nashville* (1955).

13. Doyle, 1985: 239. My analysis of these developments owes much to Doyle.

14. Ibid., 242.

15. Ibid., 246.

16. The actions of the National Guard in this incident recalls a famous shooting in Tennessee in 1974, when two Memphis police officers fatally shot Edward Garner, a fifteen-year-old black boy, in the back of the head. He had been fleeing from police with a stolen wallet containing ten dollars. The U.S. Supreme Court eventually heard the civil suit stemming from this killing and held that the fleeing felon rule upon which the police officers relied was unconstitutional. See *Tennessee v. Garner*, 471 U.S. 1 (1985).

17. One of the most comprehensive airings of the police side of the story emerged at the filing of a civil lawsuit in U.S. District Court. Leon Fisher's mother

and the three women with whom he had children each sued Sergeant Hickerson for $750,000 for using excessive force. See the *Tennessean*, July 7, 1998: 5B, "Officer details events before shooting; suspect was trying to steal his gun, he says in filings," by Catherine Trevison. An internal police review board hearing unanimously concluded that Hickerson justifiably shot and killed Fisher. An attorney close to the civil suit told me guardedly that he or she had requested that plaintiffs' attorneys provide concrete evidence from actual witnesses that police handcuffed Fisher before shooting him, as was claimed. To date (May 10, 2000), no witness has attested to Fisher's being handcuffed before being shot. The attorney also told me that the autopsy report suggested that police did not handcuff Fisher before shooting him. An attorney for the plaintiffs told me that he did not believe police handcuffed and then shot Fisher (telephone conversation May 17, 2000). He saw the shooting simply as a "big mistake." See *Fisher v. Hickerson, 3: 98–0481*, pending in U.S. District Court in Nashville, filed June 1, 1998, under federal civil rights law, Title 42, §1983.

18. The Nashville police media relations officer, Don Aaron, told reporters that the initial crowd that gathered in the aftermath of the shooting numbered fewer than one hundred people, with "only a handful" throwing objects at the police. See the *Tennessean*, August 11, 1997: 1A, "Police link arson, shooting," by Jon Yates.

19. *Tennessean*, October 15, 1998: 1B, "Arson defendants acquitted: No other suspects in 1997 Dollar General fire."

20. Ibid.

21. *Tennessean*, September, 17, 1997: 1B, "Sam Levy resident testifies about 2 teens burning store," by Kirk Loggins.

22. *Tennessean*, October 14, 1998: 8B, "Judge acquits 1 of Dollar Store arson charge," by Kirk Loggins.

23. Two other area residents, Juerno Brown, twenty-two, and Roxanne Williams, nineteen, pleaded guilty to burglary and theft charges stemming from the looting of the store.

24. According to data from the Metropolitan Development and Housing Agency, 247 of Sam Levy residents receive welfare, 79 social security, 108 disability, and 143 are employed. Communication dated February 25, 2000.

25. "Police link arson, shooting," by Jon Yates.

26. "Sam Levy resident testifies," by Loggins.

27. "Police link arson, shooting," by Yates.

28. Myrdal, 1944, 2: 541–542. Myrdal goes on to note that "white policemen are also a great portion of all whites killed by Negroes. . . . The white policeman in the Negro community is in danger, as the high casualty figures show, and he feels himself in danger. In the mind of the quick-trigger policeman is the fear of the 'bad nigger.' "

29. Fyfe, 1982: 721.

30. Walker, Spohn, and DeLone (2000: 96, and Table 4.2) scrutinized police shootings in Memphis from 1985 to 1989 and found no unarmed or nonassaultive suspects of any race shot and killed by police. This compared with one white and thirteen black unarmed and nonassaultive suspects killed from 1969 to 1974.

31. Ibid., 97. However, these authors also acknowledge the difficulty in obtaining systematic data on fatal shootings by police.

32. The National Crime Victimization Survey (NCVS) of 1994 revealed that

victims perceived the offender to be black in 51.7 percent of single-offender robberies and 23 percent of all assaults. Cited in Walker, Spohn, and DeLone, 2000: 100. See also Hawkins, Laub, Lauritsen, and Cothern (2000: 3), who summarize the research on race, ethnicity, and serious and violent crime. Citing the 1998 Uniform Crime Reports data, they note, "Black youth, when compared with white youth, were most overrepresented in arrests for robbery (54 percent and 43 percent respectively) and murder and non-negligent manslaughter (49 percent and 47 percent respectively)" this work assumes that black youth make up 15 percent of the youth population and white youth 79 percent.

33. Smith, Visher, and Davidson, 1984.

34. Petersilia, 1983.

35. *New Yorker*, April 29/May 6, 1996: 62, "Black and Blue," by Jervis Anderson. Cited by Russell, 1998: 35.

36. *New York Times*, March 5, 2000, "Squads That Tripped Up Walking the Bad Walk," by Jane Fritsch.

37. "Police link arson, shooting," by Yates.

38. Ibid.

39. The results of those tests showed that Fisher's DNA matched that found at the Bradley crime scene. This does not, of course, mean that Fisher shot and killed Bradley.

40. Additional indictments (not dispositions) included failure to appear for a hearing, April 16, 1997; criminal trespass, March 11, 1997; disorderly conduct, February 21, 1997; assault, February 19, 1997; resisting arrest, February 19, 1997; evading arrest, February 19, 1997; disorderly conduct, February 19, 1997; selling drugs, February 19, 1997; resisting arrest, July 18, 1996; vandalism, July 18, 1996; driving on a suspended license, July 18, 1996; criminal trespass, July 18, 1996; possession of drugs, March 24, 1996; resisting arrest, January 24, 1996; driving on a suspended license, December 12, 1995; criminal trespass, November 1, 1995; tampering with evidence, November 1, 1995; assault, November 1, 1995; selling drugs, November 1, 1995; resisting arrest, November 1, 1995; vehicle theft, October 12, 1994; evading arrest, October 12, 1994; criminal trespass, October 12, 1994; failure to appear, October 12, 1994; driving with a suspended license, March 28, 1994; unlawful possession of a weapon, September 20, 1993; and criminal trespass, April 29, 1993.

41. "Police link arson, shooting," by Yates.

42. *Tennessean*, August 20, 1997: 8B. "Officer photographs group protesting police shootings," by Joe Rogers.

43. *Nashville Scene*, October 21, 1999: p. 1, "Above the Law: How rogue guards at a Nashville security firm terrorized Hispanics they were paid to protect," by Willy Stern. The controversial series of articles was based on interviews with seventeen Detection Services employees and three dozen Hispanic residents. There are approximately 45,000 to 50,000 Hispanics in Nashville, and estimates suggest that up to 40 percent are living there illegally.

44. "Judge acquits 1," by Loggins.

45. Cases noted in the *Tennessean*, January 1, 1997: 1A, "Murder in black and white: Behind the statistics, many see Nashville's homicide rate as a symptom of lost hope," by Deborah Highland.

46. Consider, for example, the killing of Elton Maupins, a black man aged forty-

three, who was murdered at his home during a robbery. Maupins and his wife, Christine, were watching television in their bedroom when robbers entered their home and shot him through his bedroom door. Also consider the beating death of Samuel Featherstone, a black man aged forty-two, who was severely beaten, stabbed, and robbed in his home. Before the killing, Featherstone and the suspect had been smoking crack cocaine. And the death of Christopher Waters, a black man aged thirty-five, who died when someone who entered his apartment stabbed him, striking the femoral artery. Cases noted in "Murder in black and white," by Highland.

47. See the *Tennessean*, December 3, 1997: 4B. According to official statistics, the number of homicides declined from 112 in 1997, to 97 in 1998, to 68 in 1999.

48. "Murder in black and white," by Highland.

49. *Tennessean*, November 29, 1997: 1B, "Crime rises as night falls and police exit Sam Levy," by Tim Chavez.

50. "Police link arson, shooting," by Yates.

51. Ibid.

52. James Warfield and Mary Riley, cited ibid.

53. Le Bon, 1960 (original 1895).

54. Rudé, 1973: 28–29.

55. E. P. Thompson, 1971: 78.

56. Rudé, 1973: 26–27.

57. Cohen, 1988: 283. Italics in the original.

58. Hawkins, 1987.

59. Cohen, 1988: 279.

60. In 1997 the Sam Levy projects were home to 463 families and a total of 1,583 individuals. Of these residents, 91 percent were black. The rest were white. See the *Tennessean*, August 12, 1997: 1A, "Levy residents vent anger at meeting."

61. *Tennessean*, September 14, 1997: 5D, "It shouldn't take tragedy to waken us," by Jon Yates.

62. Hirst, 1979: 144.

Notes to Chapter 4

1. See Morris, 1999; Clinton, 1994; A. Davis, 1983; hooks, 1984. Catherine Clinton (1994: 140) notes that even after Emancipation most freedwomen did not bring agents from the Freedmen's Bureau into their domestic lives. At the same time, "White observers condemned husbands who considered wife-beating a 'right' and resisted bureau intervention."

2. Gutman, 1976: 318, 319.

3. It was not until the early 1960s that we began to see the significant rise in female-headed households in the black community.

4. For similar accusations about Asian battered women, see Wang, 1996, discussed in Websdale, 1999: 37–39; for Native American battered women, see Zion and Zion, 1993.

5. As we saw in chapter 1, the tension, conflict, and violence between police agencies and the black community dates back to slavery. The fact that the criminal

justice system has brutalized blacks affects the willingness of some black women to call police during domestic violence conflicts.

6. Donnell Stewart (2000) makes a similar observation from his experience as a therapist working with batterer treatment groups in Boston through the EMERGE program. I am most grateful to David Adams for passing on these materials to me and sharing his insights regarding domestic violence and men and women of color. Personal conversation, July 12, 2000.

7. See Websdale, 1999: 153.

8. Websdale, 1999: 216. In my 1994 research into domestic homicides in Florida, I found that 1.58 black women per 100,000 kill their intimate black male partners, compared with 0.23 Latinas and 0.15 white women. I found the black intimate-partner homicide rate in Florida to be six times that of whites and two and a half times that of Latinos. These findings are consistent with those of numerous other researchers; for example, see Centerwall, 1984, 1995.

9. Centerwall, 1984, 1995.

10. Cazenave and Straus, 1995: 326–327. They speculate (1995: 336) "that there may be some effects of racial oppression which are independent of income and which may cause marital stress and tensions that may erupt in violence." For a recent discussion of these issues of race, class, and woman battering, see Ptacek, 1999.

11. Bureau of Justice Statistics (BJS), 1998; 2000. Nonlethal intimate violence includes rape, sexual assault, robbery, and aggravated and simple assault.

12. For men, the rate of victimization by an intimate was about one-fifth the rate for women. However, it is important to note that these figures do not address the context of violence, the nature of injuries received, or the meaning of the violence to the men and women involved. Between 1993 and 1998, 11.1 per 1,000 black women experienced violence by an intimate, compared to 8.2 per 1,000 white women. Over the same period, 2.1 per 1,000 black men and 1.3 per 1,000 white men reported intimate violence perpetrated by females (see BJS, 2000, Appendix Table 4: 10).

13. Websdale, 1999: 216–232.

14. Websdale, 1999.

15. Renzetti and Maier (1999: 12, 13) report similar fear among women living in public housing in Camden, New Jersey. None of the thirty-six women interviewed by Renzetti and Maier reported feeling safe in her neighborhood at night. When asked about their biggest problem, "every woman mentioned personal safety concerns and fear of crime." Like the women I interviewed in Nashville, many of the Camden women reported "often" hearing gunshots outside their units at night.

16. Websdale, 1999: 202.

17. Germane did most of her work with Latinas, some of whom had entered the United States illegally. In the cases of battered illegal-immigrant Latinas, Germane noted the peculiar complexity of any pending divorce or separation and the way she had to work on the immigration issues to establish legal immigrant status before addressing the divorce issue. For a discussion of the plight of immigrant battered women, see Websdale, 1999: 178; Orloff and Rodriguez, 1997.

18. hooks, 1984: 85.

19. Chesney-Lind, 1999.

20. Goetting, 1999: 4, 5. Under this feminist definition, "there can be no battered men: men can be treated unfairly and even brutally by women, but they cannot be battered because to be battered requires a social order antagonistic to one's particular gender."

21. J. Davis, 1976. See also Websdale, 1999: 7–8.

22. Although work on the intersection of race/ethnicity and battering is sparse, there is evidence that physically abusive African American, Latino, and Asian American men "explain and contextualize their abusive behavior in different ways, and their sense of manhood differs from that of European Americans" (Mederos, 1999: 141).

23. This observation is consistent with Donnell Stewart (2000: 125, 127), who notes that most batterer treatment programs draw upon traditional examples of white male privilege when talking about power imbalances that promote the abuse of women. However, as Stewart notes, when it comes to black males, they "have little experience with social entitlement per se. . . . Yet black men sometimes use their perceived lack of male privilege along with their feelings of powerlessness in society as a justification of abuse against their partners. In a hierarchical, male-dominated world, they have to be, theoretically, 'on top' in some venue. Black women and children are the only ones left to subordinate." In a similar vein, Stewart notes that black batterers who turn to dealing drugs may rationalize exposing their families to this violent world by seeing dealing as a solution to their unemployment and general economic malaise. This kind of "rationalization," if indeed that is what we should call it, may not be seen as such by the black man with no way of supporting his children other than dealing drugs. However, whatever the beliefs of men in these situations, there is no doubt that from time to time young children do get caught in the cross fire of the drug trade. For example, two-year-old D. J. Cherry Jr. was shot and killed, while sitting in his car seat, by a drug dealer after a deal initiated by his father turned sour. This killing evoked enormous outcry in the community. See the *Tennessean*, January 23, 1997: 1B, "Neighbors get involved in solution," by Tim Chavez.

24. In his therapeutic group work with African American batterers, Donnell Stewart (2000: 122) notes that "clients wanted validation that job discrimination, unemployment and a host of economic and social ills negatively impacted their behavior."

25. The historical record documents that patriarchal relations existed among black Africans before the slave trade. For example, bell hooks (1984: 16) observes, "White male observers of African culture in the 18th and 19th centuries were astounded and impressed by the African male's subjugation of the African female. They were not accustomed to a patriarchal social order that demanded not only that women accept an inferior status, but that they participate actively in the community labor force." See also Fox-Genovese, 1988.

26. The unit officially opened August 1, 1994.

27. Legislators removed the requirements of proving the victim's emotional distress, thus making prosecution easier. The new stalking law also increased the penalty for multiple stalking offenses from a class E felony (a one- to two-year sentence) to a class C felony (three to fifteen years and a $10,000 fine). For a discussion of

stalking, see *Christian Science Monitor*, November 10, 1995, "How Police Stalk Stalkers in Nashville," by Elizabeth Spaid.

28. By the time the Nashville DVU emerged, its counterpart in San Diego had overseen a 70 percent fall in domestic homicides since its creation. We cannot necessarily attribute these decreases to the work of the DVU. For further information, see the *Tennessean*, July 24, 1996: 1B, "Metro Shines Light on Domestic Abuse."

29. From 1990 to 1995, domestic violence–related killings accounted for 112 of the 412 (27 percent) homicides in Nashville.

30. See "Metro Shines Light."

31. Domestic violence calls increased from 18,359 in 1993 to 22,024 in 1995.

32. "Metro Shines Light."

33. According to a COPS office memo, the Nashville Police Department postponed a "Threat Assessment" grant they had been awarded. According to my sources, the grant never started and the paperwork had not cleared City Hall. Given that the department was due to receive $500,000, one wonders why. Memo dated July 10, 2000, and distributed to COPS grantees at a conference in Minneapolis.

34. Websdale, 1998, 1999.

35. Having attended a focus group at Bessie's program at night, I too saw people dealing drugs in the run-down streets. Coincidentally, there were two police patrol vehicles in the parking lot opposite the program premises, just a few blocks from the drug activity.

36. See Chesney-Lind, 1999: 128; M. Fullilove, Lown, and R. Fullilove, 1992: 277; Hirsch, 2001.

37. U.S. Department of Housing and Urban Development, 1996: 1; cited in Renzetti, 2001: 2.

38. Renzetti, 2001: 6.

39. See Osthoff, 2001.

40. Brenda Ross, a black woman who counsels Haitian victims of domestic violence in Spring Valley, New York, reported the same phenomenon at a recent meeting of COPS grantees in Minneapolis (July 10, 2000).

41. Gutman, 1976: 136.

Notes to Chapter 5

1. Elijah Anderson (1999: 316–317) notes, "In their social isolation, an oppositional culture, a subset of which is the code of the street, has been allowed to emerge, grow, and develop. . . . In such communities there is not only a high rate of crime but also a generalized diminution of respect for law."

2. Ibid., 1999: 114.

3. J. Wilson, 1983: 260.

4. The Harrison Drug Act (1914) mistakenly classified cocaine as a narcotic. However, cocaine is a stimulant, whereas heroin and the opiates have a depressant effect on the central nervous system.

5. These pleasurable sensations result from the increase of dopamine levels in the brain. However, chronic use depletes dopamine, leading to the craving for more cocaine. Classic lows follow the rush produced by crack, and cravings can become

intense. An increase in heart rate and blood pressure, an elevation in body temperature, and dilation of the pupils accompany addiction to crack. Heavy use of cocaine can lead to postuse depression and paranoia.

6. Reinarman and Levine, 1995: 148.

7. See Reinarman and Levine, 1995. The *Tennessean* is not immune to this kind of distortion. For example, in 1997 an article noted that Tennessee was "in the grips of a serious crack cocaine problem" (*Tennessean*, November 24, 1997, "Spread of meth labs sparks alarm," by Jon Yates). Another article mentioned "the disintegrating future for a growing number of Metro children under siege of this *epidemic*" (emphasis added) and stated, "Crack is unlike any other drug in hooking its victims. It is cheap, and its pleasure is similar to sex. The only effective strategy is to keep people from even trying it" (*Tennessean*, May 8, 1997, "More grit than grins in drug war," by Tim Chavez). See also the *Tennessean*, March 6, 1996, "Crack: The worst drug since heroin." In this article, Sumner County drug task force chief Richard Barton is quoted as saying, "Crack is the worst thing that's ever happened to society."

8. Reinarman and Levine (1995: 165) cite National Institute on Drug Abuse data (1993) to support this point. In a household survey conducted in 1992, the NIDA found that even among the age groups most frequently using crack (eighteen to thirty-four), only about 3 percent reported "ever using" crack. Only one-third or so of these told surveyors they had used crack in the preceding year (0.9–1.1 percent of the total sample). Of these, around one third (0.4 percent of the total sample) reported use during the preceding month. Reinarman and Levine conclude, "NIDA's general household surveys indicated that the lifetime prevalence of crack use began low and declined thereafter. And, despite all the claims that it is 'instantaneously addicting,' a clear majority of those who did try it did not continue to use it."

9. Recent evidence suggests that drug cartels have recently begun to exploit the South African underclass, which, as its U.S. equivalent did in the 1980s, finds itself sufficiently desperate to buy the cheap and addictive drug. South African police made their first arrest for crack distribution in 1995 and arrested 230 suspected dealers in 1997 and nearly twice that number in 1999. See the *Guardian Weekly*, August 24–30, 2000, "South Africa develops dangerous taste for crack," by Jon Peter.

10. Cited in Russell, 1998: 133. Russell notes that "Congress voted 332–82 to overrule the recommendation of the Sentencing Commission."

11. Christie, 1993; see also Chambliss (1994: 184), who notes that state expenditures on criminal justice increased 150 percent between 1972 and 1988. The increase in educational expenditures for that period was only 46 percent.

12. *Tennessean*, August 12, 1997: 1A, "Levy residents vent anger at meeting."

13. *Tennessean*, November 29, 1997: 1B, "Crime rises as night falls and police exit Sam Levy," by Tim Chavez.

14. Bourgois, 1995. For commentary on the case of a female crack dealer see Dunlap, Johnson, and Manwar, 1994.

15. Crack cocaine is the most common drug in the subterranean economy in Nashville. However, it appears that heroin may be making something of a comeback. Heroin was the drug of choice among Nashville's poor in the 1970s and early 1980s. Crack eclipsed heroin in the later 1980s. A 1996 drug bust netted a significant stash

of heroin. A five-month undercover investigation resulted in the confiscation of $25,000 worth of heroin, two semiautomatic handguns, and $1,200 in cash. Although the four suspected dealers lived in upmarket Antioch, most of the trading occurred in and around John Henry Hale Homes. The defendants in this case were Ronald Lee McKinley Sr., fifty-one, charged in federal court with armed trafficking of narcotics and possession of narcotics; his son, Ronald Lee McKinley Jr., twenty-six, charged in state court with delivering heroin; Charles Wayne Pitts, thirty-eight, charged in federal court with armed trafficking of narcotics and possession of narcotics; Shirley Marie Green, twenty-eight, charged in state court with selling heroin. See the *Tennessean*, July 12, 1996: 3B, "Drug, gun probe yields four arrests."

16. By running numbers I refer to various forms of gambling, such as betting on the numerical value of the Dow Jones at the end of a certain period of time, and so on.

17. *Tennessean*, March 21, 1998: 7B, "Drug sting nets 18 suspects," by Trine Tsouderos.

18. *Tennessean* October 29, 1995: 1A, "Crack stronger than a mother's love: Growing problem of addiction splits families, overwhelms system," by Wendy Kurland.

19. Darrell faced a sentence of twenty-seven to thirty-three and a half years. His moneyman, Linus Leppink, counted the McQuiddys' money and laundered the profits by providing Darrell with vehicles and what appeared to be a legitimate job at a diet clinic Leppink owned. For more details, see the *Tennessean*, August 23, 1997: 8B, "Federal indictments unsealed," by Hector Becerra; February 18, 1998: 1B, "Pleading guilty, 2 men detail life in drug ring," by Catherine Trevinson.

20. Among a sample of ninety-two prostitutes arrested in 1998, fourteen tested positive for HIV and fifteen for syphilis. See the *Tennessean*, May 2, 1998: 3B, "Police padlock motel suspected as sex, drug haven," by Jon Yates.

21. Police posing as prostitutes on Dickerson Road apprehended sixty-six men. Of those, 41 percent were married, 82 percent were over the age of twenty-six, and more than half were high-school or college graduates. See "Police padlock motel," by Yates.

22. See the *Tennessean*, October 21, 1997: 1B, "Police close down motel: Complaints of drug activity lead to shutdown, 14 arrests at lodge near Trinity Lane Area," by Jon Yates.

23. Halberstam, 1998: 275.

24. Ibid., 278.

25. Tannenbaum, 1990: 265.

26. "Pleading Guilty," by Trevinson.

27. "Police close down motel," by Yates.

28. See the *Tennessean*, January 2, 1998: 1A, "Addicts find help is scarce," by Duren Cheek. This article cites the testimony of the Reverend Hank Myers about the lack of drug treatment for the poor. He also noted the prevalence of forty-eight-hour detoxification programs instead of more-appropriate interventions, and the replacement of inpatient treatment programs by inadequate outpatient programs. Specifically, the article notes, "The state's alcohol and drug programs were the biggest losers when the state inaugurated its TennCare program on Jan. 1, 1994, to take a

money-saving managed-care approach to providing health services to its citizens dependent on Medicaid. Funds for alcohol and drug services were slashed dramatically."

29. See, for example, the *Tennessean*, January 14, 1999:1B, "Clash with police just a symptom," by Tim Chavez.

30. See J. Miller, 1996: 115–125.

31. Smith, Visher, and Davidson, 1984; Petersilia, 1983.

32. Horton, convicted of murder in 1975, failed to return from a June 12, 1986, furlough. The next year he broke into a home in Maryland, raped the occupant, and stabbed her companion. Lee Atwater, presidential candidate George Bush's campaign strategist, used Horton as a poster child for Democrat Michael Dukakis's softness on crime. See Tonry, 1995: 11–12.

33. J. Miller, 1996: 48.

34. *Tennessean*, September 25, 1995: 1A, "Tough crack law targeting blacks? 29-year-old who sold crack at Sam Levy waits to be sentenced," by Laura Frank. To its credit, the *Tennessean* ran a computer-assisted analysis of federal sentences given to white and black criminals in general, finding that "on average, blacks' sentences were 10% longer than whites' when their crimes were the same and they had similar criminal records."

35. Chambliss, 1994; J. Miller, 1996.

36. For a good recent example, see the calls from Gary Johnson, the Republican governor of New Mexico, reported in the *New York Times*, August 20, 2000, "He Just Said No to the Drug War: The iconoclastic governor of New Mexico, Gary Johnson, is the highest-ranking official ever to call for partial legalization. How did a Republican trip over this issue?" by Matthew Miller. In the article, Governor Johnson says, "Half of what we spend on law enforcement, half of what we spend on the courts and half of what we spend on the prisons is drug related. Our current policies on drugs are perhaps the biggest problem that this country has." The reporter goes on to note that, regarding drugs, Johnson told an audience, "Nearly 80 million Americans have tried them, including more than half of this year's graduating high school class." Johnson added, "No one condones this . . . but do we really want our kids to be branded 'criminals' for having experimented with drugs? If they're not driving or stealing while high, where is the harm?" In the preceding year, Johnson pointed out, alcohol killed 150,000 people, 450,000 died from smoking cigarettes, another 100,000 from prescription drugs, and perhaps only 5,000 from heroin and cocaine combined. Johnson went on to say, "Yet we are arresting 1.5 million people a year in this country on drug-related crime. Half those arrests are for marijuana, and half those arrested are Hispanics. Tell me that half the users of marijuana in the United States of America are Hispanic! I don't think so. We ought to legalize marijuana. We need to stop 'getting tough' with drugs." California Republican representative Tom Campbell, who is running for the Senate, puts it this way: "Look at our drugs war over the last 20 years and measure drug availability by the street price of heroin and cocaine. This price is one-quarter of what it was 20 years ago. Since 1980 the number of drug overdose deaths has increased by 540%. The proportion of high school seniors reporting that drugs are readily available has doubled. Incarceration for drug offenses has risen tenfold. The purity of heroin on the streets has increased more than four

times. We've spent a quarter of a trillion dollars since 1980 . . . and this war on drugs is a failure" (cited in the *Guardian Weekly*, September 14–20: 14, "Admit it: The war on drugs is a failure," by Peter Preston). In a similar vein, John DiIulio Jr., a senior fellow at the Manhattan Institute and at one time a staunch supporter of increasing incarceration, recently questioned the virtue of further increasing the number of prisoners, especially those held for drug-related offenses. He argues, "The justice system is becoming less capable of distributing sanctions and supervision rationally, especially where drug offenders are concerned. . . . Current laws put too many nonviolent drug offenders in prison." Referring to a study of incarcerated drug offenders in Massachusetts, DiIulio remarks, "Most of the state's drug offenders had no known record of violence." Turning to studies in New York state, he notes, "It appears that at least a quarter of recent admissions to the state's prisons are 'drug-only offenders,' meaning felons whose only crimes, detected or undetected, have been low-level, nonviolent drug offenses" (*Wall Street Journal*, March 12, 1999). For a more detailed statement of DiIulio's position against mandatory minimum sentences for drug offenses, see the *National Review*, May 17, 1999: 46, 48–51, "Against Mandatory Minimums: Drug sentencing run amok."

37. In June 2000 the U.S. Supreme Court reaffirmed that police must issue the Miranda warning informing citizens of their rights upon arrest. Chief Justice William Renquist said, "We . . . hold that Miranda and its progeny in this court govern the admissibility of statements made during custodial interrogation in both state and federal courts." In assuming this stance, the Court refused to replace the Miranda warning with "a less stringent federal law allowing voluntary confessions even when police fail to give the warnings" (*New York Times*, June 26, 2000, "Supreme Court reaffirms that police must warn criminal suspects of Miranda rights," by John DiIulio Jr.). According to the *New York Times*, the Supreme Court's decision was "one of its most important criminal law rulings in decades."

38. See the *Tennessean*, January 2, 1998: 1B, "Court says weapon 'pat down' has limits: opinion says drugs seized illegally after search of man," by Kirk Loggins.

39. Kennedy, 1998: 78–79.

40. Thompson, 1975a: 265.

41. Gilroy, 1982: 146.

Notes to Chapter 6

1. Fanon, 1963: 253.

2. *Tennessean*, September 25, 1995: 1A, "Tough crack law targeting blacks?: 29-year-old who sold crack at Levy Homes waits to be sentenced," by Laura Frank.

3. Wilson and Kelling, 1982.

4. Walker, 1984.

5. Kelling, Pate, Dieckman, and Brown, 1974.

6. See Goldstein, 1977: 110.

7. Sherman, 1990.

8. Grinc, 1998: 167.

9. Trojanowicz, 1993.

10. See Parenti (1999) for a discussion of the nationalization of U.S. police

through various governmental initiatives, especially the establishment of the Law Enforcement Assistance Administration.

11. *Tennessean*, October 1, 1996: 1A, "50 new cops on the beat on paper," by Linda A. Moore.

12. *Tennessean*, November 14, 1997: 1B, "Gore focuses on community policing: In town tomorrow for town hall meeting to talk about program," by Jon Yates. By December 1997 another sixty new police officers were sworn in to the Nashville Police Department. Federal community policing grants paid for forty-seven of these positions. See the *Tennessean*, December 21, 1997: 5B, "New metro law officers are sworn in," by Jon Yates.

13. *Tennessean*, November 16, 1997: 1A, "Gore touts community policing," by Jon Yates.

14. Niederhoffer, 1967.

15. Westley, 1970.

16. Even when minority officers join the ranks of police departments, the evidence suggests that their occupational role as police officers and their commitment to the police code and subculture take precedence over their loyalties to the minority communities from which they came. For a recent explanation of this issue, see the *Philadelphia Inquirer*, July 29, 2000, "Police culture seems stronger than ethnicity, experts say," by Huntly Collins. Collins notes that of the fifty-nine kicks or punches delivered by police to Thomas Jones, a forty-one-year-old fleeing black man suspected of carjacking, just three officers delivered them, two of them black and one white. Such a subculture or code of blue seems to militate against police opening themselves up to feedback from communities, especially communities where officers perceive themselves and fellow officers to be in danger.

17. The latest National Crime Victimization Surveys reveal that between 1993 and 1999 the rate of violent crimes declined 32.7 percent. Robbery with injury dropped 38.5 percent, aggravated assault decreased 41.2 percent, and rape fell 40 percent. Property crime rates continue on a twenty-five-year downward trend. See the report in the *Washington Post*, August 27, 2000, "Violent Crime Continues to Decline, Survey Finds," by Warren Leary.

18. *Tennessean*, October 26, 1999: 1A, "Police's renewed battle gets crime under control: Metro says it must be aware of 'peaks and valleys' in rate," by Beth Warren, Jon Yates, and Thomas Goldsmith.

19. Ibid. In 1998 a combination of DART (Drug Abuse Response Team) and FLEX officers confiscated 158 guns and 34 other weapons, and made 4,409 arrests. The 112 homicides of 1997 had declined to 97 in 1998. See also the *Tennessean*, June 13, 1999: 1A, "Homicides in Metro fall by half: Other major crime rates are declining," by Beth Warren.

20. *Tennessean*, September 19, 1998: 1A, "New policing takes hold: Sectors find different ways to fight crime," by Jon Yates.

21. *New York Times*, September 19, 1999. "Crack's Legacy: A special report," by Timothy Egan.

22. *New York Times*, June 25, 2000, "View from New York Streets: No Retreat by Police." This article was reported by David Barstow, C. J. Chivers, Juan Forero, Sarah Kershaw, and Nina Siegal and written by Mr. Barstow.

23. "Crack's Legacy," by Egan.

24. Qtd. in ibid.

25. Qtd. in ibid.

26. *New York Times*, March 4, 2000, "Cities Reduce Crime and Conflict without New York–Style Hardball," by Fox Butterfield.

27. Citing criminologist Alfred Blumstein from Carnegie Mellon University in Pittsburgh, Butterfield notes that the murder rate in U.S. cities fell most precipitously in San Diego (76.4 percent decline), followed closely by New York (70.6 percent) and Boston (69.3 percent). Robbery rates in the three cities also declined dramatically over the same period: San Diego, 62.6 percent; New York, 60.1 percent; and Boston, 50.2 percent.

28. Similar approaches to that adopted in Boston have evolved in High Point, N.C., Indianapolis, New Haven, Memphis, and Portland, Oregon.

29. "New policing takes hold," by Yates.

30. J. Miller, 1996: 33, citing the U.S. Department of Justice, 1992: 91.

31. Miller, 1996: 34, citing the U.S. Department of Justice 1993: 5.

32. Miller, 1996: 34, citing the U.S. Department of Justice, 1993a:13.

33. Miller, 1996: 36.

34. Bureau of Justice Statistics, 1986. See also Buzawa and Buzawa, (1990: 54–65) for other factors that work against the prosecution of men who beat women.

35. Zinn, 1980: 195.

36. Oshinsky, 1996:14.

37. Friedman, 1993: 95.

38. Qtd. in Zinn, 1980: 282.

39. Ibid., 286.

40. On the same day the Supreme Court gave its decision in *Munn v. Illinois*, it also released similar decisions in other so-called Granger cases, including *Peik v. Chicago and Northwestern Railroad* (1886), *Chicago, Burlington and Quincy Railroad v. Iowa* (1886), and *Winona and St. Peter Railroad v. Blake (1886).*

41. The Supreme Court retreated from these positions in 1886 and 1889, and in *Chicago, Milwaukee and St. Paul Railroad Co. v. Minnesota* (1889), rate regulation of the railroads by a state commission was invalidated.

42. Kennedy, 1998: 87. The case was *Ratliff v. Beale*, 74 Miss. 247, 265, 266–267 (1896), cited ibid., 413, n. 40.

43. Ibid., 88.

44. *Hunter v. Underwood* 471 U.S. 222 (1985), cited by Kennedy: 413, n. 42.

45. Gunnar Myrdal (1944: 452) notes: "A new movement to disfranchise the Negroes by more effective legal means—starting with the Mississippi Constitutional Convention of 1890 and continuing with the adoption of new constitutions in seven other states between 1895 and 1910—drew its main arguments from the danger of a break in white solidarity, demonstrated by the agrarian revolt. When Populism declined, and it did so rapidly after 1896, and the unity between the Populists and the Democrats became restored, the main dish at the love feasts was the disfranchisement of the Negro."

46. Zinn, 1980: 285.

47. This revolution also greatly increased the corporate acquisition of infor-

mation about people for marketing and sales purposes. Consultants who safeguard the privacy rights of computer users have reported a substantial increase in the use of what they call "spyware," designed to funnel information to huge corporate databases. The spyware is attached to various software programs people install onto their hard drives. It reports various idiosyncrasies of users, including their Web-surfing habits. The commercial utility of electronic eavesdropping is yet another example of the erosion of privacy rights; an erosion that parallels the loss of Fourth Amendment rights on the streets. See the *Guardian Weekly*, July 29–August 2, 2000: 29, "Your computer is watching you," by Ariana Eunjung Cha.

48. Oshinsky, 1997: 40. For example, Oshinsky (1997: 41) cites the case of "Lewis Luckett of Canton, Mississippi, 'a pure and simple negro, black as the ace of spades,' who received a two-year sentence for the theft of a hog."

49. Blassingame, 1977: 652.

50. Bureau of Justice Statistics, 1995.

51. Michalowski and Carlson, 2000.

52. Erlich, 1995: 3. "Prison Labor: Workin' for the man," http://burn.ucsd.edu/archives/ats-1/1995.Nov/0047.html, November 1, 2000.

53. Bureau of Justice Statistics, 1995a.

54. See articles by Dwight Lewis in the *Tennessean*: October 25, 1998: 5D, "Laws to erase a felon's vote hits African Americans hard," and January 30, 1997: 7A, "How black vote is diluted by number of men in jail."

55. For convictions occurring after June 30, 1996, only those for the crimes of murder, rape, treason, or voter fraud preclude restoration of voting rights (Public chapter number 898, 1996, Amending Tennessee Constitutional Amendments, 40-29-105). However, the voting-forfeiture laws still disproportionately affect blacks in Tennessee to a huge extent. Among adult whites, only 2.4 percent are disenfranchised because of their status as ex-felons; the comparable percentage for blacks is 14.5. Of the total of 97,800 disenfranchised felons, 38,300 are black.

56. "Laws to erase a felon's vote," by Lewis. I do not want to suggest that the backlash against extending suffrage to significant sectors of the black population was the same during the nineteenth-century redemption of the South (1877–1896) and twentieth-century redemption of the Reagan-Bush-Clinton era (1980–2000). Clearly, in the earlier period women did not have the vote, the labor power of the black poor was a much needed commodity, and American capitalism was just beginning to expand as the western frontier was settled and eyes turned to the war with Spain in 1898.

57. Cited in the *Arizona Daily Sun*, September 26, 2000: A4. See also the U.S. Census Bureau: http://www.census.gov.

58. Luttwak, 1999: 60. Among these corporations, Luttwak identifies Xerox, Hoffman-LaRoche, Delta Air Lines, Digital Equipment, and Chevron.

59. Luttwak, 1999: 218. See also Zweig, 2000.

60. For a discussion of the altercations between police and protesters in Seattle and the broader concerns of both environmentalists and labor unions about the WTO, see *Socialism Today*, January 2000, issue 44, "WTO under siege." The article quotes Clyde Prestowitz, head of Washington's Economic Strategy Institute, who observed, "There is a widespread view abroad that globalization is being forced on

the world by American corporations, that globalization is Americanization. So there is a banding together to protect the national essence." The failure of the Seattle meetings to proceed was perhaps more a product of long-standing transatlantic tensions over issues such as agriculture and the growing power of the world's developing nations than it was about the effects of protesters' actions. See the *Guardian Weekly*, June 8–14, 2000: 24, "Seattle was a wake-up call to governments—and to established NGOs," by Charlotte Denny. For commentary on the disturbances in Prague in October 2000, see the *Guardian Weekly*, October 5–11, 2000: 23, "Protesters open doors for moderates: The noise on the streets is filtering through to the inner sanctums of capitalism," by Charlotte Denny. For insights into the beating of protesters in Prague after they had been jailed, see the *Guardian Weekly*, October 12–18, 2000: 5, "Czech police beat jailed protesters," by Kate Connolly. See also Cockburn and St. Clair (2000), who make the point that protest was passive and peaceful in Seattle. The violence and intimidation were started by the police.

61. See, for example, the jury decision finding Greenpeace demonstrators not guilty of destroying genetically modified crops in Norfolk, England (*Guardian Weekly*, September 28–October 4, 2000: 9. "Greenpeace activists cleared in GM crop case: Future of tests in doubt as farmer says jury's verdict gives 'green light to trespass and vandalism,' " by Paul Kelso).

62. *Guardian Weekly*, September 21–27, 2000: 14, "World Bank report on poverty censored, say aid agencies," by Charlotte Denny.

63. Cited ibid.

64. See W. Wilson, 1996, p. 249, Appendix C, Table 2, "Percentage who are members of union (1969–1987)."

65. Western and Beckett, 1999: 1033 and Table 1.

66. Luttwak, 1999: 32.

67. See Finnegan, 1998.

68. Western and Beckett, 1999: 1034.

69. Gordon, 1990: 239, 9, 239.

70. Western and Beckett, 1999: 1052.

REFERENCES

Anderson, Celestine. 1979. "The Invention of the Professional Municipal Police: The Case of Cincinnati, 1877–1900." Ph.D. dissertation, University of Cincinnati, Cincinnati, Ohio.

Anderson, Elijah. 1991. "Neighborhood Effects on Teenage Pregnancy." In C. Jencks, and Paul E. Peterson, eds., *The Urban Underclass*. Washington, D.C.: Brookings Institution, 375–398.

———. 1999. *Code of the Street: Decency, Violence, and the Moral Life of the Inner City*. New York: W. W. Norton.

Bartlet, David W. 1993. "Housing the Underclass." In Michael B. Katz, ed., *The Underclass Debate*. Princeton, N.J.: Princeton University Press, 118–157.

Bassuk E. L., L. Weinreb, J. Buckner, A. Browne, A. Salomon, and S. Bassuk, 1996. "The Characteristics and Needs of Sheltered Homeless and Low-Income House Mothers." *Journal of the American Medical Association* 276: 640–646.

Beccaria, Cesare. [1764.] 1801. *An Essay on Crimes and Punishments*. 5th ed. London: J. Bone.

Bennett, Lerone, Jr. 1968. *Before the Mayflower: A History of the Negro in America, 1619–1964*. Baltimore: Pelican.

Blassingame, John. W. 1972. *The Slave Community*. New York: Oxford University Press.

———, ed. 1977. *Slave Testimony*. Baton Rouge: Louisiana State University Press.

Bogue, Donald. 1963. *Skid Row in American Cities*. Chicago: Universtiy of Chicago Press.

Bourgois, Philippe. 1995. *In Search of Respect: Selling Crack in El Barrio*. New York: Cambridge University Press.

Bowden, Tom. 1978. *Beyond the Limits of the Law*. Harmondsworth, Eng.: Penguin.

Boyer, Richard O., and Herbert Morais. 1955. *Labor's Untold Story*. New York: United Electrical Radio and Machine Workers of America.

Braudel, Fernaud. 1979. *The Structures of Everyday Life: Civilization and Capitalism, 15th–18th Century*, vol 1. New York: Harper and Row.

Browning, Sandra Lee, Francis Cullen, Liqun Cao, Renee Kopache, and Thomas Stevenson. 1994. "Race and Getting Hassled by the Police: A Research Note." *Police Studies* 17: 1–11.

Bunyan, Tony. 1976. *Political Police in Britain*. London: Julian Friedmann.

Bureau of Justice Statistics, U.S. Department of Justice. 1986. *Preventing Domestic Violence against Wives*. By Patrick Langan and Clive Innes. Washington, D.C.: Government Printing Office.

———. 1992. Criminal Victimization in the United States, National Crime Victimization Survey Report. NCJ-139563, December. Washington, D.C.: Government Printing Office.

———. 1993. *Felony Sentences in State Courts, 1990*. By Patrick Langan and John M. Dawson. NCJ-1441872, March. Washington D.C.: Government Printing Office.

———. 1993a. *Felony Defendants in Large Urban Counties, 1990*. By Pheny Z. Smith. NCJ-1441872, May. Washington, D.C.: Government Printing Office.

———. 1994. *Criminal Victimization in the U.S., 1994*. Washington, D.C.: Government Printing Office.

———. 1995. *Criminal Victimization in the United States, 1993*. Washington, D.C.: Government Printing Office.

———. 1995a. *Sourcebook of Criminal Justice Statistics*. Washington, D.C.: Government Printing Office.

———. 1997. *Corrections Statistics. 1997*. Washington, D.C. Government Printing Office.

———. 1998. *Violence by Intimates: Analysis of Data on Crimes by Current or Former Spouses, Boyfriends, and Girlfriends*. NCJ-167237, March. Washington, D.C.: Government Printing Office.

———. 2000. *Intimate Partner Violence*. By Callie Marie Rennison and Sarah Welchans. NCJ-178247, May. Washington, D.C.: Government Printing Office.

Butterfield, Fox. 1995. *All God's Children: The Bosket Family and the American Tradition of Violence*. New York: Avon Books.

Buzawa, E. S., and C. Buzawa. 1990. *Domestic Violence: The Criminal Justice Response*. Newbury Park, Calif.: Sage.

Carson, W. G. 1981. "White Collar Crime and the Institutionalization of Ambiguity: the case of the early Factory Acts." In M. Fitzgerald, G. McLennan, and J. Pauson, eds., *Crime and Society: Readings in History and Theory*. London: Routledge and Kegan Paul, 134–147.

Cashmore, Ellis, and Eugene McLaughlin, eds. 1991. *Out of Order? Policing Black People*. London and New York: Routledge.

Cazenave, Noel A., and Murray Straus. 1990. "Race, Class, Network Embeddedness, and Family Violence." In Murray Straus and Richard Gelles, eds., *Physical Violence in American Families*. New Brunswick: Transaction Publishers, 321–339.

Cei, C. B. 1975. *Law Enforcement in Richmond: A History of Police-Community Relations, 1737–1974*. Ph.D. dissertation, Florida State University, Tallahassee, Fla.

Centerwall, Brandon S. 1984. "Race, Socioeconomic Status and Domestic Homicide, Atlanta, 1971–1972." *American Journal of Public Health* 74: 813–815.

———. 1995. "Race, Socioeconomic Status, and Domestic Homicide." *Journal of the American Medical Association* 273, 22 (June 14): 1755–1758.

Center for Research on Criminal Justice. 1975. *The Iron Fist and the Velvet Glove*. Berkeley: CRCJ.

Chaiken, Jan, Peter Greenwood, and Joan Petersilia. 1977. "The Rand Study of Detectives." *Policy Analysis* 3, 2: 187–217.

Chambliss, William. 1994. "Policing the Ghetto Underclass: The Politics of Law and Law Enforcement." *Social Problems* 41, 2: 177–194.

Chesney-Lind, Meda. 1999. "Media Misogyny: Demonizing 'Violent' Girls and Women." In J. Ferrell and N. Websdale, eds., *Making Trouble: Cultural Constructions of Crime, Deviance and Control*. Hawthorne, N.Y.: Aldine de Gruyter, 115–140.

Christie, Nils. 1993. *Crime Control as Industry: Towards Gulags, Western Style*. London and New York: Routledge.

Clinard, Marshall B., Peter C. Yeager, Jeanne Brisette, David Petrashek, and Elizabeth Harries. 1979. *Illegal Corporate Behavior*. Washington, D.C.: Law Enforcement Assistance Administration, U.S. Dept. of Justice.

Clinton, Catherine. 1994. "Bloody Terrain: Freedwomen, Sexuality, and Violence during Reconstruction." In Catherine Clinton, ed., *Half Sisters of History: Southern Women and the American Past*. Durham: Duke University Press, 136–153.

Cockburn, Alex, and Jeffrey St. Clair. 2000. *Five Days That Shook the World*. New York: Verso.

Cohen, Stanley. 1988. *Against Criminology*. New Brunswick: Transaction.

Coffey, Brian, and J. Clarke Gocker. 1998. "Racial Disparities in Mortgage Lending: the Example of Urban Ohio." *Social Justice* 25, 3: 115–127.

Daniels, Christine, and Michael V. Kennedy, eds. 1999. *Over the Threshold: Intimate Violence in Early America*. New York and London: Routledge.

Davis, Angela. 1983. *Women, Race, and Class*. New York: Vintage.

Davis, John A. 1976. "Blacks, Crime and American Culture." *Annals of the American Academy of Political and Social Science* 423 (January): 89–98.

Dicerson, Ellen Ann. 1977. "The Nashville Housing Authority, 1938–1941: A Case Study of Public Housing under the New Deal." M.A. thesis, Vanderbilt University, Nashville, Tenn.

Dobash, R., and R. Emerson Dobash. 1981. "Community Response to Violence against Wives: Charivari, Abstract Justice and Patriarchy." *Social Problems* 28, 5: 563–581.

Doyle, Don H. 1985. *Nashville Since the 1920s*. Knoxville: University of Tennessee Press.

Dunlap, Eloise, Bruce D. Johnson, and Ali Manwar. 1994. "A Successful Female Crack Dealer: Case Study of a Deviant Career." *Deviant Behavior* 15: 1–25.

Edin, Kathy. 2000. "Few Good Men: Why Poor Mothers Don't Marry or Remarry." *American Prospect* (January 3): 26–31.

Edin, Kathy, and Jencks, Christopher. 1990. "The Real Welfare Problem." *The American Prospect* (Spring).

———. 1992. "Reforming Welfare," In Jencks, *Rethinking Social Policy*. Cambridge: Harvard University Press, chapter 5.

Edwards, Susan. 1989. *Policing Domestic Violence: Women, the Law and the State*. Newbury Park, Calif.: Sage.

Fanon, Franz. 1963. *The Wretched of the Earth*. New York: Grove Press.

Finnegan, William. 1998. *Cold New World: Growing Up in a Harder Country*. New York: Random House.

Fogel, Robert William, and Stanley L. Engerman. 1974. *Time on the Cross: The Economics of American Negro Slavery.* Boston: Little, Brown.

Foucault, Michel. 1977. *Discipline and Punish: The Birth of the Prison.* London: Tavistock.

———. 1980. "Prison Talk." In C. Gordon, ed., *Power/Knowledge: Selected Interviews and Other Writings, Michel Foucault, 1972–1977.* Brighton, Eng.: Harvester Press.

Fox-Genovese, Elizabeth. 1988. *Within the Plantation Household: Black and White Women of the Old South.* Chapel Hill: University of North Carolina Press.

Fridell, Lorie, and Arnold Binder. 1992. "Police Officer Decision Making in Potentially Violent Confrontations." *Journal of Criminal Justice* 20: 385–399.

Friedman, Lawrence M. 1993. *Crime and Punishment in American History.* New York: Basic Books.

Fullilove, Mindy, Anne Lown, and Robert Fullilove. 1992. "Crack Hos and Skeezers: Traumatic Experiences of Women Crack Users." *Journal of Sex Research* 29, 2: 275–287.

Fyfe, James. 1982. "Blind Justice: Police Shootings in Memphis." *Journal of Criminal Law and Criminology* 73: 707–722.

Genovese, Eugene. 1976. *Roll, Jordan, Roll: The World the Slaves Made.* New York: Vintage.

Gerber, David A. 1976. *Black Ohio and the Color Line.* Urbana: University of Illinois Press.

Giddens, Anthony. 1989. *Sociology.* Cambridge, Eng.: Polity.

Gilroy, Paul. 1982. "Police and Thieves." In Centre for Contemporary Cultural Studies, *The Empire Strikes Back.* London: Hutchinson, 143–182.

———. 1987. *There Ain't No Black in the Union Jack.* London. Hutchinson.

Glazer, S. 1997. "Declining Crime Rates: Does Better Policing Account for the Reduction?" *CQ Researcher* 7, 13 (April 4): 289, 291–308.

Goetting, Ann. 1999. *Getting Out: Life Stories of Women Who Left Abusive Men.* New York: Columbia University Press.

Goldstein, Herman. 1977. *Policing a Free Society.* Cambridge, Mass.: Ballinger.

Gordon, Diane R. 1990. *The Justice Juggernaut: Fighting Street Crime, Controlling Citizens.* New Brunswick: Rutgers University Press.

Gottfried, Robert S. 1983. *The Black Death: Natural and Human Disaster in Medieval Europe.* New York: Free Press.

Grinc, Randolph. 1998. "Angels in Marble: Problems in Stimulating Community Involvement in Community Policing." In David Karp, ed., *Community Justice: An Emerging Field.* Lanham, Md.: Rowman and Littlefield, 167–202.

Gutman, Herbert. 1976. *The Black Family in Slavery and Freedom, 1750–1925.* New York: Pantheon.

———. 1976a. *Work, Culture, and Society in Industrializing America: Essays in Working-Class and Social History.* New York: Alfred Knopf.

Hacker, Andrew. 1992. *Two Nations: Black and White, Separate, Hostile and Unequal.* New York: Random House.

Hacker, Barton C. 1969. "The U.S. Army as a National Police Force: The Federal Policing of Labor Disputes, 1877–1898." *Military Affairs* (April).

Halberstam, David. 1998. *The Children*. New York: Ballantine.

Hanmer, Jalna. 1978. "Violence and the Social Control of Women." In Gary Little-john, B. Smart, J. Wakefield, and N. Yuval-Davis, eds. *Power and the State*. London: Croom Helm.

Hanmer, Jalna, J. Radford, and E. Stanko, eds. 1989. *Women, Policing, and Male Violence: International Perspectives*. New York: Routledge.

Hanmer, Jalna, and Sheila Saunders. 1984. *Well-Founded Fear: A Community Study of Violence to Women*. London: Hutchinson.

Haralambos, Michael, and Martin Holborn. 1995. *Sociology: Themes and Perspectives*. London: Collins.

Harring, Sidney. 1976. "The Development of the Police Institution in the U.S." *Crime and Social Justice* (Summer): 54–59.

———. 1977. "Class Conflict and the Enforcement of the Tramp Acts in Buffalo during the Depression of 1893–1894." *Law and Society Review* 11: 873–911.

———. 1983. *Policing a Class Society*. New Brunswick: Rutgers University Press.

Harring, Sidney, and L. McMullin, 1975. "The Buffalo Police, 1872–1900." *Crime and Social Justice* (Fall/Winter): 5–14.

Hawkins, Darnell. 1987. "Devalued Lives and Racial Stereotypes: Ideological Barriers to the Prevention of Family Violence among Blacks." In R. L. Hampton, ed., *Violence in the Black Family*. Lexington, Mass.: Lexington Books, 189–205.

Hawkins, Darnell, John H. Laub, Janet L. Lauritsen, and Lynn Cothern. 2000. "Race, Ethnicity, and Serious and Violent Juvenile Offending." U.S. Department of Justice, Bureau of Justice Statistics, Juvenile Justice Bulletin (June).

Hawkins, Homer, and Richard Thomas. 1991. "White Policing of Black Populations: A History of Race and Social Control in America." In Ellis Cashmore and Eugene McLaughlin, eds., *Out of Order? Policing Black People*. London and New York: Routledge, 65–86.

Hay, Douglas. 1975. "Property, Authority and the Criminal Law" and "Poaching and the Game Law on Cannock Chase." In Douglas Hay, Peter Linebaugh, John G. Rule, E. P. Thompson, and Cal Winslow, eds., *Albion's Fatal Tree: Crime and Society in Eighteenth-Century England*. New York: Pantheon, 17–63, 189–253.

Henry, H. M. 1914. "The Police Control of the Slave in South Carolina." Ph. D. dissertation, Vanderbilt University, Nashville, Tenn.

Higginbotham, Evelyn Brooks. 1993. *Righteous Discontent: The Women's Movement in the Black Baptist Church, 1880–1920*. Cambridge: Harvard University Press.

Hirsch, Amy. 2001. "The World Was Never a Safe Place for Them: Abuse, Welfare Reform, and Women with Drug Convictions." *Violence against Women*, 7, 2: 159–175.

Hirst, Paul Q. 1975. "Marx and Engels on Law, Crime and Morality." In I. Taylor, P. Walton, and J. Young, eds. *Critical Criminology*. London: Routledge and Kegan Paul, 203–230.

———. 1979. *On Law and Ideology*. London: Macmillan.

Hobsbawm, Eric J. 1965. *Primitive Rebels: Studies in Archaic Forms of Social Movement in the 19th and 20th Centuries*. New York: W. W. Norton.

———. 1972. "Distinctions between Socio-political and Other Forms of Crime." *Society for the Study of Labour History Bulletin* 25 (Autumn): 5–6.

Hobsbawm, Eric J., and George Rudé. 1985. *Captain Swing*. Harmondsworth, Eng.: Penguin.

Hoffman, Dennis Earl. 1979. "An Exploratory Analysis of the Response of Urban Police to Labor Radicalism." Ph.D. dissertation, Portland State University, Portland, Ore.

Hoffman, D. E., and Vincent J. Webb. 1986. "Police Response to Labor Radicalism in Portland and Seattle 1913–19." *Oregon Historical Quarterly* (Winter): 341–366.

Honeycutt, Todd C., Linda L. Marshall, and Rebecca Weston. 2001. "Toward Ethnically Specific Models of Employment, Public Assistance, and Victimization." *Violence against Women* 7, 2: 126–140.

hooks, bell. 1984. *Ain't I a Woman?* London: Pluto Press.

———. 1984a. *Feminist Theory: From Margin to Center*. Boston: South End Press.

———. 1996. *Outlaw Culture: Resisting Representations*. London: Routledge.

Horan, J. D., and H. Swiggert. 1951. *The Pinkerton Story*. London: Putnam.

Irwin, John. 1985. *The Jail: Managing the Underclass in American Society*. Berkeley: University of California Press.

Jargowsky, Paul A. 1994. "Ghetto Poverty among Blacks in the 1980s." *Journal of Policy Analysis and Management* 13: 288–310.

Jargowsky, Paul A., and Mary Jo Bane. 1991. "Ghetto Poverty in the United States, 1970–1980." In Christopher Jencks and Paul E. Peterson, *The Urban Underclass*. Washington, D.C.: Brookings Institution Press, 235–273.

Jencks, Christopher, and Paul E. Peterson. 1991. *The Urban Underclass*. Washington, D.C.: Brookings Institution Press.

Johnson, Bruce C. 1976. "Taking Care of Labor: The Police in American Politics." *Theory and Society* (Spring): 89–117.

Katz, Michael B., ed. 1993. *The Underclass Debate*. Princeton, N.J.: Princeton University Press.

Kautsky, Karl. 1918. *Dictatorship of the Proletariat*. Ann Arbor: University of Michigan Press.

Kelling, George, Tony Pate, Duane Dieckman, and Charles E. Brown. 1974. "The Kansas City Preventive Patrol Experiment." Reprinted in Carl B. Klockars and Stephen D. Mastrofski, eds., *Thinking about Police: Contemporary Readings*. New York: McGraw-Hill, 1991: 139–163.

Kennedy, Randall. 1998. *Race, Crime, and the Law*. New York: Pantheon.

Kerner Report. 1968. Report of the National Advisory Commission on Civil Disorders. New York: Bantam Books.

Klockars, Carl B. 1991. "The Rhetoric of Community Policing." In Carl B. Klockars and Stephen Mastrofski, eds., *Thinking about Police: Contemporary Readings*. New York. McGraw-Hill, 530–542.

Klockars, Carl B., and Stephen D. Mastrofski, eds. 1991. *Thinking about Police: Contemporary Readings*. New York: McGraw-Hill.

Kornblum, William. 2000. *Sociology in a Changing World*. Orlando, Fla.: Harcourt Brace.

Lane, Roger. 1967, *Policing the City: Boston 1822–1905*. Cambridge: Harvard University Press.

Le Bon, Gustave. [1895.] 1960. *The Crowd: A Study of the Popular Mind*. New York: Viking Press.

Lein, Laura, Susan E. Jacquet, Carol M. Lewis, Patricia R. Cole, and Bernice B. Williams. 2001. "With the Best of Intentions: Family Violence Option and Abused Women's Needs." *Violence against Women* 7, 2: 193–210.

Lenin, V. I. [1902.] 1975. *What Is to Be Done?* Beijing: Foreign Languages Press.

Linebaugh, Peter. 1975. "The Tyburn Riot against the Surgeons." In D. Hay et al., eds., *Albion's Fatal Tree: Crime and Society in Eighteenth-Century England*. New York: Pantheon, 65–117.

Lombroso, Cesare. 1876. *L'Uomo delinquente*. Milan, Italy: Hoepli.

Lovett, Bobby L. 1999. *The African-American History of Nashville, Tennessee, 1780–1930*. Fayetteville: University of Arkansas Press.

Luttwak, Edward. 1999. *Turbo-Capitalism: Winners and Losers in the Global Economy*. New York: Harper Collins.

Mann, Kirk. 1992. *The Making of an English Underclass*. Milton Keynes, Eng.: Open University Press.

Manning, Peter. 1997. *Police Work*. Prospect Heights, Ill.: Waveland Press.

Marx, Karl. [1852.] 1969. "The Eighteenth Brumaire of Louis Bonaparte." In Friedrich Engels and Karl Marx, *Basic Writings on Politics and Philosophy*. L. S. Feuer, ed. New York: Doubleday.

Marx, Karl, and Friedrich Engels. 1970. *Selected Works*. New York. International Publishers.

Massey, Douglas, and Nancy A. Denton. 1993. *American Apartheid: Segregation and the Making of the Underclass*. Cambridge: Harvard University Press.

Mayhew, Henry. [1861.] 1968. *London Labour and the London Poor*. Vol. 4, *Those That Will Not Work*. New York: Dover Publications.

Mederos, Fernando. 1999. "Batterer Intervention Programs: The Past, and Future Prospects." In Melanie F. Shepard and Ellen Pence, eds., *Coordinating Community Responses to Domestic Violence: Lessons from Duluth and Beyond*. Thousand Oaks, Calif.: Sage.

Michalowski, Raymond J. 1985. *Order, Law, and Crime*. New York: Random House.

Michalowski, Raymond, and Susan Carlson. 2000. "Crime, Punishment, and Social Structures of Accumulation." *Journal of Contemporary Criminal Justice* 16, 3: 272–292.

Miller, Jerome G. 1996. *Search and Destroy: African-American Males in the Criminal Justice System*. New York: Cambridge University Press.

Miller, Susan L. 1999. *Gender and Community Policing: Walking the Talk*. Boston: Northeastern University Press.

Miller, Wilbur. 1977. *Cops and Bobbies: Police Authority in New York and London, 1830–1870*. Chicago: University of Chicago Press.

Mintz, Sidney W. 1986. *Sweetness and Power: The Place of Sugar in Modern History*. New York: Penguin

Model, Suzanne. 1993. "The Ethnic Niche and the Structure of Opportunity: Immigrants and Minorities in New York City." In Michael B. Katz, ed., *The Underclass Debate*. Princeton, N.J.: Princeton University Press, 161–193.

Monkkonen, Eric. 1981. *Police in Urban America, 1860–1920*. New York: Cambridge University Press.

Montgomery, David. 1978. "Gutman's 19th-Century America." *Labor History* 19: 416–429.

Morison, Samuel Eliot, Henry Steele Commager, and William E. Leuchtenburg. 1983. *A Concise History of the American Republic*, 2d ed. New York: Oxford University Press.

Morris, Christopher. 1999. "Within the Slave Cabin: Violence in Mississippi Slave Families." In Christine Daniels and Michael V. Kennedy, eds., *Over the Threshold: Intimate Violence in Early America*. New York and London: Routledge, 268–285.

Myrdal, Gunnar. 1944. *An American Dilemma*. Vols. 1 and 2. New York: Harper.

Niederhoffer, Arthur. 1967. *Behind the Shield*. Garden City, N.Y.: Doubleday.

Omolade, Barbara. 1994. *The Rising Song of African American Women*. New York: Routledge.

Orloff, Leslye, and Rachel Rodriguez. 1997. "Barriers to Domestic Violence Relief and Full Faith and Credit for Immigrant and Migrant Battered Women." In Byron Johnson and Neil Websdale, eds., *Full Faith and Credit: A Passport to Safety*. Reno, Nev.: National Council of Juvenile and Family Court Judges, 130–148.

Oshinsky, David M. 1996. *Worse Than Slavery: Parchman Farm and the Ordeal of Jim Crow Justice*. New York: Free Press.

Osthoff, Sue. 2001. "When Victims Become Defendants: Battered Women Charged with Crimes." In C. M. Renzetti and L. Goodstein, eds., *Women, Crime and Criminal Justice*. Los Angeles: Roxbury, 232–242.

Parenti, Christian. 1999. *Lockdown America: Police and Prisons in the Age of Crisis*. New York: Verso.

Parks, Roger B., Stephen D. Mastrofski, Christina Dejong, and M. Kevin Gray. 1999. "How Officers Spend Their Time with the Community." *Justice Quarterly* 16, 3: 483–518.

Pate, T. Bowers, R. A. Ferrara, and J. Lorence. 1976. *Police Response Time: Its Determinants and Effects*. Washington, D.C.: Police Foundation.

Patterson, Sheila. 1922. *Dark Strangers*. Harmondsworth, Eng.: Penguin.

Pearson, Jessica, Esther Ann Griswold, and Nancy Thoennes. 2001. "Balancing Safety and Self Sufficiency: Lessons on Serving Victims of Domestic Violence from Child Support and Public Assistance Agencies." *Violence against Women* 7, 2: 176–192

Pepys, Samuel. 1985. *The Shorter Pepys*. Edited by Robert Latham. London: Bell and Hyman.

Petersilia, Joan. 1983. *Racial Disparities in the Criminal Justice System*. Santa Monica, Calif.: Rand Corporation.

Pleck, Elizabeth. 1987. *Domestic Tyranny*. New York and London: Oxford University Press.

Popkin, Susan J., Victoria E. Gwiasda, Dennis P. Rosenbaum, Jean M. Amendolia,

Wendell A. Johnson, and Lynn M. Olson. 1999. "Combating Crime in Public Housing." *Justice Quarterly* 16, 3: 519–557.

Popkin, Susan J., Victoria E. Gwiasda, Lynn M. Olson, Dennis P. Rosenbaum, and Larry Buron, eds. 2000. *The Hidden War: Crime and the Tragedy of Public Housing in Chicago.* New Brunswick: Rutgers University Press.

Preston, William. 1963. *Aliens and Dissenters: Federal Suppression of Radicals 1903–33.* Cambridge: Harvard University Press.

Ptacek, James. 1999. *Battered Women in the Courtroom.* Boston: Northeastern University Press.

Quadagno, Jill. 1994. *The Color of Welfare: How Racism Undermined the War on Poverty.* New York: Oxford University Press.

Rabinowicz, N. H. 1980. *Race Relations in the South, 1865–1890.* Urbana: University of Illinois Press.

Radzinowicz, Leon. 1968. *A History of English Criminal Law.* Vol. 4. London: Stevens.

Rand Corporation Report. 1990. *Money from Crime: A Study of the Economies of Drug Dealing in Washington D.C.* R-3894-RF. Santa Monica, Calif.: Rand Corporation.

Raphael, Jody. 1996. "Prisoners of Abuse: Policy Implications of the Relationship between Domestic Violence and Welfare Receipt." *Clearinghouse Review* 30, 3: 186–194.

Reiman, Jeffrey. 1990. *The Rich Get Richer and the Poor Get Prison.* 3d ed. New York: Macmillan.

Reinarman, Craig, and Harry Levine. 1995. "The Crack Attack: America's Latest Drug Scare, 1986–1992." In Joel Best, ed., *Images of Issues: Typifying Contemporary Social Problems.* 2d ed. New York: Aldine de Gruyter, 147–186.

Renzetti, Claire. 2001. "One Strike and You're Out: Implications of a Federal Crime Control Policy for Battered Women." *Violence against Women* 7, 6 (June): 685–697.

Renzetti, Claire, and Shana L. Maier. 1999. " 'Private' Crime in Public Housing: Fear of Crime and Violent Victimization among Women Public Housing Residents." Paper presented at the annual meeting of the Academy of Criminal Justice Sciences, Orlando, Florida (March).

Richardson, J. 1970. *The New York Police: Colonial Times to 1901.* New York: Oxford University Press.

Richie, Beth E. 1996. *Compelled to Crime: the Gendered Entrapment of Black Battered Women.* New York: Routledge.

Roberts, Dorothy. 1997. *Killing the Black Body: Race, Reproduction, and the Meaning of Liberty.* New York: Pantheon.

Rossi, Peter H., and James D. Wright. 1989. "The Urban Homeless: A Portrait of Urban Dislocation." In William Julius Wilson, ed., *The Ghetto Underclass.* 1993. Newbury Park, Calif.: Sage, 149–159.

Rudé, George. 1964. *The Crowd in History.* New York: Wiley.

———. 1973. *Paris and London in the Eighteenth Century.* New York: Viking.

Rule, John G. 1975. "Wrecking and Coastal Plunder." In Douglas Hay et al., eds.,

Albion's Fatal Tree: Crime and Society in Eighteenth-Century England. New York: Pantheon, 167–188.

Russell, Kathryn. 1998. *The Color of Crime.* New York: New York University Press.

Scharf, Peter, and Arnold Binder. 1983. *The Badge and the Bullet: Police Use of Deadly Force.* New York: Praeger.

Scull, Andrew. 1984. *Decarceration.* New Brunswick: Rutgers University Press.

Sherman, Lawrence. 1990. "Police Crackdowns: Initial and Residual Deterrence." In Carl B. Klockars and Stephen D. Mastrofski, eds., *Thinking about Police: Contemporary Readings.* New York: McGraw-Hill, 188–210.

———. 1997. "Policing for Crime Prevention." In Department of Criminology and Criminal Justice, University of Maryland, ed., *Preventing Crime: What Works, What Doesn't, What's Promising.* Washington, D.C.: Office of Justice Programs, 8–58.

Silver, Alan. 1967. "The Demand for Order in Civil Society: A Review of Some Themes in the History of Urban Crime, Police and Riot." In David Bordua, ed., *The Police: Six Sociological Essays.* New York: John Wiley and Sons, 1–24.

Skocpol, Theda. 1991. "Targeting within Universalism: Politically Viable Policies to Combat Poverty in the United States." In C. Jencks and Paul E. Peterson, eds., *The Urban Underclass.* Washington, D.C.: Brookings Institution Press, 411–436.

Skogan, Wesley. 1990. *Disorder and Decline: Crime and the Spiral of Decay in American Neighborhoods.* Berkeley: University of California Press.

Skogan, Wesley G., and Susan M. Hartnett. 1997. *Community Policing: Chicago Style.* New York: Oxford University Press.

Skolnick, Jerome H., and James J. Fyfe. 1993. *Above the Law: Police and the Use of Deadly Force.* New York: Free Press.

Smith, Douglas A., Christy Visher, and Laura A. Davidson. 1984. "Equity and Discretionary Justice: The Influence of Race on Police Arrest Decisions." *Journal of Criminal Law and Criminology* 75 (Spring): 234–249.

Solomos, John, Bob Findlay, Simon Jones, and Paul Gilroy. 1982. "The Organic Crisis of British Capitalism and Race: The Experience of the Seventies." In Centre for Contemporary Cultural Studies, ed., *The Empire Strikes Back.* London: Hutchinson, 9–46.

Spitzer, Steven. 1981. "The Political Economy of Policing." In David Greenberg, ed., *Crime and Capitalism.* Palo Alto, Calif.: Mayfield, 314–340.

Stack, Carol. 1975. *All Our Kin: Strategies for Survival in a Black Community.* New York: Harper and Row.

Stewart, Donnell Lassiter. 2000. "Specialized Groups for African American Clients." In *Emerge Batterers Intervention Group Program Manual.* Cambridge, Mass.: Emerge, 122–133.

Stone, Lawrence. 1977. *The Family, Sex and Marriage in England, 1500–1800.* London: Penguin.

Storch, Robert D. 1981. "The Plague of Blue Locusts: Police Reform and Popular Resistance in Northern England, 1840–57." In M. Fitzgerald, G. McLennan, and J. Pauson, eds., *Crime and Society: Readings in History and Theory.* London: Routledge and Kegan Paul, 86–115.

Styles, John. 1980. "Our Traitorous Money Makers: the Yorkshire Coiners and the

Law, 1760–83." In John Brewer and John Styles, eds., *An Ungovernable People: The English and Their Law in the Seventeenth and Eighteenth Centuries*. London: Hutchinson.

Susser, Mervyn W., William Watson, and Kim Hopper. 1985. *Sociology in Medicine*. New York: Oxford University Press.

Sutherland, Edwin. 1949. *White Collar Crime*. New York: Dryden Press.

Tannenbaum, Frank. 1990. "Definition and the Dramatization of Evil." In Delos Kelly, ed., *Criminal Behavior*. New York: St. Martin's, 265–269.

Terkel, Studs. 1970. *Hard Times: An Oral History of the Great Depression*. New York: Pocket Books.

Thomas, Hugh. 1997. *The Slave Trade: The Story of the Atlantic Slave Trade: 1440–1870*. New York: Simon and Schuster.

Thompson, E. P. 1971. "The Moral Economy of the English Crowd in the Eighteenth Century." *Past and Present* 50 (February): 76–136.

———. 1975. "The Crime of Anonymity." In Douglas Hay et al., eds., *Albion's Fatal Tree: Crime and Society in Eighteenth Century England*. New York: Pantheon, 255–308.

———. 1975a. *Whigs and Hunters*. Harmondsworth, Eng.: Penguin.

Tonry, Michael. 1995. *Malign Neglect: Race, Crime, and Punishment in America*. New York: Oxford University Press.

Trevelyan, G. M. 1926. *History of England*. London: Longmans.

Trojanowicz, Robert. 1989. *Preventing Civil Disturbances: A Community Policing Approach*. Community Policing Series no. 18, National Center for Community Policing, Michigan State University.

———. 1993. *Community Policing Survey of Jurisdictions over 50,000 People*. East Lansing: Michigan State University.

U.S. Department of Housing and Urban Development. 1996. *Final Report: Public Housing Anti-crime Summit*. Washington, D.C.: Government Printing Office.

Walby, Silvia 1990. *Theorizing Patriarchy*. Oxford, Eng.: Basil Blackwell.

Walker, Samuel. 1984. "Broken Windows and Fractured History." *Justice Quarterly* 1: 57–90.

Walker, Samuel, Cassia Spohn, and Miriam DeLone. 2000. *The Color of Justice: Race, Ethnicity, and Crime in America*. Belmont, Calif.: Wadsworth.

Walvin, J. 1992. *Black Ivory: A History of British Slavery*. London: Harper-Collins.

Wang, Karin. 1996. "Battered Asian American Women: Community Responses from the Battered Women's Movement and the Asian American Community." *Asian Law Journal* 3: 151–185.

Websdale, Neil. 1992. "Female Suffrage, Male Violence and Law Enforcement." *Social Justice* 19, 3: 82–106.

———. 1993. "Making Sense of Civil Service Reform: Policing, Politics and Power in Eugene, Oregon, during the Great Depression." *Policing and Society: An International Journal of Research and Policy* 3: 91–119.

———. 1994. "Non-policing, Policing and Progressivism in Eugene, Oregon." *Policing and Society: An International Journal of Research and Policy* 4: 131–173.

———. 1998. *Rural Woman Battering and the Justice System: An Ethnography*. Thousand Oaks, Calif.: Sage.

———. 1999. *Understanding Domestic Homicide*. Boston: Northeastern University Press.

Weinstein, James. 1969. *The Decline of Socialism in America, 1912–1925*. New York: Vintage.

West, Cornel. 1988. "Marxist Theory and the Specificity of Afro-American Oppression." In Cary Nelson and Lawrence Grossberg, eds., *Marxism and the Interpretation of Culture*. Urbana and Chicago: University of Illinois Press, 17–33.

Western, Bruce, and Katherine Beckett. 1999. "How Unregulated Is the U.S. Labor Market? The Penal System as a Labor Market Institution." *American Journal of Sociology* 104, 4: 1030–1060.

Westley, William. 1970. *Violence and the Police*. Cambridge: MIT Press.

Williams, William Appleman. 1961. *The Contours of American History*. Cleveland and New York: World Publishing.

Willis, Paul. 1990. *Common Culture*. Milton Keynes, Eng.: Open University Press.

Wilson, James Q. 1983. *Thinking about Crime*. New York: Vintage Books.

Wilson, James Q., and George Kelling. 1982. "The Police and Neighborhood Safety: Broken Windows." *Atlantic Monthly* 127 (March): 29–38.

Wilson, William Julius. 1987. *The Truly Disadvantaged: The Inner City, the Underclass, and Public Policy*. Chicago: University of Chicago Press.

———. 1993. *The Ghetto Underclass*. Newbury Park, Calif.: Sage.

———. 1996. *When Work Disappears: The World of the New Urban Poor*. New York: Alfred A. Knopf.

Winslow, Cal. 1975. "Sussex Smugglers." In Douglas Hay et al., eds., *Albion's Fatal Tree: Crime and Society in Eighteenth Century England*. New York: Pantheon, 119–166.

Wintersmith, Robert F. 1974. *Police and the Black Community*. Lexington, Mass.: Lexington Books.

Wish, Harvey. 1937. "American Slave Insurrections before 1861." *Journal of Negro History* 22 (July): 299–320.

Wood, Gordon. 1992. *The Radicalism of the American Revolution*. New York: Knopf.

Wrong, Dennis. 1961. "The Oversocialized Conception of Man in Modern Sociology." *American Sociological Review* 26, 2 (April): 183–193.

Wycoff, Mary Ann, and Wesley K. Skogan. 1993. "Community Policing in Madison: Quality from the Inside Out." Final Summary Report Presented to the National Institute of Justice.

Ziegler, Philip. 1969. *The Black Death*. New York: Harper and Row.

Zinn, Howard. 1980. *A People's History of the United States*. New York: Longman.

Zion, J. W., and E. B. Zion. 1993. "Hozho s Sokee Stay Together Nicely: Domestic Violence under Navajo Common Law." *Arizona State Law Journal* 25, 2 (summer): 407–426.

Zorza, Joan. 1991. "Woman Battering: A Major Cause of Homelessness." *Clearinghouse Review* 24, 4: 421–429.

Zweig, Michael. 2000. *The Working Class Majority: America's Best Kept Secret*. Ithaca, N.Y.: Cornell University Press.

INDEX